I0794645

CLOSING TIME

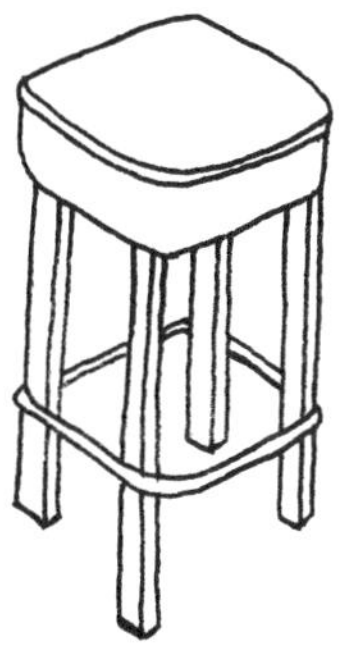

Closing TIME

SALOONS, TAVERNS, DIVES, AND WATERING HOLES OF THE TWIN CITIES

BILL LINDEKE and ANDY STURDEVANT

MINNESOTA HISTORICAL SOCIETY PRESS

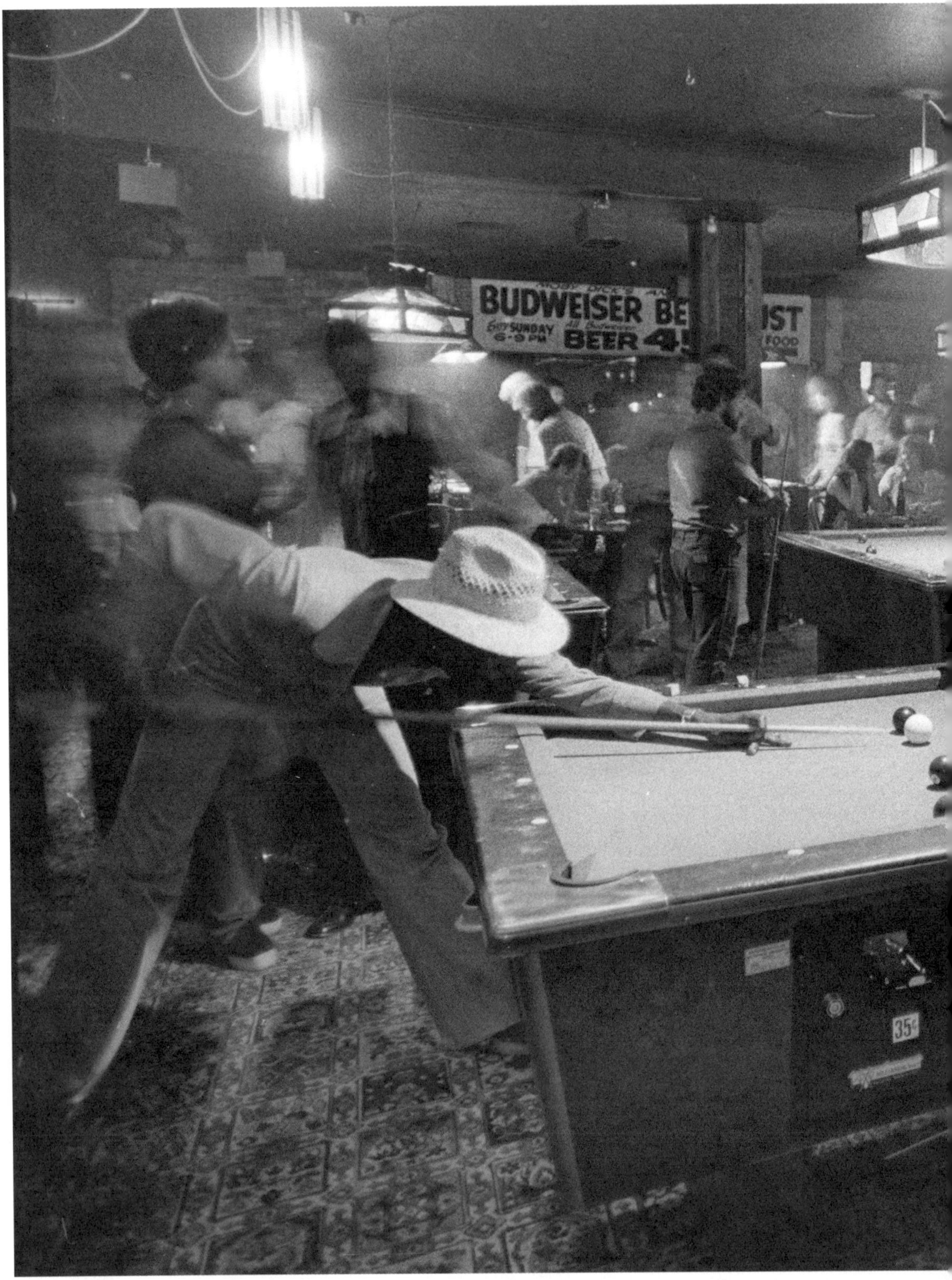
BUDWEISER
SUNDAY
6-9 PM
BEER
FOOD
35¢

mnhspress.org

The Minnesota Historical Society Press is a member
of the Association of University Presses.

Manufactured in the United States of America

10 9 8 7 6 5 4 3 2 1

∞ The paper used in this publication meets the minimum requirements of the American National Standard for Information Sciences—Permanence for Printed Library Materials, ANSI Z39.48-1984.

International Standard Book Number
ISBN: 978-1-68134-137-8 (hardcover)
ISBN: 978-1-68134-144-6 (e-book)

Library of Congress Cataloging-in-Publication Data
Names: Lindeke, Bill, author. | Sturdevant, Andy, author.
Title: Closing time : saloons, taverns, dives, and watering holes of the Twin Cities / Bill Lindeke and Andy Sturdevant.
Description: Saint Paul, MN : Minnesota Historical Society Press, [2019] | Includes bibliographical references and index. | Summary: "In *Closing Time,* Bill Lindeke and Andy Sturdevant dive into tales from famous and infamous drinking establishments from throughout Twin Cities history. Readers are led on a multigenerational pub crawl through speakeasies, tied houses, rathskellers, cocktail lounges, gin mills, fern bars, social clubs, singles bars, gastropubs, and dives. Featuring beloved bars like Matt's, Palmer's, the Payne Reliever, and Moby Dick's, the book also resurrects memories of long-forgotten establishments cherished in their day. Lindeke and Sturdevant highlight neighborhood dives, downtown nightspots, and out-of-the-way hideaways, many of which continue to thrive today. *Closing Time* brings together stories of these spaces and the people who frequented them"—Provided by publisher.
Identifiers: LCCN 2019028849 | ISBN 9781681341378 (hardcover) | ISBN 9781681341446 (ebook)
Subjects: LCSH: Bars (Drinking establishments)—Minnesota—Minneapolis Metropolitan Area—History. | Bars (Drinking establishments)—Minnesota—Saint Paul Metropolitan Area—History. | Minneapolis (Minn.)—History. | Saint Paul (Minn.)—History.
Classification: LCC TX950.57.M6 L56 2019 | DDC 647.95776/579—dc23
LC record available at https://lccn.loc.gov/2019028849

This and other Minnesota Historical Society Press books are available from popular e-book vendors.

On the previous pages: Interior of Moby Dick's, on Block E in downtown Minneapolis, 1978.
Photo from the Star Tribune, *Minnesota Historical Society Collections*

CONTENTS

PRACNA
1890
Historic Dining Saloon
WELCOME

INTRODUCTION

The two of us met, in a bar, about ten years ago. It was Pracna, on St. Anthony Main across the river from downtown Minneapolis. Pracna is a beautiful old saloon in a historic stone building that bears the words *Pracna 1890* on its crown. We don't remember what we had to drink: Bill probably had a beer; Andy probably had a cocktail.

Pracna is one of those places that people like to tell you is the oldest saloon in town, possibly because they read it on a menu while waiting for their order. It's not untrue, exactly, but there are a lot of asterisks. Frank Pracna did open a saloon on the site in 1884 and constructed the present-day building six years later. So, in one sense, to have a drink at Pracna today is to imbibe in a space that dates back more than a century, and it certainly feels that way. But Pracna's original bar closed sometime in the 1930s, and it was only reopened again in the 1970s, by an unrelated set of entrepreneurs. The new bar's main selling point was the restored nineteenth-century building, and today's Pracna reflects a sort of manufactured nostalgia—although it feels right if you sit with it for a while. The proximity to downtown ensures that it's frequently full of young professionals and visitors to the city, all eager for some local Minneapolis lore. In its 130-year-old building, Pracna is an extension of old Minneapolis, experienced through the masonry and the wood fixtures and the way you can hear nearby St. Anthony Falls if you're sitting on the patio.

Plenty of joints in this book have been continuously serving alcohol since the days when Frank Pracna was behind the bar on Main Street—Cuzzy's Bar on Washington Avenue, for example, or the Spot Bar in St. Paul, though

in both cases the names have been changed many times over. Waldmann's Saloon dates back to territorial days, though it had a 140-year interruption of service. And there are a handful of Pracna-era places scattered around the Twin Cities that didn't make it into this book: Neumann's, Brunson's, the Monte Carlo, the Schooner, Whitey's, Joe and Stan's. It's not because we don't love them, but there's only so much room.

At the same time, new bars are constantly opening around town, in spaces new and old, including trendy joints in recently gentrified areas as well as classic neighborhood corner bars. Many of these notable newer bars of the last fifteen or so years, sadly, didn't make the book, either (or, in a few cases, closed before the book went to press): Marvel Bar, La Belle Vie, the Pi Bar, Parlour, the Bull's Horn, the Rabbit Hole, the 331, others.

Above: Patrons at a saloon on West Seventh Street in St. Paul, circa 1900. *Minnesota Historical Society Collections*

Opposite, top: Ribbon badge from the Minnesota Anti-Saloon League convention of 1904. The temperance and prohibition movements were powerful forces throughout the state's history. *Minnesota Historical Society Collections*

Opposite, bottom: Block E in Minneapolis was ground zero for much of the debate over morality and urban identity in the 1970s, with Moby Dick's bar at the heart of it. *Hennepin County Library*

Page viii: Pracna sits in an 1890 building on St. Anthony Main, evoking an old-school saloon in twenty-first-century Minneapolis. *Photo by Ed Kohler, CC-BY-SA-2.0*

Each bar in the Twin Cities, or anywhere for that matter, has its own story, and each one has stories that we tell about it. Yet the rich history of our bars, saloons, taverns, and clubs doesn't always fit neatly into the larger picture we like to paint of Minneapolis and St. Paul: cities where urban bustle is tempered by nature and livability; where downtown density is offset by ample lakes, trees, and parks; where the raw edges of industry are diluted by bourgeois civility. Still, for nearly two centuries, thousands of bars have thrived amidst the enclaves of respectability in the downtowns, neighborhoods, and fringes of Minneapolis–St. Paul. This tension over urban identity has been played out in the many regulations, restrictions, and crackdowns that punctuate the story of Twin Cities booze, and bars so often mark the edges and intersections of race and class, identity and geography.

The initial decades of European settlement in the Twin Cities during the nineteenth century were laced with tensions around alcohol. Most of these battles were staged around the relatively new idea of the "saloon," a term that hadn't even been in common use until the 1870s; prior to this, men (and it was mostly men) drank in hotels, taverns, inns, and taprooms. *Saloon* came along from the French by way of England, and initially the term had a whiff of euphemism about it. A saloon was a classier place than a tavern. (The terms are used somewhat interchangeably in this book.)

Hot on the heels of the whiskey-soaked tavern keepers, the Yankee teetotalers, led by divine providence, brought Minnesota into its first, albeit short-lived, prohibition era. All the way back in 1852, Minnesota enacted laws prohibiting the sale and consumption of alcohol, and although the prohibition only remained in place for a brief six months, the battle lines between east and west, old and new, temperance and intoxication were drawn. These battles would be a constant presence in the Twin Cities, from the 1884 "liquor patrol limits" to the demolition of downtown skid rows to the 1970s war on smut to the regulatory meddling over Sunday sales. Minneapolis and St. Paul, each in their own ways, maintained their tenuous relationship with alcohol, which, it must be said, remains an addictive drug that ruins lives.

Wrapped up in all of this, too, is the specter of what you'll find referred to as the "3.2 bar" throughout these pages, as well as in everyday conversation—although not so much these days as compared to the not-too-distant past. The 3.2 bar is a distinctly Minnesotan institution that dates to the years

The Left Guard in Bloomington was a popular spot for singles looking to mingle in the swinging seventies. *Photo from the* Star Tribune, *Minnesota Historical Society Collections*

after Prohibition. These bars, typically neighborhood joints, were prohibited from serving anything stronger than beer brewed at 3.2 percent alcohol by weight. (For context, a typical American lager these days falls in the five percent range, while some craft beers can range as high as eight to ten percent or more.) Until the 1970s, nearly every Minneapolis bar outside of the liquor patrol limits sold only 3.2 near beer; even in St. Paul, which didn't have official liquor zones, permits and liquor licenses were granted more liberally to 3.2 joints than to establishments that served stronger drink. In practice, 3.2 bars usually turned a blind eye to people bringing in their own bottles of more potent booze to consume. As of 2019, there is only one 3.2 bar left in the city: the T-Shoppe in far North Minneapolis.

Throughout the decades, bars and saloons and taverns were the battlegrounds in the struggle over morality and the norms of everyday life, each establishment a small skirmish in the larger war. In the cracks in the urban facade, or sometimes at the very center, these places to drink aligned in different ways with the urban geography of social class. Bars formed a backdrop for clashes between labor and capital, political wrangling between Republicans and Democrats, and so many smaller struggles that were a constant amid the city's schizophrenic neighborhood geography.

At the same time, for many Twin Cities communities, the bars offered a sense of place. Taverns served as a social crossroads for countless ethnic,

Cassius Bar in Minneapolis was an important gathering place for African Americans arriving and settling in the Twin Cities. *Photo by John F. Glanton; courtesy of Hennepin County Library and the children of John Glanton*

cultural, and immigrant groups, as they continue to do today. Whiskey saloons became waystations for itinerant speculators and wayward opportunists. Nightclubs offered lifelines of escape from the humdrum. Singles bars provided opportunities to alleviate midwestern loneliness. Taverns became the place where factory workers bonded, brawled, or organized. Dives were dim havens for artists and crooks. Wherever there were thriving communities in Minneapolis or St. Paul, there was often a great bar at the center of it.

The stories about these places tend to be found, in the best of circumstances, in yellowed newspaper columns, written by a regular contributor who'd drop in for some local color when a deadline was approaching. Or, in more recent times, tales of city nightlife are the currency of review sites, social media, semi-abandoned internet forums, and anywhere else people online exchange opinions about what's great, what's terrible, where you should go, and where you should avoid. For the most part, the best of these are the oral histories, tales taken right from the source; the gossip, rumors, tall tales, firsthand memories, and other stories from uncles, aunts, and grandparents ring the truest. That's the type of history you only hear at a barstool, and it's rarely written down. Once those stories vanish, they vanish forever.

Many of these tales travel far beyond the Twin Cities, too. In this part of the country, at the edge of the Great Plains, Minneapolis and St. Paul might have the only big-city corner bars for a long, long distance. Moe Emard, who owned the CC Club for many years, recounted how he had heard stories about the place while growing up in the Dakotas, how it was one of the best-known spots in the Upper Midwest; later, the legend of the CC Club would be passed down by punk-rock fans for decades. If you were a young African American arriving from the South during the Great Migration of the mid-twentieth century, the downtown Minneapolis bar owned by Anthony B. Cassius might be your first stop, because you'd heard he was the guy to talk to to get yourself established.

Every bar has a story, shared by bartenders and patrons alike. *Photo courtesy of Tim Gallivan*

So, what makes a Twin Cities bar different from a bar anywhere else? There are the superficial things, of course. For one thing, you're more likely to find frozen pizza cut into squares. You're more likely to pass through a cold-weather vestibule to knock the snow off your boots before entering the bar proper. You'll probably find coat hooks under the bar for the ten pounds of winter gear you're wearing. You may even find that you're drinking 3.2 beer: check the label. You'll likely see a pull tab lady in a plexiglass booth reading a pulp novel, discarded tabs piled up in baskets. You'll see neon signs for all the local brands of beer, past and present, the great and not so great, like Grain Belt and Hamm's and Schmidt and Summit. You're also sure to see paraphernalia on the walls for Michelob Golden Light, which, for reasons unclear to nearly everyone, remains intensely popular in the entire state despite not having any real local connection. If there's a TV, during certain times of the year you're more likely to see high school hockey on the screen than the local professional teams.

But many of these things you'll find in rural Minnesota bars, too. Looking closer, what distinguishes a bar here from anywhere else in the United States has more to do with the things you notice when you walk into a place, and those aren't so neatly classified or codified. They vary from neighborhood to neighborhood, too—a bar in Northeast Minneapolis that's been serving full-strength lager and whiskey for seventy-five years feels a lot different than one down in the quieter neighborhoods of south Minneapolis that serves wine and beer and has a sign by the door that says, "Please respect our neighborhoods by exiting quietly," because it's the only bar within a square-mile radius.

A quick checklist for a Twin Cities bar trip looks much like the one you'd use anywhere: What celebrity photos did the owners choose to hang on the walls? Which newspaper reviews did they frame? What trophies are displayed? What sort of artwork is on the walls, and who made it? When you walk into the bar, the mood or vibe of the place might shift subtly upon your entrance. Maybe you're confronted with a barrage of skeptical stares, with the proverbial needle scratching across a record. Maybe you're greeted like a long-lost family member. Or maybe no one cares at all. Spend enough time in a bar in Northeast or the West Bank or Frogtown or downtown St. Paul, and you'll start to recognize the cues.

This book includes only a few of the thousands of bars, taverns, nightclubs, saloons, and dives that are part of the rich history of these cities we love. Some details are a little hazy, or perhaps someone we talked to embellished a bit. We hope that's okay with you. You can correct the record over drinks with us sometime. You can tell us what the place was *really* like, what really happened within the walls of your favorite drinking establishment.

Palmer's Bar has been a cornerstone for more than a century in the ever-evolving Cedar-Riverside neighborhood on Minneapolis's West Bank. *Photo by Anna Botz*

Drawn from remembrance of a physiognomist.

PIERRE PARRANT, OR "OLD PIG'S EYE."

First settler in St. Paul, in 1838.

“His old crooked eye scowling at me.”

PIG’S EYE PARRANT’S SALOON

1839–1841

LOCATED NEAR 2595 CROSBY FARM ROAD FOR 1839–1840, THEN DOWNTOWN BY JACKSON AND SHEPARD

The most remarkable thing about Pig’s Eye Parrant’s saloon was that it achieved such legendary status despite its short lifespan. To this day, all throughout St. Paul, from dives to boardrooms, people recount the story of Pig’s Eye and his whiskey shack, and his visage is invoked as a symbol of shame or perseverance or both. Historical pariah and underground antihero, Pig’s Eye is a symbol of the tension between St. Paul’s nineteenth-century moral self-image and the persistent forces of merriment, forces as strong today as they were a hundred and fifty beers ago.

With that in mind, the scant historical traces of Parrant’s saloon hardly live up to the legend, for Pig’s Eye’s place was as short-lived as his legend is long. What follows is the best story of Pig’s Eye’s you are likely to find.

Pierre “Pig’s Eye” Parrant was a retired fur trader who began squatting around the outskirts of Fort Snelling in 1832. Lawrence Taliaferro, the head Indian agent at Fort Snelling, described him simply as “a foreigner, prohibited from the trade.” Taliaferro’s journals make it clear that Parrant routinely flouted this prohibition and, like a nuisance, made his name selling whiskey on the borders of the Indian lands.

Opposite: Illustration of Pierre “Pig’s Eye” Parrant from circa 1840. *Minnesota Historical Society Collections*

What else is clear is that Pig’s Eye’s particular combination of personality and appearance made him the perfect scapegoat for the territory’s power players. The nickname “Pig’s Eye” referred to Parrant’s physical deformity: one eye was blind, with a white ring around the pupil and puffy pink skin around that. The askew visage combined with his rough voyageur manners personified frontier vice and symbolized all that stood in the way of decency and progress. Writer J. Fletcher Williams, in the first definitive history of St. Paul, explains: "It must be related, that he bore not the most enviable character. It was hinted that he left Sault Ste. Marie on account of some irregularities of conduct that were distasteful to the good people there."

Parrant set up camp near the Mendota settlement. At the time, everything outside the fort's boundaries was still Dakota land, and settling there or doing business required permission from the Indian agent. Also living around the fort were scores of civilians who had fled the doomed Selkirk colony on the Red River in today's Manitoba. They worked for the military or sold produce and livestock to the garrison, farming on the military reservation near Coldwater Spring or staying at Mendota. One imagines Parrant among these settlers, buying and selling whiskey or other valued commodities to soldiers and other customers, eking out an existence at the margins of the fort's official society.

That all changed in 1837, when rumors of a new treaty with the Dakota began to spread. With land claims on the horizon, the fort's commander, Major Joseph Plympton, decided it was long past time to redraw and expand the lines of the military reservation, evicting the traders on the grounds of maintaining moral purity. As historian Mary Lethert Wingerd describes, the link between traders and whiskey was a convenient pretext to keep the traders out and ensure that any nearby land claims remained in the hands of military leadership. The Canadians were caught in the crossfire.

Anticipating eviction, many of the Selkirkers moved east of the Mississippi to what was called Rumtown, today's Highland Park. Parrant himself moved farther downriver, setting up shop next to Fountain Cave, a well-known cavern in the bluffs three and a half miles downstream. He made the cave his new home and, by the summer of 1838, had built a small but highly visible building where he peddled his homemade whiskey.

Fountain Cave was an attraction all in itself, a huge cavern extending deep into the bluffs underneath what is today Davern Street. One of the earliest known events at the cave involving Euro-American residents took place on July 4, 1831, years before Parrant showed up. An army adventurer named Joseph Brown celebrated the relatively young holiday by bringing a cannon into the cave and shooting a tribute out its mouth. According to one account, the blast almost brought the cave entrance crumbling down.

Thankfully for Parrant, the cave held up, and he settled outside the mouth a few years later. Passersby heading down the river would stop to make discreet purchases of Pig's Eye's booze and, if they wanted some added adventure, wander into the dark abyss of the cave to enjoy their new wares.

Illustration of St. Paul's Fountain Cave, near the site of Pig's Eye Parrant's saloon, circa 1850. *Minnesota Historical Society Collections*

J. Fletcher Williams's early history of the state describes a typical occurrence at Parrant's place:

> *But we must not lose sight of old* PARRANT, *located at the cave. During all this time he was driving a flourishing trade, selling whisky to both Indians and whites. Occasionally a party of soldiers, bound on a spree, would come down to his ranch, get soaked with his red-eye and tangle-foot brands, and fail to report next day. Hence a guard would have to hunt them up, and the poor fellows would sojourn in the guardhouse, or wear a ball and chain for a period. Two or three times the officers at the fort threatened to tear his shanty down, but never executed the threat at that time. His place was searched once or twice, with the intention of demolishing all liquor found, but the old fox was too sly to be caught that way. He didn't keep much stock in sight. The rest of it was buried near by, where no one but himself could find it. Some say he used to hide it in the cave.*

Pig's Eye's shop at the mouth of Fountain Cave did not last long. Only a year later, Parrant put up his land claim as collateral on a loan, and a year after that he lost his stake due to lack of payment on the debt; what's more, the final lines of the expanded military reservation took in Rumtown and the cave, as well. Displaced again, Pig's Eye moved a few miles farther downstream, made another land claim in 1839, and opened another whiskey saloon in today's downtown St. Paul.

This one lasted a bit longer. Located in a prime location at the base of the river bluffs, Parrant's place proved to be the first of many saloons, stores, and cabins that collected in what would eventually become St. Paul's lower landing. Parrant's new saloon was a landmark for the growing community of squatters, refugees, and adventure seekers just east of the military boundaries. One can imagine the simple wooden shack, folks drinking and watching the river for any sign of incoming travelers.

Pig's Eye's lasting fame stems largely from a story of a Canadian named Edmund Brissett, who had stopped near the landing for a few days during his travels. Brissett was passing time at Parrant's tavern and wanted to send a letter to a man he knew downriver on Grey Cloud Island, only he did not know how to address his epistle.

Brissett's journal includes the following account of that fateful afternoon: "I looked up inquiringly at Parrant, and seeing his old crooked eye scowling at me, it suddenly popped into my head to date it at Pig's Eye, feeling sure that the place would be recognized, as Parrant was well-known along the river. In a little while an answer was safely received, directed to me at Pig's Eye. I told the joke to some of the boys and they made lots of fun of Parrant. He was very mad, and threatened to lick me, but never tried to execute it."

And thus the town of Pig's Eye was born, a frontier joke poking fun at a disfigured, irascible crank, albeit one with a small gift for opportunism.

By 1841, the "town of Pig's Eye" had been renamed by the newly arrived Catholic priest Lucien Galtier, who did not think much of the collection of saloons by the landing. By then, Pig's Eye's place had been surpassed in stature by better-funded settlers and, for the second time, he lost his land claim in a legal dispute. Soon afterward, Pig's Eye Parrant disappeared into both legend and the northern forests of Wisconsin, taking, as an early writer noted, "his fame, trade, name and carcass" to parts unknown. Some said he died of disease; others said he perished in a fight.

Nevertheless, his image thrived in the ensuing decades. His saloon grew in reputation with each new recollection, for example, this one from "Dakota Land; or the Beauty of Saint Paul," by a New York writer painting a bifurcated picture of the new territory:

> *But a very baneful influence was retarding the happy results labored for by the priest [Galtier]. . . . One Pierre Parrant, who was in the service of the fiend, opened a temple for his followers to worship in. Parrant was a*

Canadian voyageur, who acquired some notoriety from a facial deformity not very dissimilar to that of Caliban. Many people believed he had but one eye. That was a mistake. He had two eyes. But the singularity of defect in his optical expression was so swinish, that even the Indians as well as the whites, unanimously bestowed upon him the derisive title of "Pig's Eye." Yet he cared not for that so long as they were his deluded slaves. He had a miserly heart, and loved nothing better than gold.

Parrant's temple became a popular resort. There was no sign over the door, nor any emblem of Deity or God to be seen upon the outside of the temple; and yet it was thronged with Dakotas and pale-faces who thirsted for minne-wakan*—which is called "whisky" in our less poetical vernacular idiom. Parrant was a frontier rum-seller. No excise law could reach his jugs, his kegs, or his barrels. Business was lively in his groggery. It was lively during the day, and more than lively at night. . . .*

The Dakotas, couriers de bois, voyageurs, bois brule, *and degraded adventurers hanging around, soon elevated Parrant to the exalted position of chief liquor merchant in the place. Numerous other white skins, with heart-feelings figuratively darker than the color of their mangy hides, also established groggeries hard by. But none of them were patronized so liberally as Parrant. And indeed, if the recollection of my informant is correct, all the merchants who first opened stores in the settlement, sold as much whiskey as they could.*

Thus did the short-lived whiskey saloon of Pierre "Pig's Eye" Parrant become the symbol of moral turpitude, worthy of scorn and indignation, and a legend that foretold the birth of a new city on the ruins of one old man's attempt to find a place to trade.

One postscript: Pig's Eye's name was resurrected in the bars of St. Paul in the 1990s in an attempt to keep the old Schmidt Brewery on West Seventh Street afloat. A new company was founded selling a pale lager beer under the Pig's Eye brand, and St. Paul City Council member Dave Thune posed as the image of Pierre Parrant for the label. Though the brand lasted for less than two decades, the signs advertising Pig's Eye beer can still be seen hanging over the doors of select St. Paul dives, a symbol of an unpretentious good time.

"Every comfort and convenience that an establishment of the kind can afford."

ALEXIS CLOUTIER'S BOWLING SALOON

1850–1852

MARSHALL STREET AT DANA STREET (NOW FIFTH AVENUE NORTHEAST), ST. ANTHONY (NOW MINNEAPOLIS)

Alexis and Theodose Cloutier arrived in the Minnesota Territory in 1843, about the same time that Pig's Eye Parrant sold his claim on the lower levee. Alexis Cloutier, like Pig's Eye, was born in Canada, spoke French as his first language, and was eager to make a living in the liquor business. He was a generation younger than Pig's Eye, arriving in the territory with his young family amid a group of other French Canadians from Quebec via the Red River and Pembina settlements. The Cloutiers settled for a time in St. Paul and then moved upriver to the village of St. Anthony, on the east bank of the Mississippi River at St. Anthony Falls.

The village of St. Anthony, despite being just a few miles up the road, was very unlike the city of St. Paul.

St. Anthony did not boast a particularly wild atmosphere, nor did its sister city of Minneapolis on the other side of the falls, with which it would merge in 1867. Most of the inhabitants likely would have agreed with the assessment of the *Minnesota Register* in 1849 that "the number of retail liquor establishments in St. Paul and other towns in the Territory is a LEETLE too great for a sound and healthy State of public morals," concluding that it was "the subject of remark by strangers and gives us a bad name at home and abroad to say nothing of its evil effects upon society."

In 1850, when Alexis Cloutier opened his bowling saloon at Marshall and Dana Streets, near the steamboat landing, his was the only saloon in a town of forty-five hundred people. There were seven churches, nine sawmills, two newspapers, and a pervasive spirit of Yankee rectitude among the New Englanders who settled the city. There was not much tolerance for the brand of amusement and gaiety Cloutier was interested in. "We have a small police force organized, that we may be fully equipped," proclaimed the introduction to the city directory that year, "but there is not much for them to do. The people are well disposed, love to go in the way of usefulness, rather than in the way of vice and immorality."

Cloutier was probably aware of this. Shortly after he opened his saloon, he took out an ad in the *St. Anthony Express*, making a case for his new place in exceptionally genteel terms: "Alexis Cloutier begs leave to inform his friends and the public generally that he has completed a new Bowling Saloon at the Falls (near the Steamboat Landing), and he now flatters himself that all who feel inclined to patronise him will find every comfort and convenience that an establishment of the kind can afford."

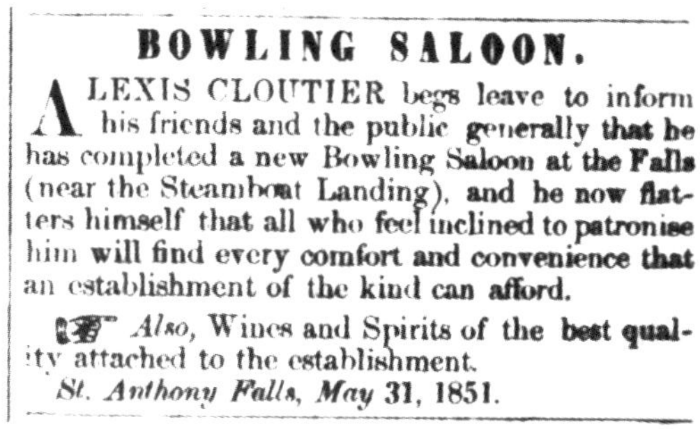

BOWLING SALOON.

ALEXIS CLOUTIER begs leave to inform his friends and the public generally that he has completed a new Bowling Saloon at the Falls (near the Steamboat Landing), and he now flatters himself that all who feel inclined to patronise him will find every comfort and convenience that an establishment of the kind can afford.

☞ *Also*, Wines and Spirits of the best quality attached to the establishment.

St. Anthony Falls, May 31, 1851.

Newspaper item announcing the opening of Alexis Cloutier's Bowling Saloon near Steamboat Landing in St. Anthony, May 1851. *Minnesota Historical Society Collections*

Almost as an afterthought, he added: "Also, Wine and Spirits of the best quality attached to the establishment."

Cloutier's only St. Anthony–based industry peer was the German immigrant John Orth, who'd arrived from Alsace-Lorraine in 1848. That year, he opened the state's second brewery (after Yoerg's in St. Paul), located at Marshall Street and what would soon become known as Brewery Street. Orth took out an announcement right above Cloutier's in the *Express*: "I am now prepared to supply the citizens of the Territory with Ale and Beer, which will be found equal—yes superior—to what is brought from below. I am now demonstrating that malt liquors of the very best quality can be manufactured in Minnesota." Orth succeeded wildly: his brewing company was the largest in the region by 1875, operating eighteen breweries across the state. Brewery Street is now known as Thirteenth Avenue, but it's still the site of the imposing Grain Belt Brewery building, formerly the home of the Minneapolis Brewing Company, successor to Orth's original company.

Residents of and visitors to St. Anthony could also get a drink at Cheever's Tower, a ninety-foot lookout tower and tourist attraction a bit farther downriver. Cheever boasted a ladies' saloon on the first floor, offering ice cream and sparkling water, and a second-floor men's saloon serving good old-fashioned American hard cider and—improbably—featuring a small menagerie consisting of two raccoons.

That was about it, though. And while Orth sold his product all over Minnesota, not just St. Anthony, and Cheever's Tower was less a neighborhood destination than an attraction for travelers and tourists, Cloutier's saloon was right in the heart of the village, stumbling distance from Main Street and the burgeoning milling and commercial district. Bowling saloons were popular in the East in the 1840s, and you could find beautifully appointed examples as far west as Illinois and Wisconsin. During this period, the bowling saloon straddled the line between respectability and vice. They were very masculine spaces, thick with cigar smoke and lined with spittoons. Gambling was common. Visiting New York City in 1842, Charles Dickens made note of "a painted lamp direct[ing] you to the Bowling Saloon or Ten Pin alley, Ten Pins being a game of mingled chance and skill invented when the legislature passed an act forbidding Nine Pins." Because of this association with gambling and games of chance, bowling in all of its iterations was frequently a target of legislation. It was banned outright in McLeod County in central Minnesota.

In spite of—or because of—this tinge of illicitness, Minnesota men enjoyed visiting bowling saloons like Cloutier's. The English writer Laurence Quincy traveled through Minnesota in 1855 and paid a visit to a bowling saloon in St. Paul. His description gives a sense for what Cloutier's place may have been like: "The roughest characters from all parts of the West between the Mississippi and the Pacific collect here and from morning till night shouts of hoarse laughter, extraordinary and complicated imprecations, the shrill cries of the boy-markers calling the game and the booming of the heavy bowls are strangely intermingled, and you come out stunned with noise and half blinded with tobacco smoke." He also gives a glimpse into the polyglot crowd you might have found in such a saloon: "Of course the Anglo-Saxon language in its varied modifications of Yankee English, Scotch and Irish prevails, but there is plenty of good French and the voyageur *patois,* Chippewa or Sioux, German, Dutch and Norwegian."

Quite a few St. Anthonyites were not pleased with this sort of commotion in the heart of their industrious community. In 1852, the *St. Anthony Express* inaccurately claimed that its city did not have a single "drinking saloon, or a whiskey grocery, or a grog shop" in town. "We have no room for those who frequent such places," sneered the editorialist. The decade of the 1840s and early 1850s saw a wave of temperance agitation in the Minnesota Territory. Activists took cues from New England, then a hotbed of prohibitionist sentiment. After the state of Maine passed the most comprehensive anti-liquor legislation in the nation in 1851, completely outlawing the manufacture and sale of alcohol in the state, the Minnesota Territory soon followed suit. On April 5 of the following year, a territory-wide referendum was held on the question of prohibition. It passed 853–662. Minnesota would be, as of May 5, 1852, a dry territory. Church bells rang throughout the territory—even in St. Paul, as booze-soaked a city as anywhere in the old Northwest.

Cloutier must have watched these developments with unease. However, though he was a barkeeper, he was also no Pig's Eye Parrant, no pariah who'd be run out of town. He served as a county commissioner a few years later, and by 1852, he likely had already cultivated some political connections. He knew whom to call on.

On April 29, a week before the law was to take effect, Cloutier paid a visit to two county commissioners, who issued him a liquor license good for "one year." To what degree these two elected officials were acting in good faith, or even if they were in agreement with one another, isn't clear; when Cloutier was later brought before the courts, the opposing counsel contended that it was "a fact notoriously public that the only one of the Commissioners who could write his name, or read and understand the Law, protested against the giving of this and other licenses."

Regardless, Cloutier got his license. That gave him time to figure out his next move. Gambling, smoking, and bowling went on as per usual throughout May and June on the corner of Marshall and Dana.

Sometime in June, three of Cloutier's neighbors went to the city police to complain. Sheriff George Brott stopped by with a warrant, arrested Cloutier, and confiscated three barrels of booze. He was said to be "threatened with formidable resistance" from some of Cloutier's patrons, "red shirted lumbermen from the Falls," but Brott rolled the barrels out of the saloon and into a storage warehouse a few blocks away. Cloutier appeared in court shortly thereafter and pleaded not guilty. His attorney argued that his right to continue to sell liquor was not based on abstract permission, but rather on an authorized, physical piece of paper from the commissioners, which he presented to the judge, asserting, "There is no dodging it, no getting behind it, nor before it." Nevertheless, Cloutier was found guilty and fined either twenty or twenty-five dollars, depending on which account you believe.

Cloutier appealed the case to Justice H. Z. Hayner, newly appointed to the territorial supreme court. There, a funny thing happened.

Hayner, after reviewing the case and another one like it involving a St.

Anthony commission merchant, ruled that the law under which Cloutier had been charged was unconstitutional. In short, territorial legislative power was vested in the legislative assembly and governor, and they had, in the words of a contemporary account, "no right or authority to delegate it to any body of persons—not even to the people of the Territory." The results of the referendum were overturned, and prohibition fervor in the territory dissipated for the immediate future. Sheriff Brott was left in the embarrassing situation of having to return Cloutier's product to him. "After Heyner's [*sic*] decision was made," he recalled decades later, "I went to return the liquors but found that some one had gotten under the building and bored a hole through the floor and casks and drawn off all the liquors; consequently I had to pay."

"I was not sorry when I had no more seizures to make in that line," he added. Hopefully, Cloutier had the decency to buy him a drink.

In the months leading up to the passage of nationwide Prohibition in 1919, Cloutier and Justice Hayner were fondly recalled by wet sympathizers as two nearly forgotten individuals who'd held off the cause of prohibition in the state for two generations.

Cloutier remained in the saloon business through at least 1860. He owned and operated a bar near St. Peters and St. Martin's Streets (Ninth and Tenth Avenues Northeast), a few blocks from the site of the bowling alley. He eventually moved to Dayton, Minnesota, where he lived a quiet life on a farm until his death in 1881.

Cloutier was a man devoted to his family and his trade. On the occasion of her eighty-sixth birthday in 1936, more than fifty years after Alexis died, his youngest daughter, Harriet, celebrated by uncorking and enjoying a sort of family heirloom. It was a bottle of wine made from elderberries her father had picked along the banks of the Mississippi River in Minneapolis in 1859, not far from his bowling saloon.

"Gemütlichkeit!"

WALDMANN'S SALOON

1857–1863

445 SMITH AVENUE NORTH, ST. PAUL

Through its first decades, from 1840 into the 1850s, St. Paul was notorious for saloons and whiskey, and visitors to the small city on top of the Mississippi River seemed to compete to describe the drunkenness that gripped St. Paul's citizens every day. The best comes from an 1848 fur company executive, whose account captures the proper finger-wagging tone: "Almost every house is either a shop or a grocery [aka tavern], and certainly a grocery keeper cannot complain that he has had no patronage, for drinking whisky seems to occupy at least half the time of the worthy citizens of St. Paul's [*sic*] while the balance of their time is employed in cheating each other or imposing upon strangers."

Heading into the boom years of the 1850s, St. Paul was an elastic proposition, a mercurial port at the far northern reaches of the Mississippi that was transforming into a dynamic mix of frontier diversity and an influx of the new, especially speculators, vagabonds, and European immigrants. The city's population shrank or grew with the stark seasons, and winter was hard. Workers migrated south when the ice stopped up the river—the city's lifeline—and sidelined the hundreds of riverboats that brought travelers to the city in temperate months. After the spring thaw, St. Paul leapt back to life. Boats streamed up to the upper and lower landings to unload passengers and every type of cargo and supply before being filled with firewood for the return trip downstream.

In 1852, there weren't even ten thousand people living in St. Paul, puny by St. Louis standards, but by the end of the decade, the population had tripled, bursting with German, Irish, and other immigrants fleeing hardship and political repression. Inspired by the ubiquitous ads in the eastern press, they arrived in Minnesota for the promises of opportunity and land. The city's slapdash wooden buildings filled with newcomers, and the population boom fueled real estate speculation and interest in every kind of business venture. For better and worse, St. Paul was ripe with opportunity.

At the same time, the influx of the mostly Catholic immigrants transformed the liquor politics of the state, as many of these newcomers were amenable to beer and whiskey and did not view the consumption of alcohol as an inherent moral failing. The dreams of the early domestic settlers, mostly Yankee Protestants, quickly vanished, along with the chances of enforcing the so-called Maine Law, a prohibition on booze. In a quirk of political timing and judicial activism, the prohibition era in nineteenth-century Minnesota lasted only six months, quickly vanishing even in moralistic Minneapolis as a new alcohol culture arrived along with the beer-loving Germans.

Notably, the *Deutsches* migrants packed with them the recipe and yeast needed for bottom-fermenting lager beer, and a "lager beer craze" transformed the Upper Midwest. St. Paul itself offered fertile ground for the new brew, as the city's older saloons had been serving primarily whiskey or other strong spirits. Perhaps they might have had wine, mead, or a selection of beer, all of which would have been the dark English-style ales. In contrast, the German-style beers were lighter in body and had the appearance, at least, of being less intoxicating than the dark ales and whiskeys.

The first brewery in the area was called Yoerg's, near the upper landing. Just upstream from downtown, the Christopher Stahlmann Brewing Company (the site of the Schmidt Brewery complex today) popped up along the bluff shortly afterward, making its famous "Cave Lager." By the mid-1850s, a handful of breweries, like Funk's, Worm's, and Banholzer, were clustered around the edges of St. Paul, especially in the fast-growing German neighborhoods along the bluffs.

This 1883 map of St. Paul shows the location of Waldmann's saloon on Forbes Street (now Smith Avenue). *Minnesota Historical Society Collections*

Emigrants from Bavaria, Anton and Wilhelmina Waldmann were some of the new faces in town, arriving together from St. Louis on a riverboat into Minnesota Territory in 1856. During their first few summers in the city, the Waldmanns made a not insignificant pile of money selling hardwood to steamboat captains desperate for fuel for the return trip downriver. Anton leased a new limestone building on Forbes Street in 1857 and soon began running a saloon there. The gray stone building, with its three-foot-thick walls, was one of the more stately German lager saloons in St. Paul at the time, and the nicest beer joint in the Forbes Street neighborhood, but it was just one of a dozen new German saloons that had begun serving lager in the years before the Civil War.

For a few years, Waldmann had the perfect spot from which to ply his trade. Waldmann's Saloon was right on the busy mostly unplatted oxcart

SUMMIT AVE.
VIRGINIA
LAUREL
NELSON
LOUIS
CARROLL
SUMMIT AVE
FIFTH
AVE.
CHESTNUT
PLEASANT
SHERMAN
OAK ST.
WALNUT
ST.
LISBON
SMITH
DOUGLAS
ST.
LEECH ST.
Mc BOAL
WILKIN ST.
GOODRICH
FORBES
BANFIL ST.

road leading from St. Paul and the river landings to points west, like Fort Snelling, St. Anthony, Shakopee, or the distant Red River settlements. The road zigged and zagged its way along the edge of the river bluffs toward the ferry over the Mississippi, and the street outside Waldmann's bustled with coaches, horses, oxen, and cart drivers on their way out of town.

The saloon itself was a solid two-story building erected from gray Platteville limestone. Two entrances opened onto a wide planked sidewalk fronting the dirt of Forbes Street; the left entrance went upstairs to the Waldmanns' private apartment, and the right led into the small two-room saloon. It was a remarkably sturdy structure for a saloon; most of the other lager joints or Yankee saloons elsewhere in town were made of wood.

If you walked into Waldmann's on an autumn afternoon, you likely would have found the low-ceilinged, bare-planked-floor saloon half full of men sitting around wooden tables, talking business or politics and smoking cigars or pipes. Cheap lithographs would be mounted on the wall depicting various heroes of failed European rebellions, and the men would be nibbling on pickles, wurst, and pig's feet. There would surely be a cask of cool lager fresh from the cellar, and if you were lucky, there might be an older Bavarian playing folk tunes on a zither. Notably, during the day, you might even find women taking their places among the men, joining in the conviviality, some with their children on the floor, sampling food off china plates.

Waldmann's Saloon reached its peak on Sundays, when St. Paul's burgeoning German community came together under the banner of *gemütlichkeit*—an idealistic pan-German attitude of welcoming good cheer—and on weekends, Waldmann's became a biergarten for a day or two. Coming straight from church, dressed in their finest attire, optimistic *Deutsches Volk* gathered around long tables and beer barrels to toast their forthcoming prosperity in the new country and to exchange all kinds of gossip. There might have been a brass player or two wandering around, playing Bavarian and Prussian folk songs, and new cousins might appear in old suits.

Sundays were when St. Paul's Germans were on full display, much to the displeasure of the city's temperance community, which had a while back passed a Sunday temperance law. The law read: "That such saloon, house or place shall be closed on and during Sunday, and at and after 12 o'clock at night, of each day, and that therein no spirituous or intoxicating liquors shall be sold, given to or disposed of to any person then being intoxicated, or who shall be a habitual drunkard, or to any minor or any person of unsound mind."

Thankfully for saloonkeepers like Waldmann, the rule was rarely enforced within St. Paul's borders.

As the new German folk faced off against the old guards—both the

Yankee teetotaler tradition and the whiskey-soaked frontier culture—defending the morality of German lager became a big issue in local politics. Ambitious Minnesota politicians who wanted the support of the rapidly growing German population had to weigh carefully how tightly they embraced temperance, prohibition, or the legacy of frontier slavery.

Waldmann's Saloon lasted only six years. The end of Waldmann's began when the building's once-prime location on Forbes Street became a liability. For years in booming St. Paul, there had been plans to straighten the winding "Fort Road." For city leaders, running the road in a straight line from the city's core out to the fort ferry crossing represented a big leap forward. The catch had always been figuring out how to buy the land rights off the landholders, exchanging deeds for land titles at the edge of the city like so many poker chips.

The current incarnation of Waldmann Brewery and Wurstery.
Photo by Anna Botz

Then the deep national recession of the late 1850s changed everything. Following the Panic of 1857 and the crash of the banks, real estate speculation tanked. Landowners who had been stubborn holdouts soon became eager sellers, and in 1860 the city leaders put their plans for the new Fort Road into action. By the early 1860s, the parade of wagons and wanderers heading back and forth between St. Paul and the fort were following the new road that shot like an arrow through the grid of old streets toward the Fort Snelling ferry. Sadly for Waldmann, the route passed a few blocks away from the saloon's impressive stone building, isolating it from the steady flow of traffic.

Soon after the road was completed, Anton Waldmann sold the building and opened up a grain and seed business closer to downtown. The Waldmanns lived upstairs for a time before moving back to their German homeland in 1886. By then, the railroad had arrived at the base of the river bluff. While it connected St. Paul to points west, the new tracks and the large retaining wall separated the neighborhoods around Forbes Street from the river below. The limestone building that had once held Waldmann's Saloon eventually became housing as business shifted to the bustling Fort Road a few blocks away. After the city built a bridge to the West Side in 1889, the corner of McBoal Street and the now-renamed Smith Avenue became busy again. But by then, the old saloon was a distant memory.

However, the saloon's geographically marginal location proved a boon in the end. Thanks in part to its isolation from the rhythms of the city's economic progress, the old saloon building remained standing through more than a century of neighborhood transitions. Today, behind the painstaking work of preservationists, the building has been restored to its previous incarnation as a saloon, and the Waldmann Brewery is open for business, operating a taproom serving traditional German American lagers to the public once again. You can visit it today and imagine what it might have been like in the 1850s, at the beginning and the end of an era.

“First and last chance for the West Siders.”

CANTIENY’S SALOON

1874–1883

1 NICOLLET AVENUE, MINNEAPOLIS

As was the case in most American cities in the late nineteenth century, Minneapolis and St. Paul were home to a handful of so-called last chance saloons. This was a common name given to saloons situated between two different municipalities, especially those with two different sets of vice laws. The first and the most prominent locally was Bill Bircher’s on the West Side of St. Paul, but there were others by the end of the 1870s. Mostly, they were clustered along the borders of the two cities, such as Como Avenue between Minneapolis and St. Paul or North Washington Avenue heading out west. By the early decades of the next century, last chance saloons were considered a convention of the late nineteenth century, and the name appeared on a wistful list published in the *Minneapolis Star* in 1930 alongside tintypes, square dances, opry houses, sunbonnets, town drunkards, and fallen women as memory markers of the era.

Casper Ober Cantieny and his son Antony operated such a saloon. Cantieny’s last chance saloon wasn’t fundamentally different from the 114 other licensed saloons in Minneapolis in 1875, but it had one big advantage: Cantieny’s had the best street address in town. It was located at No. 1 Nicollet Avenue, in Bridge Square, right at the foot of the Hennepin Avenue suspension bridge. “First and last chance for the West Siders,” it was said, at a time when memories of St. Anthony and the East Side as a distinctly different municipality were fresh in people’s minds. As early as 1874, the location of Cantieny’s saloon was listed in the city directory as simply “Nicollet Avenue near the bridge.”

Cantieny's Saloon, located in the building on the right in this 1877 photo, was Minneapolitans' last chance for a drink before crossing over into the once separate city of St. Anthony. *Minnesota Historical Society Collections*

That bridge, built in 1851, was, according to an 1855 headline in the St. Paul *Daily Minnesotan,* the first to cross the Mississippi anywhere along the river. It was elegant, in a crude, timber-framed sort of way, but the second Hennepin Avenue Bridge, built in 1876, was a real beauty. It was the city showing off a little civic muscle: made with stone, the bridge rose above the river like a storybook castle. Any photograph of the new Hennepin Avenue Bridge was an advertisement for Cantieny's—there it was, prominently appearing to the right of the bridge when photographed. Cantieny was a carpenter by trade, and he might very well have built the saloon with his own hands.

The two-story saloon was nothing special, but it looked like a comfortable place to spend a few hours. It was a classic western-style false front structure, the kind romanticized by Hollywood a half century later, a gabled building hiding behind a whitewashed wood façade crowned by a parapet. In 1875, all but ten of Minneapolis's saloonkeepers lived upstairs over their establishments, and the Cantienys were no exception. To the right of the building, a covered stairway led to the family's upstairs apartment. No written record of the interior of Cantieny's saloon survives, but it likely looked and felt much like other saloons around the Cities, with a long bar and a mirror and spittoons. It probably served oysters, sardines, and pig's feet, and whiskey and Orth beer. It likely had, in the words of one historian writing ninety years later about the American neighborhood saloon, "a fusty, musty odor, damp and clammy, an odor compounded of sawdust, tobacco juice, malt, metal polish and whiskey."

Maybe Casper Cantieny's modesty prevented him from putting up a huge "Last Chance" sign outside to take advantage of the real estate. But hell, it was located at No. 1 Nicollet Avenue, occupying the block halfway between the new city hall and the new bridge. Anyone walking by was a potential customer, and people were always walking by. There were no fewer than seventy-five saloons to choose from in Bridge Square in 1875, within a block of Casper's place, but Cantieny's was the first chance and the last chance for the West Siders.

Casper was born in the Swiss canton of Graubünden in 1807. He arrived in America in his mid-forties, moving from Ohio to Illinois to Minnesota, where there was already a sizable Swiss immigrant community. Casper married later in life, to another Swiss native named Mary, at age fifty-one. His daughter Mary was born in 1857 and Antony, or Tony, the next year. Swiss immigrants to Minnesota were noted as master carpenters and brewers, and Casper worked in both fields. Before running a saloon, he made a living as a carpenter, and he brought up his son in the same trade. Despite his advanced age, Casper served in the Civil War in the cavalry.

By the 1870s, Casper and Tony had built the saloon at No. 1 Nicollet, selling cigars and candy along with liquor. Casper dealt with the usual occupational hazards. He was occasionally fined for selling liquor to a minor. Sometimes, he'd be fined for letting people in on Sunday, when saloons were required by law to be closed. Sunday was usually the day the floors were cleaned, and the back doors of saloons all over town were left open to air out the rooms. Surely there was no harm in letting a thirsty friend wander in through the back door for a quick drink, even if it was the Sabbath? "A good prayer at church in the forenoon balances the afternoon sales and squares accounts with God," wrote one "Handy Andy" in the *St. Paul Globe* about this time. If you got caught by a passing patrolman, you might receive a small fine.

Generally, though, Casper had a good reputation around the city. He was the kind of guy you'd like to find behind the bar. He looked much younger than his years, seeming "to have borne his life easily," according to one contemporary.

Tony was said to strongly resemble his father, but the son did not inherit his father's easygoing disposition or his good reputation. "A home bred rough," according to some accounts. "A tough" and "a desperado" elsewhere. "One of the nerviest and most brutal toughs ever known by the Police," according to yet another. Tony had been sent to reform school at age fourteen for larceny. Through his young adulthood, he was in and out of prison, holding down intermittent work as a carpenter and behind his father's bar. He seemed to be looking for trouble. In 1884, he found it.

A few minutes before midnight on July 25, 1884, Tony wrapped up a shift at Cantieny's and headed out with two friends to go "on a tare" [*sic*] around some after-hours bars in the neighborhood. At some point, Tony returned to Cantieny's and pocketed a pistol that one of the regulars, a lumberman, had pawned for some cash earlier in the day. A central gathering place for the community, neighborhood saloons saw a great deal of informal lending and banking at the time. Some lumberman probably wanted money for a drink, and Casper was happy to oblige by holding on to his pistol as collateral until payday. Tony and his friends went out again, "raising cain." At about 4 AM, they made their way home, thoroughly drunk.

Somewhere on North Washington, they ran into a police officer named Laughlin. All parties were vaguely acquainted; Tony and his boys thought of Laughlin as a real Yankee bumpkin, fresh out of the backwoods of Maine. Laughlin himself had only been on the force for two months; before serving as a police officer, he'd been an undertaker, riverboat clerk, and cook, and he had even run a saloon himself. Words were exchanged, and some kind of altercation followed. Then Laughlin attempted to arrest the gang. Tony and his boys ran, and Laughlin pursued. Whistles were blown; reinforcements were called in. Laughlin may have fired on Tony. Tony turned, yelled, "You can't arrest me, you son of a bitch," and shot blindly back at the officer with the lumberman's pistol. He managed to hit Laughlin's torso. Tony then fled the scene, threw the pistol into nearby Bassett's Creek, and headed back to Cantieny's to clean up. There he was arrested a few hours later. Laughlin, gravely wounded, was rushed to the hospital. He made his statement on his deathbed, accusing Tony of the crime. Shortly thereafter, he died. Laughlin is believed to be the first police officer killed in the line of duty in the city of Minneapolis.

When Tony was arraigned the next day, he didn't seem worried. He was smiling, joking, and puffing a cigar. The mood darkened quickly, though. Word spread throughout the city about the slaying of the police officer, and people were furious. A mob formed around the county jail. It consisted mostly of young men, "small boys and riff raff . . . without a leader," according to an eyewitness account. The youth yelled for Tony, demanding he be hanged and offering to do it themselves. At some point, the mob rushed the prison, broke down the front doors, and were only held off from carrying Tony out and hanging him by a number of police officers armed with rifles. A full-fledged riot broke out, and the situation was serious enough that the mayor requested assistance from the state militia. "They're a pack of cowardly damned fools," Tony was reported to yell toward the mob. "I ain't afraid of no crowd like that." After things had cooled down a bit, Tony was quietly transferred to St. Paul to await trial.

Tony pled self-defense. He was charged with second-degree manslaughter and sentenced to seven years at Stillwater prison.

Casper Cantieny spent years courting politicians for a pardon, spending huge amounts of money in the process, and becoming tangled up in a number of lawsuits himself. He ultimately persuaded Governor Andrew McGill of his case, and Tony was released in 1888, having served only four years. He seemed genuinely penitent. "I never should have done it if I'd been sober," he told the press upon leaving prison.

Penitent or not, both the Cantienys were ruined. Tony ran another saloon for several years on High Street and First Avenue, very close to the Hennepin Avenue Bridge in what had become by then a rapidly deteriorating part of the city, in the heart of its red-light district. He died in 1907 at the age of forty-nine.

Right up until he died in 1896, Casper also remained in the saloon business, moving farther out of the downtown core after he lost ownership of the building by the bridge. His last saloon and residence was at 815 Washington Avenue North. Just before the trouble with Tony began, he'd been evicted from No. 1 Nicollet Avenue to make room for the Minneapolis Union Depot that was being built at the confluence of Nicollet, Hennepin, and the bridge. The old saloon building was razed, and the 1 Nicollet Avenue address disappeared for good with Casper and Tony Cantieny's last chance saloon.

“High words in very low language”

AMERICAN HOUSE SALOON

1860s–1883

301 WABASHA STREET, ST. PAUL

In 1873, the American House sat in a prime location. The two-and-a-half-story wooden hotel, one of the block’s larger buildings, centered on its saloon, with swinging wooden doors that opened up on the corner of Wabasha and Fourth Streets in downtown St. Paul. Its wide wooden frontier sidewalks lifted pedestrians over the dirt and mud of the downtown streets, and the windows were opened in the warm months. As St. Paul’s growing population boomed, the streets overflowed, and the rooms of the American House filled with travelers to the new heart of the young Northwest. Wabasha Street itself led to the great St. Paul bridge, a spindle of iron road angling sharply down from the bluff to the west side of the river. Fourth Street was just far enough from the river and its bustling riverboat landings to offer some respite from the din of the packet boats and the smoke of the new railroads. That made the American House saloon a prime destination for the boosters, speculators, traders, adventure seekers, and various hucksters who flowed through St. Paul like flotsam down the Mississippi.

The name of the hotel itself is somewhat misleading to today’s ears. In the 1870s, the term *American* carried a specific identity and weight. In those days, it was the “American” House in contrast to the German House or the Irish or the Swedish. There were hotels called American House in towns and cities all over Minnesota, in Glencoe, Wabasha, Princeton, and elsewhere. Each was independent, but they shared a familiar, symbolic identity.

If you wanted a reputation as a frontier gent, the American House was the place to hole up, a natural address for the ambitious to board between stops out to the forest, the farm, or the territories to the west. Visitors arriving in St. Paul with a business idea and a few dollars in their pockets would put an ad in the paper for a land sale, an exchange of goods, or work wanted, listing their contact information only as American House. The city directory was full of these itinerant men (and, more rarely, women)—stagecoach drivers, clerks, cigar makers, printers, confectioners, and more—and the American House was their home in the city at the edge of the growing American empire. The hotel's saloon was the living room where men exchanged gossip, directions, sales pitches, insults, and blows—swimming in the timeless, mercurial mix of opportunity and limbo that marks any great hotel bar. They sang around the piano—one newspaper account described a pianist who "hammered the American House piano as if he foresaw he should never again see a musical instrument"—or sat around the backroom tables playing cards. And always, the men ran up tabs drinking great quantities of whiskey. One imagines the row of bottles behind the bar, the bartender continually filling smudged glasses or pouring small mugs of brown ale delivered by the handful to the wooden tables around the room, the clinking of glasses and the constant murmur of stories and laughter.

The American House, at the corner of Wabasha and Fourth Streets in St. Paul, circa 1873. *Minnesota Historical Society Collections*

The American had the additional good fortune of being just up the block from the offices of the *St. Paul Daily Globe,* a dramatic and opinionated rag brimming with ribald tales of daily comings and goings. The *Globe* published dozens of accounts of brawls and scandals that passed through the rooms of the American House. On slow days, *Globe* reporters might stop in the American House to grab a glass of whiskey and hunt for a lead for the front page. One such article from 1878—bearing the headline "GILL-FILLER GOBBLED"—told the story of one night at the American House around Election Day:

> *A knock down drag out row [with] parties engaged in the passage of the complements of the early morn. Tom McGovern, an employee of the water*

> *works, had been out all night electioneering. The fatigues of the nights' work forced McGovern to go into the bar room of the American House to brace up. There he met Kelly. Kelly's eyes wooed up as if he too had been electioneering, or more likely, as if he had been electioneered. They discussed the situation and slightly differed as to which was the true policy to be adopted in running the governmental machine. High words in very low language led to blows. . . . In the struggling they got into an adjoining card room. The door was locked, and they proceeded with their fun all alone, depriving several bystanders of the delight of the exhibition. In the midst of the political discussion, officer Kennaly came along and arrested both disputants, before the argument had been fully completed. Kelly seemed to have some strong points, and McGovern also appeared to have responded with force.*

Such was the state of late-night political debate at the American House saloon.

Another story describes the long jury sequestration for an infamous murder trial. The men involved were receiving two dollars a day for their juridical trouble and, as such, were apparently in no hurry to decide the fate of the accused. They were forcibly sequestered in the American House for the duration, and despite the sheriff's official rules prohibiting the consumption of whiskey during the deliberations, the *Globe* tells how the jury smuggled liquor through the second-story hotel windows using ropes and accomplices on the street. They'd drink the whiskey from teacups to fool the sheriff, who must not have cared all that much, and "debated" the verdict playing cards, getting drunk, and earning a living. It was six weeks before they finally convicted the suspect.

The American House saloon was kept by a fellow named Gil Pottgeiser, who tried but often failed to run a tight ship in a town full of frontier alcoholics. Through the doors passed a constant parade of speculators, fortune seekers, traders, and, for one week in 1878, a dozen raw recruits for the Seventh Calvary—General Custer's old regiment.

Pottgeiser had owned a few different saloons in St. Paul's early days, and the American House was the finest of them. Like any saloonkeeper, Pottgeiser had a stern demeanor. One *Globe* story from 1880 tells of a famous bouncing accident:

> *A few minutes to 4 o'clock yesterday afternoon, young Albertson, which is one of the properties of the C. O. D. Laundry, called at the American House with regard to some clothing. He passed from the office to the bar room and called for drinks. The remark was made that he was already*

> *indebted for drinks to the extent of 85 cents and that he must settle the old score before receiving additional accommodations. He replied that such was not the case, but that the House owed him for laundry work. However this may be, Albertson became noisy and vituperative. . . .*
>
> *During the talk between Albertson and the barkeep, Gilbert Pottgeiser entered the saloon and asked what the trouble was about. Words ensued, and it is said that the former called Pottgeiser some very hard names.*
>
> *The men each held a beer glass, and, becoming riled, Pottgeiser threw his glass at Albertson, which in passing struck a wooden screen and was broken, a fragment of the glass striking Albertson in the neck and inflicting the wound. When Albertson reached the street he turned and broke two panes of glass in the window with his fists.*
>
> *[Pottgeiser] states, however, that in throwing the glass he did not intend to hit Albertson, but merely to strike the screen and frighten him out of the saloon. It is said that Albertson has the reputation of being a wild young man with a quick and quarrelsome temper. But that is neither here nor there. The deed has been done, and the free use of hard names is no justification for assaults of this kind, which have become fearfully common in St. Paul. It is time for public sentiment to stamp with its victim the severest condemnation on affairs of this kind, and show the hot blooded gentry that vagrant passion cannot be exercised in so wanton a manner with impunity.*

By the time the 1880s arrived, along with the bustling new railroads and thousands of new citizens, the American House and its saloon were becoming a thing of the past. The city's frontier days gave way to a new era of industrial expansion, and the new buildings downtown were dwarfing the old wood hotels. Gil Pottgeiser died in 1883, and by October, his estate was auctioned off.

Today, the site remains in the heart of downtown St. Paul. The massive brick Lowry Building, onetime home of the Oz nightclub and today a classy bar and restaurant called Grey Duck, sits on the same corner, still serving whiskey and hosting late-night political debate.

"The last of the frontier hangouts"

JUMBO SALOON

1885–1910

208–210 SOUTH WASHINGTON AVENUE, MINNEAPOLIS

Captain Al Schaefers was the toast of Minneapolis on the evening of the Fourth of July, 1886. His saloon, the Jumbo, had the most beautiful outdoor garden in the city, and, with the patriotic zeal of a relatively recently arrived immigrant, he was hosting a blowout birthday party for the Republic.

"Captain" seems to have been a mostly ceremonial designation, but Albert Schaefers was very active in local Democratic politics. He led an independent Democratic organization composed at its peak of about a thousand so-called Mugwumps who'd bolted from the Republican Party in disgust at the perceived corruption and nativism of James G. Blaine, the party's candidate for president in the 1884 election. Although the Mugwumps had failed to sway Minnesota's seven electoral votes to Grover Cleveland, Captain Al made quite a show leading a division of Mugwumps and Democrats in a victory parade for President Cleveland down Washington Avenue in subzero temperatures and howling snow that November. The cohort of men, kitted out in improvised uniforms, toted fireworks, brass instruments, torches, and banners reading "Honesty Will Rule" and "Our Adopted Country Forever."

Schaefers was also well liked among the higher-ups in Mayor A. A. "Doc" Ames's notoriously corrupt Democratic Party machine. Captain Al incorporated a political organization at his saloon called the Jumbo Club, devoted to the advancement of Democratic politics in the ward—and of his own fledgling political career.

As involved as he was in politics, Schaefers was at heart a saloonkeeper, a lover of pageantry, spectacle, and excess. After immigrating to Minnesota from the Rhine-Hesse region of Germany, he got his start running a saloon on the outskirts of Minneapolis, where he lived with his wife, Dina, and their son, John. They were known for serving beer in earthenware mugs marked, in a Teutonic blackletter script, "COFFEE," either as a joke, an elaborate effort to circumvent liquor laws, or a little of both.

In 1885, he acquired a second saloon in downtown Minneapolis, a converted two-story farming machinery warehouse described by contemporary viewers as "barnlike." The saloon originally had opened as Orchestrion Hall in 1873, a venue that served German lager and housed a German-made orchestrion that played popular tunes of the day. A few years later, a group of cigar makers acquired the hall and tried to expand on the German concept by installing a beer garden. Upright (and uptight) Yankee Minneapolis perhaps wasn't ready, because it quickly failed. Schaefers redubbed the cavernous wooden barn the Jumbo—the famed elephant had died that year, and his name had become synonymous with gargantuan scale. Schaefers retained the German-style beer garden, and though it hadn't been his idea, he was the one who made it work. Within the year, the garden became one of the hottest spots in Minneapolis—and the target of the local chapter of the Woman's Christian Temperance Union, which frequently sent protestors to read biblical tracts and proselytize on-site, sometimes disguising themselves as members of the "undercrust" to gain entry and spring songs and sermons on the tipplers.

But in a provincial prairie town dominated by industry and the church, Schaefers's Jumbo was a fun, colorful place to relax, get a drink, and hear some music. On the Fourth of July, 1886, the garden was packed to capacity. The fireworks display Schaefers had rigged up was, according to the local paper, "one of, if not the finest in the city. . . . All manner of pyrotechnics were exploded."

"The scene," it added, "was a lively one."

A series of 1885 newspaper ads—taken out not in the Republican-leaning *Minneapolis Tribune* but in the Democratic-leaning *St. Paul Globe,* all the way across the river—gives a sense of the sort of snappy conversation Schaefers hoped you might find there:

> *"Have you seen Jumbo?"*
> *"What, Barnum's Jumbo?"*
> *"No; no; Schafer's* [sic] *new Jumbo, at 208 and 210 Washington avenue south. It has been elegantly fitted up and is just the place to spend a pleasant evening."*

Illustration from the *St. Paul Globe* depicting "the ladies and gents" at Jumbo Saloon, February 28, 1890

Depending on your priorities and social position within the community, you might regard the Jumbo in starkly different terms. Decades later, reminiscences of the Jumbo still appeared occasionally in print when the old days were being evoked. In the 1920s, evangelist and writer Reuben Archer Torrey recalled it as "the lowest saloon in the city," a place where alcoholic losers ended up, the last way station from respectability to the gutter. "One of the hell holes of Minneapolis," noted an elected official (and a Democrat, at that).

Others remembered it as "the famous Jumbo," last of the "frontier hangouts," where you might as easily be robbed in the alley as meet up with some colleagues. A railroad clerk named A. G. Long recalled years later about a fight between a gang of drunks and a "dude" in a silver-buttoned jacket who'd slipped in a mud puddle and was being laughed at—the dude took a run at the group, only to be interrupted when a bunch of other men suddenly ran out of the Jumbo past *him* in order to take hold of a passing streetcar and throw it off the tracks. The streetcar workers were on strike at the time, and the clientele of the Jumbo was sympathetic to the cause. Captain Al may well have been among them.

Such public images are built on unstable ground, though. Schaefers was, by 1887, a pillar of the local community, but he also appeared to be keeping some secrets about his financial solvency. Sometime that year, he skipped town, never to return. The Orth Brewing Company, to which he owed a great deal of money, first discovered his disappearance. They hired a detective agency to recover the debt or, failing that, the thousands of dollars' worth of barrels of wine and booze he'd acquired from them. They found instead mostly empty barrels that had been spirited away at different hiding locations around town. Schaefers had left, it was said, "numerous creditors, abandoned liabilities, and little or no assets." Where was he? Colorado or New Mexico, it was reported. It was even rumored he'd fled to the Democratic stronghold of St. Paul and landed in a hospital after drinking himself into a stupor.

Eventually, his old friends at the *Globe* reported he was "enjoying the cool breezes of California and writing to Minneapolis friends that he will probably remain there." It's not clear if he brought his family with him or not. His creditors, it was said with some amusement, "are undergoing several kinds of torment as to how they are going to get their money." They probably never did. A few years later, Captain Schaefers was reported to be in California with another saloonkeeper named Colonel Jacob Becker, "amassing wealth rapidly" in an unnamed town. The Jumbo, the article wryly noted, "did not prove a goldmine" to Schaefers "during his brief administration."

It was not a goldmine for Schaefers, nor for anyone else. After his flight to the West Coast, the Jumbo went through a variety of owners—the local paper recounts a parade of hapless proprietors coming aboard, only to be run out or succeeded in short order by another, including a shadowy cabal referred to only as "Eastern capitalists." Orth Brewing took the business into receivership after Schaefers's disappearance, then sold it to another man, who turned it over to a nice mustachioed fellow named H. H. Brown (described in a newspaper profile as "good-natured and rotund"). Brown reverted to the Orchestrion Hall name and had big plans for cleaning the place up. He didn't last a year on the job.

In true Twin Cities fashion, people continued to refer to the saloon as "the Jumbo" long after that was the name in the city directories. But no longer were the orchestrion—still apparently functional after twenty hard years—and beer garden its main attractions. Instead, the Jumbo had become one of the premier houses of ill repute in Minneapolis, a space known for solicitation and a recruiting ground for vulnerable young women. It was generally regarded by moral members of the public as a place for "scarlet women and vile men." Located on the outskirts of the city's fast-growing red-light district to the east of Bridge Square, the Jumbo was one of the few establishments in the city where you'd find a mixed crowd of men and women drinking together—perhaps not on the first floor, but certainly on the second, which was advertised as "Ladies' and Gents' dining room and ice cream parlors." A contemporary description laid out the first floor like this: "The main theatre floor contains about 50 heavy oak tables with four chairs grouped about each table. The frequenters are supposed to put in their time drinking beer. In the dozen boxes surrounding the stage, bleached and painted women were installed whose sole business was to work fool patrons of beer." Upstairs, you bought a ten-cent ticket for entrance to a smoky auditorium, featuring performances by a mixed crowd of singers and dancers. The auditorium was flanked on either side by small rooms where—well, who knows what went on in there. Ice cream consumption, no doubt.

In an article from 1890, the *Minneapolis Journal*—passing judgment while also hinting that these spaces could be a respite for those left out of the mainstream of polite middle-class society—summed up much of the clientele: "Young unhappy girls of the poorer and more ignorant classes, unfortunate and deserted wives, working women whose lives and dismal homes make the glitter, the excitement and the free love-making of the place a fascination and a solace." The writer describes "four blank beer-stained walls," but that same year, his opposite number across the river at the *Globe* painted the scene at the Jumbo in a more appealing way: done up in "evergreens and bunting, and as the white wood-work is kept fairly clean, the place is not altogether uninviting."

The end was coming, though. By 1890, public panic about prostitution and "white slavery" was ramping up. "There is a feeling in the air that the Jumbo saloon has not long to live as a free and easy concert hall and beer garden," reported the *Tribune* in 1891. There had been a sense that the Jumbo was protected by powerful interests in the police department and local government; indeed, the evident indestructibility of Jumbo's liquor license was a frequently discussed topic in the press, at the saloons, and on the streets. However, pressure from temperance organizers and reformers prompted action from the authorities. It was about this time that the city passed an ordinance banning music in open gardens with liquor, with an eye on the Jumbo. This effectively put an end to the only other thing besides the orchestrion and prostitution that the Jumbo was known for.

In 1894, saloon and dance hall proprietor John C. Sodini stepped in, hoping to add the Jumbo to his vast portfolio of drinking establishments. Whatever dubious reputation the Jumbo might have had previously, the saloon completely tanked when Sodini came in. "It is very rare that a day

A "typical group" at Jumbo Saloon, according to this illustration from the February 28, 1890, edition of the *St. Paul Globe*

passes without the police having some trouble with Sodini, the Italian, and his numerous resorts," the *St. Paul Globe* scowled in 1892—and that was one of the more sympathetic comments the local press had about him. His specialty, it was said, was "lewd resorts where women show their nether limbs for the delectation of wayfaring lumbermen and itching harvest hands."

Sodini knew the Jumbo well, having operated a bar called the Casino across the alley on the same block for years—the local cops referred to the Jumbo and Casino as "Big Casino" and "Little Casino." Sodini received, after a few attempts, a liquor license for the Jumbo. He was said to be eager to employ "female beer jerkers" to work the bar. It didn't matter much who was jerking the beer, because in 1894, the tired old structure burned to the ground.

Sodini reopened a "New Jumbo" on the same site, which then went through another series of name changes to emphasize its usefulness as a theater: first the Jumbo Theater, then the Tivoli, then the Columbia, then the Empire. Sodini sold it and fled to St. Paul, but the joint's bad reputation lingered. Vaudeville came in, and the new ownership took a stab at capitalizing on that. However, when one actress murdered another backstage one evening—allegedly beating her to death with a chair—most people lost much interest in the place as anything other than an endlessly self-renewing source for seedy gossip. Whatever was on the marquee, most people continued to refer to the building at the corner of Washington Avenue South and Second Street as "the Jumbo" and the alley behind it as Jumbo Alley.

By about 1910, it was all done.

The US government was looking for a site for a new post office, and Block 40, which had housed the Jumbo and its various predecessors and successors since the 1870s, was chosen. The choice was intentional and encouraged by city fathers: it was a way to level the entire block and replace it with something uniform, respectable, and elegant—not *elegant* in the way an advertisement for the Jumbo describes elegance, but in the way the White City of the 1893 World's Columbian Exposition was *elegant*. "As a wiping out of memories," the *Tribune* editorialized in 1906, "the taking of block 40 would be a better sponge than" any other site. The planners and reformers won. Today, the building that succeeded the Jumbo is listed on the National Register of Historic Places, an old City Beautiful government building where you can get passports made.

Captain Al, the Jumbo's originator, seems to have disappeared from the historical record shortly after the building's demise. In that sense, Schaefers was, like the old-timer said of his bar, one of the last of the frontier types in Minneapolis: an ambitious young person who'd landed in this tiny river town from the East and blew through a lifetime of money, booze, and political influence in a few greedy years. Once he'd extracted what he wanted, he pulled up stakes and headed west, just as Minneapolis was becoming big and respectable.

Minneapolis would have its share of big-city hustlers, grifters, and unsavory characters in the decades to come, but Captain Al Schaefers of the Jumbo Saloon is maybe the last whose exit from the scene was quite so neat and so quintessentially nineteenth century—the last one so fitting for a tiny frontier town on the edge of the prairie.

"A first-class stimulant."

SCHIEK'S

1887–1971,
with occasional revivals through 2011

49 WASHINGTON AVENUE (1887–1894);
45–47 SOUTH THIRD STREET (1894–1960);
115 SOUTH FOURTH STREET (1961–2011), MINNEAPOLIS

Schiek's was a Minneapolis fine dining and drinking fixture for so long, and it outlived so many of its late-nineteenth-century peers, it accumulated a fantastic amount of mythology over the eight or so decades it was in operation. When the original closed for the first time in 1971, in its third location since 1887, the remembrances from longtime customers were flowing in the local press. It had been serving up drinks in downtown Minneapolis since 1862, it was recalled. So central was its first proprietor, Fred Schiek, to the city's liquor trade that his Minneapolis liquor license number was "1."

None of that was true, but enough time goes by, and these sorts of things take on their own truths. The history of bars is a generations-long game of telephone, even when—*especially* when—the verifiable details are impressive enough on their own.

The long history of Schiek's can be divided into three eras, based on its three locations. Each of these three eras parallels the general trajectory of saloon culture in Minneapolis so well (and, unlike a lot of Schiek's peers, the establishment is so copiously documented in photographs, news items, and papers) that this entire book could focus solely on Schiek's, and you'd get a lot of the same stories, themes, and ideas put across.

The first era is its start on Washington Avenue in 1887, where it served as a rough-and-tumble saloon of the sort we've already visited, notable for spittoons, oysters, and whiskey. Its second and best-loved location opened in 1894 at 45–47 South Third Street, an opulent saloon and restaurant behind a theater, playing host to both locals and international celebrities like Sarah Bernhardt and Abbott and Costello until it was demolished in the first wave of urban renewal in 1960. Its third and final act was at the old Farmers and Mechanics Savings Bank, the imposing neoclassical building on Fourth Street, from 1961 through 1971. After that, the site hobbled through a few different iterations, some of which used the Schiek's name, some of which didn't: a Canadian-owned chain spaghetti restaurant (not Schiek's), a disco (Schiek's again), a strip club (not Schiek's, then Schiek's again, and then not Schiek's). As of this writing, it's occupied by the Downtown Cabaret, a high-end topless bar, and the Schiek's name has been retired since about 2011. It's certainly possible at some point the name will be revived again. It's nothing if not durable.

Schiek's Cafe on South Third Street in Minneapolis, circa 1912. *Minnesota Historical Society Collections*

Fred Schiek and his son Louis arrived in Minneapolis in the mid-1880s from Baden, Germany, via Iowa. Early on, Fred Schiek managed a German-style beer hall on Hennepin, maybe the sort of place you'd go if the Jumbo was too crowded. In 1887, he opened a saloon and liquor wholesaler on Washington Avenue and First Avenue. Initially, it wasn't particularly distinguished from the dozens of other German immigrant-owned saloons nearby.

Even early on, though, Fred clearly had bigger ambitions than slinging rotgut to farmhands and lumbermen. He had an eye for how the place *looked,* more so than the typical saloonkeeper. "The windows are brilliant lighted and the many bottles of liquors reflect their varied hues with dazzling effect," recalled one writer of the saloon's façade in the final year on Washington.

Fred also had a talent for marketing to a more rarified crowd. Few of his competitors, for example, would have thought of running an advertisement in the local paper that consisted of sworn affidavits from two professional chemists, testifying to the medicinal-grade quality of Schiek's house brand, Private Stock Perfection of Fine Whiskey. It was found to be "entirely free from the presence of fuel oil and other substances" and "a strictly first-class stimulant."

Schiek's drew a lively and diverse crowd, ranging from laborers to politicians. The Minneapolis papers of the 1890s regularly reported on court cases in which some key piece of evidence was overheard at Schiek's. You never knew whom you might be sitting next to at the bar.

In 1893, an opportunity came in the form of an eviction: Jacob Barge, the owner of the Barge Block in which the saloon was located, got into a dispute with Fred over the renewal of his lease. The case went to the high courts, a judge ruled against Fred in 1894, and the Schieks were kicked out of the space. Fred got to work formulating a plan.

He found a new location, in a former pool hall, and held a grand opening on Saturday, June 30, 1894. It was behind the brand-new Metropolitan Theater, considered one of the finest theatrical venues in town. The new Schiek's consolidated all of Fred's ideas about the right way to run a saloon. First, the design was the most important consideration: out went the spittoons, gaslight, and pig's feet; in came the mahogany, potted plants, and electric lighting. Second, it would appeal to a wide range of clientele, with a particular eye on the aspirational tastes of the second- and third-generation European immigrants. (Its proximity to the theater district ensured that it would have a steady stream of visiting entertainers and bohemians as well as a significant gay clientele in the first half of the twentieth century.) "Originally famed for its excellent German Cuisine," went one advertisement, "it now caters to the taste and appetites of all nations." Moreover, it wouldn't be just for men—or the dining rooms wouldn't, at least. An ad in the back of an 1896 Bijou Theater flyer made note of the very modern improvement of a women's entrance, with an option of bypassing the saloon entirely for a separate ladies' dining room—"Peacock Alley," as it was known. (There remained a separate women's entrance as late as the end of World War II. After the war, the management decided that what might have seemed genteel and charmingly old-fashioned one or two decades earlier was painfully out of step with the atomic age.)

In the months after opening the new saloon, Fred and Louis made a substantial purchase that they intended to use as the showpiece for the saloon. At a cost later reported to be $25,000 (close to a quarter million dollars in today's money), they allegedly purchased a twelve-foot-high mahogany bar from the 1893 World's Columbian Exhibition in Chicago and had it transported back to Minneapolis. "It is forty feet long," a contemporary newspaper account recounted, "entirely of mahogany, with the counter fitted up with the latest and most improved appliances for attendants."

"There are six huge, fluted columns in it with caps and arches beautifully hand carved," the piece continued. "Under the arches are handsome French plate mirrors. In the center of the bar is a life-sized figure piece, which must have been taken from some art salon." This was no mean dive like the Jumbo.

Staff behind the bar at Schiek's, 1934. *Minnesota Historical Society Collections*

At the bar, the selection was cosmopolitan in scope: Havana cigars; imported pilsners from central Europe; lagers from the Löwenbräu Brewery of Germany; Bass ales and stouts from England; and German, French, and Spanish wines, all offered alongside beers from the Minneapolis Brewing Company, Blatz, Hamm's, and Schmidt. A little piece of doggerel used in Schiek's later advertising speaks to the expansive offerings: "The Frenchmen love their native wine / The Germans love their beer / The English love their half and half because it brings good cheer / The Irish love their whiskey because it brings them dizziness / The American has no choice at all / So he drinks the whole darn bus-i-ness."

"Seldom equaled is the place of Fred Schiek's for beauty," noted a *Minneapolis Tribune* editorial in 1894, "never surpassed for goods."

"Call and be astonished," Fred promised in an advertisement. People were.

Nostalgia, however, much like Fred's original Private Stock Perfection of Fine Whiskey, is a first-class stimulant.

In the decades following, after ownership had moved away from the Schiek family, memories became clouded and the legend grew—not just about Fred opening the place in 1862, or him having the city's first liquor license, but details about the bar itself. Published reports of the length of the original bar would extend it from forty feet to a hundred feet. The provenance of the bar, too, became less clear in retrospect: early accounts from 1894 merely note that the bar *resembled* the famed Transportation Building at the 1893 World's Fair, not that it *came* from the World's Fair (or the 1904 St. Louis World's Fair, as was also reported). As for the "life-sized figure . . . from some art salon," she would lose all of her clothing and transform from three dimensions to two in later tellings, going from a statue behind the bar to a painting covering the entire ceiling. Nudes were such a common part of saloon décor for so long that the mistake is understandable in retrospect, even though it flies in the face of Fred Schiek's aggressively tasteful modernization program for the saloon. Would he have tolerated something as gauche as a nude on the ceiling? Seems unlikely. In fact, the figure was known as "Becky," a gilt-plastered statue of a bonneted milkmaid holding a wine goblet, who seems to have appeared behind the bar sometime in the 1890s. Her origin is unknown, as is her ultimate fate. She didn't make the transition to the new site in 1961.

Fred died in 1904, and Louis took over the business. Under his purview, the focus shifted more and more to the restaurant side of things. Louis saw Schiek's through Prohibition, and the food, entertainment, and décor were classy enough that they never had to fall back on soda pop and near beer. When the original site was demolished in 1960, an old guest registry was located, including twin entries noting "bar closed, June 30, 1919," and fourteen years later, "beer back, April 7, 1933."

Louis died in 1941, and a local theater operator named Ben Berger bought Schiek's. He established a singing sextet and began producing the small-scale musical theatrical productions for which the restaurant became well known through the 1940s and '50s.

When Berger moved into the bank building on Fourth Street in 1961, chased out of the old Gateway District by the city, he brought a portion of the old mahogany bar with him. Incredibly, through all the subsequent iterations, it's still there, in the back of the strip club. Fred Schiek would likely not be crazy about the stripping. But at least part of him would be pleased that his mahogany bar, the centerpiece that remade his saloon from a German whiskey joint to a nationally celebrated fine dining destination, is still remarked upon, a century later.

“Time brings around all things.”

THE EUREKA

1887–1899

384 MINNESOTA STREET (1887–1889);
86 EAST FIFTH STREET (1889–1891);
90 EAST FIFTH STREET (1891–1898);
384 MINNESOTA STREET (1898–1899), ST. PAUL

Thomas Jefferson Sr. and John H. Cunningham worked together in St. Paul on and off for the better part of a decade. Jefferson was the outgoing one, the front man, the dandyish former boxing champion and political figure who could command a room. Cunningham was the quiet one, the manager, the money guy who stayed out of the limelight and kept the receipts in order. Jefferson and Cunningham were, by the estimation of the *Appeal,* the city's African American newspaper of record, two of the “best known colored citizens of St. Paul.” They shared a number of interests—boxing, Democratic politics, music, real estate, and liquor—and they made some combination of all of these a part of their livelihoods at the Eureka, the saloon they opened together in 1887 and ran for twelve years.

Jefferson arrived in Minnesota first, coming from Maryland in 1880. Within a few years, he was the black heavyweight boxing champion of St. Paul, and he was training other boxers. “Headquarters for exponents of the manly arts,” proclaimed an advertisement he took out in the papers. “For exercise, go to Tom's.”

By 1883, he had been involved in the creation of a Minnesota chapter of the Odd Fellows, as well as a league for black voters and a National Guard unit. He was deeply involved in the Democratic Party at a time when the vast majority of African Americans were still loyal to the party of Lincoln.

He was, it was said, "the first colored man in Minnesota to sever his allegiance from the Republican party and cast his political fortunes with the Democratic party."

Cunningham arrived in Minnesota a few years after Jefferson, and by 1887, the two men owned a real estate business at 86 East Fifth Street, at the corner of Minnesota Street. Both would work or live on this block for the next decade.

That year, the two men purchased a failing restaurant located at 384 Minnesota Street, just a half block from the real estate office. It was called the Eureka, and they retained the name. They also acquired a precious liquor license. "There are only 312 saloons that have stood the $1,000 license," reported the *Appeal* in February 1887, referring to St. Paul's newly increased liquor licensing fee. "Of these only one the Eureka is owned by colored men." For the black community in St. Paul, Jefferson and Cunningham's saloon was a favorite gathering place, for drinking, smoking cigars, shooting pool, and—illicitly—playing craps in the back. Quite a bit of gambling went on at the Eureka.

Thomas Jefferson Sr., co-owner of the Eureka bar in St. Paul, featured in the *Appeal* newspaper, September 15, 1900. *Minnesota Historical Society Collections*

The two men pursued their various interests at 384 Minnesota Street. In 1887, they cofounded, with a few other men, the Crescent Club, a social aid and cultural society for the local African American community. In 1888, they founded the St. Paul Colored Band, occasionally known as the Eureka Band, with Jefferson as president and Cunningham as treasurer. Neither appeared to play an instrument in the group, which consisted of fourteen musicians whose musical prowess was said to "put to shame many older organizations." Cunningham hired one of Jefferson's boxing mentees, W. H. Butt, to sing and entertain at the Eureka. Political organizing also went on there: Jefferson, the more politically engaged of the two, helped recruit some of the first black officers on the St. Paul police force.

The sheer variety of activities at the saloon is a testament not just to the breadth of the two men's interests but also to the saloon's centrality to the life of African American men in the 1880s and '90s. From political debates on how the Republican Party sold out Reconstruction to a few guys fooling around on clarinets to low-stakes gambling on dice games—all of it could be found at the Eureka. Occasionally, debates would break into fights, tempers would flare, and knives or guns would be drawn and occasionally used. But the Eureka also looked after its most devoted patrons. When men working at or involved with the saloon got sick, Cunningham would provide assistance in their recovery. If things took a turn for the worse, he would pay for the funeral. "Big-hearted J. H. Cunningham," the *Appeal* called him. In lieu of a social safety net for African Americans, the saloon, along with the church, was where you could find a community of people to help support you and your family.

As the business grew, Cunningham moved the Eureka from the Minnesota Street address to the pair's old real estate office at 86 East Fifth Street. He did up the walls with pacrusta, a fashionable wall treatment technique that gave interiors a high-relief patterned surface. "Cunny is a rustler and make no mistake," the *Appeal* noted affectionately. ("Cunny" is probably not an altogether innocent nickname; that particular slang term has been used since the seventeenth century.) Two years later, the bar moved a few doors down, to 90 East Fifth, a space that was twice as large and had a second floor. Here, Cunningham commissioned frescoes for the interiors. The expanded space made more culinary options possible, and "all the delicacies the market affords" could be made to order and served out of the back room for lunch and dinner.

Cunningham ran the Eureka throughout the 1890s. Jefferson was never far away; in the mid-1890s, he ran the Damfino Saloon at 346 Minnesota, a few doors from the Eureka's first location. Its name gives a clue about the easygoing and collegial spirit of the place; *damfino* was a popular contraction in the late nineteenth century of the phrase "damned if I know."

In 1898, Jefferson and Cunningham decided to get the band back together. The reasons are not clear from the historical record. Cunningham seems to have gone through a rough spell, closing the Eureka sometime around 1895 and then going to work as a janitor for a year after. The space at 384 Minnesota, where Cunningham and Jefferson had started out ten years earlier, became available, and the pair reopened the Eureka there—most prominent of the "cluster of dives on Minnesota Street," as it was described in the press. Jefferson was the proprietor, and Cunningham was hired to manage it. They took out an ad in the city's papers: "Time brings around all things, and time has brought around again the old Eureka saloon once more," it read, then listed the names of the two men. All of these names—Eureka, Jefferson, Cunningham—were comforting and reliable to St. Paul's African American community. "The saloon was opened yesterday for business at the old stand," the *Appeal* reported in June 1898.

They may have had plans to continue the operation for decades to come, but Cunningham had been ill for a while. He was in his early fifties and in poor health. He wasn't married, though he had a common-law wife named Anna Walker. On Thursday, July 6, 1899, just over a year after the new Eureka opened, he checked into the city hospital. The next day, he passed away at the age of fifty-two.

Cunningham seems to have been a quiet man, and he retained one last secret with him in his final hours. While in bed at home, the day before he checked into the hospital, he called Anna to his side and told her that he wanted to be married. A justice of the peace was summoned to marry the two of them in a small bedside ceremony at their home. Cunningham appeared brighter following the ceremony than he had in weeks of illness. "His last words at the hospital," it was reported later, "were of his wife."

"I had no idea he was going to die nor do I think he had, for he talked of plans for the future," Walker later said, though Cunningham must have known the end was near. He had a life insurance policy of $500, which is equivalent to a little under $15,000 today. When he died, the policy went to Walker, and it was paid out by Northwestern Life Insurance a week later.

Thomas Jefferson Sr. had not been at the wedding ceremony; it seems that no one but Cunningham's and Walker's immediate families were in attendance. In fact, Jefferson hadn't even known about the wedding until a reporter told him. He was said to be "surprised to learn of the leap Cunningham had taken." Jefferson was able to participate in the massive, well-attended funeral at Mother St. James African Methodist Episcopal Church at Seventh and Robert Streets. Cunningham was buried among the city's elite in Oakland Cemetery.

Jefferson ran the Eureka for another year or so, redubbing it the Royal in 1900. He moved it a few doors down Minnesota Street, and then sold the business in 1901 to a small group of businessmen, including a colleague from his boxing days, a former champion and popular personality named Harris "The Black Pearl" Martin. Jefferson opened a theater on the site of the old Eureka in 1910. Aside from that, Jefferson seems to have stepped out of the limelight in the early years of the twentieth century. Did he ever open another saloon? It seems not, but *damfino,* as the man himself might have said.

Jefferson died in 1927, leaving a growing African American community in St. Paul centered around the institutions he'd worked to build: the Democratic Party, social aid clubs, African American fraternal societies, amateur bands, and black-owned restaurants. He was buried at Oakland Cemetery, too, not far from his friend and colleague John H. Cunningham.

"Beer, wine, and brandy were not for Norsemen."

TRIANGLE BAR

1899–1990

1822 RIVERSIDE AVENUE SOUTH, MINNEAPOLIS

There had been saloons at 1822 Riverside Avenue for years before the distinctive Triangle Bar was built on the tiny, triangle-shaped lot. There had long been saloons on that spot because there had long been Scandinavians living nearby, and Scandinavians were some of the hardest-drinking people in the state. Even by the 1960s, when most of those Danes and Norwegians and Swedes had died off or left the neighborhood, the Triangle remained a singularly good-time place fueled by music and beer, where you could both hear traditional folk music and drink in the traditional folk manner—which is to say, raucously.

It wasn't until the late nineteenth century, after a generation or two, that Scandinavians would earn their reputation as a stoic, abstaining force for moderation in the social and political life of the Twin Cities. Even at the time of the earliest saloons on Riverside Avenue, Scandinavian clergy, reformers, and organizations like Svensk Finsk Nykterhets Förening af Amerika were a major force for temperance. But the clergymen and reformers were often outnumbered by their harder-living relations.

When rural Norwegians, Swedes, and Danes began pouring into Minnesota in the 1870s, they brought a taste for *hjemmebrent* (literally, "home-burnt," a clear, pure alcohol moonshine) and *snoose,* or chewing tobacco. So prevalent was snoose in the community that Cedar Avenue, the main drag near the Triangle Bar, was colloquially known as *Snus Gatan*—Snuff Boulevard—after the rivers of tobacco-choked spit that flowed down the street. "Beer, wine, and brandy were not for Norsemen," wrote a Norwegian American novelist in the early twentieth century of the drinking culture among Scandinavians in the Midwest in the 1890s. "They weren't civilized enough. . . . They hadn't learned to indulge in such things intelligently."

By the 1880s, the neighborhood's Scandinavian residents were numerous enough and possessed enough political clout to push back against a new initiative from the city's leadership. In 1884, the city of Minneapolis passed the liquor patrol limit laws, which cordoned off bars and saloons in certain segments of the city in an effort to keep their corrosive influence out of residential neighborhoods. Initially, the idea had been to restrict saloons to the central downtown core, where police officers could more easily monitor the goings-on; one persistent urban legend is that the boundaries of the patrol limits were based on the distance a beat officer could traverse on foot over the course of a shift.

However, two residential neighborhoods outside the downtown core were incorporated into those boundaries, neighborhoods largely composed of immigrants for whom socialization in saloons was a significant part of daily life: a wet coalition of Eastern Europeans, Irish, and Germans in Northeast Minneapolis, centered around Orth's first brewery, and the largely Scandinavian West Bank.

By the turn of the century, after the patrol limits had been in place for a generation, a third of all saloons in Minneapolis were located on the West Bank. The best spot to get a drink remained stretches of Washington Avenue and Hennepin Avenue in downtown Minneapolis. But outside the downtown core, the West Bank was one of the very few neighborhoods where residents could stop in for a drink of whiskey or full-strength beer after work. These limits would shape the landscape of bars and saloons in Minneapolis for nearly nine decades following. They still shape the landscape: it remains, to this day, very difficult to find a neighborhood bar serving spirits outside downtown, the West Bank, Northeast, and the boundaries of the original liquor patrol limits.

One of the West Bank saloons was operated by Oscar B. Lyke, a New York Yankee who made his home and his fortune among the Scandinavians. He operated a small saloon known as the Little Dandy in the late 1880s, amid a cluster of small owner-occupied commercial buildings on the triangle. It's supposedly the smallest lot in the city with running water, an odd little slice of land created when Riverside Avenue cut a diagonal through the grid in 1872.

"Little dandy" was a common phrase in the parlance of the day. A dandy was "a male of the human species, who dresses himself like a doll and who carries his character on his back," according to the 1828 Webster's

dictionary. "Little dandy" was the nickname given to a teenage soldier killed at Vicksburg during the Civil War, whose maudlin story was making its way through the state's newspapers in early 1887, about the same time Lyke was picking a name for his new establishment.

The Little Dandy seems mostly to have catered to its Scandinavian neighbors: an 1890 *Globe* article about an altercation at the bar describes a group of men named Steenberg, Carlson, and Mainberg. Apparently Steenberg, the bartender, was knocked out after failing to adequately mediate an argument about some aspect of the art of homebuilding.

Lyke's immediate successor was a Norwegian-born saloonkeeper, real estate developer, former butcher, and prominent West Bank figure and ward heeler named Olaf C. Damm, born Olaf Dammrud in Norway in 1859. The building he inherited from Lyke was a modest affair, a brick and wood one-story structure surrounded by other similar buildings pressed onto the oddly sized lot. Damm had big plans for the Little Dandy.

Since about the 1880s, local brewers had been looking for innovative ways to hang on to their customers and push out competition, both local and from much larger breweries in St. Louis and Milwaukee, who were able to ship their product in refrigerated trains for the first time. The tied house was the best way to do this: a brewery would build and furnish a saloon on behalf of a local saloonkeeper, with the stipulation that the saloon would sell only that brewery's beer. The name of the saloonkeeper might not even be prominent; more likely you'd see the name of the brewer on large letters over the front door.

Gluek Brewery worked out such a deal with Damm. In 1899, Gluek pulled permits to construct a $10,000 saloon at 1822 Riverside. Better yet, Damm and Gluek managed to rope in a distinguished Minneapolis architect, Warren Barnes Dunnell. Dunnell was a progressive architect, trained in Paris and better known for churches, schools, and hospitals than saloons. His agreeing to the commission may have been out of some sense of cultural allegiance; Dunnell, like Damm, was a Norwegian immigrant.

The Triangle Bar, at the intersection of Riverside Avenue and Fourth Street in Minneapolis's West Bank neighborhood, as seen in 1972. *Minnesota Historical Society Collections*

Dunnell brought the same degree of attention and grace that he brought to projects like the imposing Fergus Falls State Hospital in Fergus Falls, Minnesota. "Buildings erected 25 years ago are illy adapted to their uses, poorly ventilated and plumbed," he told the *Tribune* in an 1898 interview about his architectural philosophy. "In a word, so unsanitary that their destruction would be a blessing."

The building he designed for Gluek and Damm was elegant and strange, a wedge-shaped building that took up the entire lot. It made use of the most contemporary materials and techniques: "Red pressed brick and ornamental brick, and cut stone, galvanized iron cornice and skylights, plate glass, iron beams and column, cement sidewalks and cellar, plumbing and steam heating," as it was described in a local trade publication. The Triangle did indeed become a destination for the first- and second-generation Norwegian American community on the West Bank; if not a point of pride for everyone, at least a highly visible landmark.

Damm sold the building a few years later, and after moving north to the Iron Range and later Canada, he made a fortune in land speculation. When he died in 1921, he was buried at Lakewood Cemetery in Minneapolis.

For some sixty years after, the Triangle Bar's clientele remained mostly working class, male, and Norwegian. Red Nelson, a University of Minnesota student and West Bank promoter from the 1960s, remembered the bars of the neighborhood at the time being filled with "hard-bitten workers and leftover Scandinavians." By the early 1960s, when the University of Minnesota began expanding into the West Bank and bringing masses of students with it, the Triangle Bar underwent another shift in identity. It became a focal point for the folk and blues revival in the city. This shift in identity drew heavily on the bar's Scandinavian roots, both consciously and unconsciously.

"As the older generation died out, there was a vacuum, and nature abhors a vacuum, as the old saying goes," Nelson said. "This vacuum drew students from across the river. Of course, the cheap housing, strong beer, and lack of supervision from the University helped, too."

Died out though they had, it was that wave of youth that kept the memory of the Triangle's Scandinavian clientele alive for another generation. Maury Bernstein—a balding, bespectacled permanent university student, folklorist, and accordion player with a bushy mustache and a sharp, ironic sense of humor—was a regular at the Triangle starting in 1963, playing raucous folk and traditional music. People were invited to "see and admire his new wrought-iron cubicle, built to protect him from over-enthusiastic customers." He presented programs of "German drinking songs, Russian gypsy songs, Italian, Irish, Scottish, Israeli, Greek, Romanian, Norwegian, Swedish, and Danish Folk Songs!" To this, he added, "Oops, we forgot French, Yiddish, Turkish, and English." Bernstein's own interest in folk music stemmed from, as he describes it, growing up in a government housing project in a multiethnic neighborhood in Minneapolis, listening to shortwave radio broadcasts from around the world. He retained a particular interest, however, in the musical and drinking culture of the West Bank's earlier Scandinavian inhabitants.

Bernstein was involved in organizing a series of Snoose Boulevard festivals in the mid-1970s, focused in part around the Triangle. These festivals brought in Scandinavian musicians, vaudeville comedians, and booze, evoking the lively immigrant spirit of the Snoose Boulevard era in a way that reflected the fading older culture but with the sensibility of the counterculture. On one hand, it spoke elegiacally to the old culture that had inhabited those West Bank bars. "People want so much to have this kind of thing," said one Snoose festival participant in 1974, before continuing sadly: "You can almost feel that the older generation tries very hard to belong to it, too, even though it's all dead."

On the other hand, the proximity to the college and to youth grounded the scene in a sort of radical sixties energy. The Snoose festivities and the accompanying scene weren't necessarily a genteel re-creation of a history textbook; in fact, it was wild enough to lead the director of the American Swedish Institute to complain that the festivals overemphasized the seamy side of the immigrant experience. Bernstein wasn't interested in museum pieces; nor was he interested in either the staid postwar culture or the radical political attitudes of the time. The niche he carved out at the Triangle championed outsiders and weirdos who had little interest in the mainstream but a great deal of interest in the cosmopolitan, the arcane, and the historical.

The musicians that followed Bernstein to the Triangle shared a similarly countercultural, eccentric outlook, and the ones who made their names there are known today as some of the founding members of the Twin Cities music scene. These are names linking the Cities' history to its status as a regional musical powerhouse: Willie Murphy, Spider John Koerner, Tony Glover. "Where all the beatniks hung out," Murphy remembered fondly of the Triangle, decades later. The focus of the folk and blues scene later shifted elsewhere on the West Bank, but the Triangle was the focal point in the early years. Dunnell's grand structure hasn't housed a bar for nearly three decades, though the building itself remains a West Bank landmark.

The voters of Minneapolis finally overturned the liquor patrol limit laws in 1974, about the same time the blues and folk scene at the Triangle was drying up. The patrol limits, in their near century on the books, served the exact function that the city fathers who'd instituted them intended—however, perhaps not in the way they intended: they kept the few neighborhoods like the West Bank cordoned off, developing a culture focused around socialization in bars that was—and remains—distinct from the city's other, sleepier residential neighborhoods. The West Bank, Northeast, and the Lower Loop were wet islands, separated from the rest of the city by invisible lines, and they were looser, wilder, and more generous in spirit. The liquor patrol limits allowed the Triangle and bars like it to develop personalities and followings quite unlike elsewhere in the city. The bohemian, cosmopolitan flavor of the city's folk scene of the 1960s was incubated on the welcoming foundations of the old Little Dandy, erected fifty years earlier by first-generation immigrants with a taste for spirits.

"One was unreservedly welcome to move in on the menu either as a gentleman or a hog."

ROGERS HOTEL BAR

1901–1932

25–29 SOUTH FOURTH STREET, MINNEAPOLIS

If there was anything that got under Tooze Rogers's thick skin, it was the free lunch ban. The question came to a head in March 1904 when, at the behest of the health commissioner, the superintendent of the Union Mission, and other supposed do-gooders, the Minneapolis City Council unanimously passed a new ordinance against the so-called free lunch, the commonplace practice of putting out food in saloons, taverns, and bars all through downtown Minneapolis.

Tooze was the famous nickname of J. E. Rogers, whose father was a minister and who worked his way up from the gritty saloons of Washington Avenue to become one of the best respected hotel proprietors in the city. Tooze stood for "Two-Z," and the nickname was represented by his famous logo, two letter Zs twinned like lightning bolts and blazoned on bottles, beer glasses, and the free drink tokens that passed as currency all over the state.

Tooze worked his way up from the heart of the Gateway District running a small bar, the Mint Saloon, and since the early days he'd catered to the tastes of the well heeled. For example, he very publicly kicked out the gamblers from his saloon after reports of illegal gambling were made public.

Minneapolis was a place of rapidly rising fortunes, and Tooze was going to ride that wave.

The ambitious Rogers pinched pennies with a fierce grip, always wary of being scammed by a bad check or fending off the Gateway bums. During the early years, he even slept with a loaded .38 under his pillow to protect the night's receipts, a fact we know because one hot summer night, Tooze was startled in the midst of a dream by sounds in his bedroom. Pulling out his revolver, he blasted the apparent intruder. Tragically, it turned out to be his own wife, who had woken up in the middle of the night and was struggling to open the window of their stuffy bedroom. Shot clear through the neck, she somehow survived and, ultimately, outlived Rogers.

Another account of the early days at the Mint Saloon captures the two sides of Rogers. It became known at city hall that an ill-mannered man named Crusader Briggs was spreading rumors that Mayor William Eustis frequented an "'aristocratic' house of ill-fame." Attempting to quash the story, Mayor Eustis publicly grilled Briggs until he testified that he'd heard the story from a certain saloonkeeper, Mr. J. E. Rogers. Rogers denied the allegation and called Briggs a liar, defending the honor of himself and his saloon.

Soon afterward, the following event transpired at the Mint:

> *Frederick Briggs, brother of Crusader Briggs, went into the Mint Saloon early last evening and asked if Tooze Rodgers [*sic*] the proprietor was in. It will be remembered that Rodgers is the man who gave Crusader Briggs the lie when the latter was called before the mayor. Frederick Briggs said to Mr. Rogers that he could lick the man who said his brother was a liar. Drawing a long knife he said, "I want blood." He got it. Rodgers rushed from behind the bar, letting go his right, smashed Mr. Briggs in the jaw. The young man fell to the floor and did not come to for ten or fifteen minutes. When he awoke he had a lump on the side of face as large as a tea cup. Pulling himself together he disappeared from the saloon. Fifteen minutes later he appeared at the entrance of the saloon with a gun. The policeman on the beat, noticing the large lump on Briggs' jaw, suspected that all was not right. He took hold of the young man and instituted a search of his clothing. In one overcoat pocket he found a revolver and in the other the knife which Briggs had threatened to carve Mr. Rogers.*

Thus was the life of Tooze Rogers.

By the turn of the century, Tooze had made it big, for a saloon man, moving onward and upward from the Mint. By then, he owned no fewer than six liquor establishments in Minneapolis and St. Paul, and the nicest of them all was the Rogers Hotel, a large and stately red brick neoclassical

The Rogers Hotel, home to Tooze Rogers's legendary saloon. *Minnesota Historical Society Collections*

building on the corner of Fourth and Nicollet, the heart of bustling Newspaper Row.

Lunch at the Rogers Hotel was legendary, the best of the free lunches that made Minneapolis's downtown saloons famous in the stories of working men and gentlemen alike. In his memoir of Minneapolis in the 1890s, Henry Broderick described the deep impression made by the Rogers's bar:

> *The good saloons were places to pause for solid citizens. There were many, but let's peek at one of the best. That would be the one conducted by Z.Z. Rogers, known as Two-Z Rogers. . . . Its chief clientele were members of the Wheat Exchange and the Corn Exchange, both of these buildings being located one block to the south. The gleaming bar was about one hundred feet long, the back sixty feet or so being devoted to a buffet lunch counter. Here was an array of silver and copper containers, presided over by two white-capped chefs dispensing roast beef, baked ham, baked beans and many other palatable items. Whether one bought a glass of beer for five cents, a shot of whiskey for ten cents, or a bottle of champagne for two dollars, one was unreservedly welcome to move in on the menu either as a gentleman or a hog. Gentlemen must have predominantly outnumbered the fellows who wanted to feast on five cents because the place made money so fast it wore out the cash registers.*

Tooze's was also the rare Minneapolis saloon where, by one account, "women could be seen without scandal." Behind his respected establishment, Rogers avidly defended the city's saloon culture. His voice was important as the fight between the saloonkeepers and the forces of temperance intensified during Minneapolis's boom years in the 1880s and '90s.

Things came to a head for Tooze when, a few years after the city's liquor patrol limit laws were instituted in 1884, the moral reformers went after the free lunches. The charge was led by city health commissioner P. M. Hall, who argued that the free food was something of a gateway to sin and sloth: "The free lunch was responsible for making saloons the gathering places of 'bums,' loafers and petty criminals, a class the saloon keepers were as anxious to get rid of as any one could be." As Hall described, the debate in the city council "was a short one and the ordinance making it a misdemeanor to serve free lunch in saloons was recommended for passage without opposition."

C. M. Stocking, superintendent of the Union Mission, agreed with Hall's perspective:

> *It is my belief that between 300 and 400 men in Minneapolis really depend upon free lunches for subsistence three or four months of the year. If the free lunch is abolished these men will be forced to leave town and go to the farms where they are needed. I think much of the purse-snatching and holdup work has been due to the fact that the vicious class can remain in Minneapolis when without money, and live on free lunches. . . . Free lunch is a tripping place in the path of many men who would brace up if the lunches were to be done away with. . . . It's a big thing for a lot of men if they are forced to go to work. Many of them are not naturally vicious, but need something to force them to straighten up.*

Tooze was having none of it, and he vigorously defended the morality, beneficence, and quality of his famous bar buffet. Others joined Rogers in the fight for free lunch, as described by Broderick: "One saloonkeeper, who conducts six liquid dispensaries and is the inventor of the famous 'auto lunch,' or nickel-and-two-boiled-eggs device, says the ordinance is a ridiculous measure, that will not be tolerated by business men. 'If I was making the laws,' said he, 'I would compel every saloon to maintain a first-class free lunch, the same as is now furnished in all the good saloons. The free lunch make for temperance, as everybody knows that beer and whisky on an empty stomach are bad for the drinker.'"

Another "prominent saloon man" voiced similar sentiment: "No one but the much-abused saloon-keeper can understand the awful shifts many poor fellows will be put to by the removal of the free lunch. Already a number of miserable men have 'touched' me for enough to get a bite with, and I expect it will be an hourly occurrence from now on. I don't care. I'll vie up to the deserving ones."

The objections were to no avail, and the era of the free lunch saloons was brought to an end in Minneapolis, though it remained a common practice in St. Paul.

Despite the ban, Rogers continued to run his high-class bar and defend saloon society, for example, by sponsoring his famous baseball team, the Toozes. News of his travels, encounters, and various ailments (appendicitis!) were printed in the paper, and he and his wife, Mae, maintained a conspicuous public presence.

In 1905, one year after the free-lunch ban passed, Tooze launched a new culinary tradition: free Thanksgiving meals for the city's newsboys. Seemingly determined to provide free food to someone, Tooze made the gesture to poke at the anti-saloon crusaders.

One 1914 account described the Thanksgiving scene: "At 5 a.m. yesterday four newsboys stopped in front of the Rogers Cafe. One was colored, another was a cripple, one of the others was redheaded and the fourth was a little Jewish boy. They were typical of the boyhood that Tooze Rogers had always befriended. At 7 o'clock the vanguard of four were pressed against the door of the café entrance by the force of a long line of boys that extended for more than half a block in each direction. At 10 o'clock the line wound around on Hennepin Avenue."

Eventually, the sound "Hoorah for Tooze Rogers" broke forth from the "hearts and stomachs" of more than five hundred newsies.

After Rogers died in 1912, Mae kept the tradition going for another eight years until she, too, passed away. Tooze's saloon lasted until 1932, when it was bought and the name changed to the Milner Hotel. The newspaper reported on the demise of the old saloon: "The once famous cafe also had come upon bad days after the death of Tooze Rogers. For a time it flourished, and then came prohibition, and its doors closed. A few times it was reopened, but success never came to it again. The lavish fittings disappeared. Last winter licenses were revoked and padlocks placed on the doors."

To this day, in certain dives and holes around Minneapolis, you can still find a Crock-Pot of taco meat, hot dogs, or sloppy joes sitting on a back table around lunchtime. Rogers would have appreciated that, despite the best efforts of the crusaders, there still is such thing as a free lunch in Minneapolis.

“One of the most artistic beauty spots in the world.”

THE GROTTO

1908–1922

153 THIRD AVENUE (NOW KELLOGG AVENUE), ST. PAUL

Of course the Grotto would be written up in a book a century later, alongside the famous and infamous establishments run by the likes of Tooze Rogers, Fred Schiek, and Pig's Eye Parrant. That's exactly what the Rileys would have expected in 1909, had you told them. The Grotto, they believed, was destined to be one of the great bars of the world, the one sight a traveler stepping off a train at Union Depot in downtown St. Paul couldn't afford to miss. That's why the Rileys had postcards printed up to sell at the bar. People wouldn't believe the stories if there weren't some kind of visual proof of the bar's splendor.

The Grotto wasn't like the dining rooms or cocktail lounges in the city's hotels, outfitted with stained glass and brass fixtures and staffed by solicitous men in white jackets. The Grotto is very unlike any bar that existed at the time, or really any bar that has existed since. The postcards featured just a black-and-white image of an occupied space, devoid of human habitation, but the otherworldliness of the bar came through loud and clear. It is, like its name indicates, a grotto, a wonderland of colored stone outcroppings hidden inside an unpromising row of commercial buildings in downtown St. Paul. It was as if you'd wandered into an undersea cavern on your way from Union Depot to your hotel.

Prior to the opening of the bar, the unit it occupied on Third Street, at 153, had been home to a fairly unremarkable series of businesses, ebbing and flowing with the growth of St. Paul as a rail town. A series of hotels had occupied the second floor, most notably the Maple Leaf, which accommodated business travelers as well as those falling somewhere outside the business class. If anything, the address was associated with lurid headlines in the *Globe,* the more sensationalistic of St. Paul's dailies. Among the tenants of 153 Third Street in the early 1900s were a woman who committed suicide by drinking carbolic acid after being jilted by her fiancé. There was also a railroad foreman who drank himself to death one night. His body was found upright in a chair in his room, fully dressed, after the man had been administered sedatives a few hours earlier by the hotel's management following an acute attack of the DTs.

Third Street was a rough place. Anywhere so many travelers were passing through was bound to be.

By the turn of the century, St. Paul's Union Depot had grown into a rail powerhouse. Built in 1881 and renovated in the late 1890s, the depot's prominent, multistory Richardsonian tower was visible to passengers arriving by train from Chicago.

Located just two blocks from the bustling depot, the storefront at 153 Third Street hosted a succession of middle-end tailors and clothiers, targeting shoppers stopping over in St. Paul. The last business in the space prior to the opening of the Grotto was a cigar maker and store run by the Iltners, an elderly man and his son. The younger Iltner also worked for the railroad as a depot agent. A lot of people in the neighborhood worked for the railroad.

The block was owned by the Riley family, who'd made their fortune in trains. Cornelius Riley was born in Ireland in 1836 and made his way to St. Paul in 1861. He set up the first newsstand in the city, selling newspapers and magazines at the downtown hotels to travelers from the East. He moved his newsstand into the Union Depot shortly thereafter, and by 1881, he was a fairly powerful cog in the machine that was the regional railroad. Newspapers located in small towns served by the Northern Pacific Railway wrote about him with a sense of awe: "He employs nearly all the train boys out of St. Paul," wrote the Warren *Sheaf* in 1881 (population of Warren at the time: 108). With his son, William C. Riley, Cornelius owned the Northern Railway Train News Company. If you bought a magazine, a book, a cigar, or a piece of fruit on a train arriving at, stopping in, or departing from Union Depot, you were putting money in the Rileys' pockets. And they had an enormous amount of money in their pockets. The block of luxurious apartments they built in the 1880s on Cathedral Hill, Riley Row, was later described by former tenant F. Scott Fitzgerald as "a museum of

Interior of the Grotto, depicted on a postcard, 1908. *Author Collection*

American architectural failures," but was then, as now, a towering symbol of the city's prosperity. When the younger Riley died in 1929, he left a million-dollar estate.

Books, magazines, and cigars weren't enough for the Rileys, however. They had bigger ambitions. In 1908, the Iltners and their cigar business got the boot from 153 Third Street, and the Rileys began a massive renovation.

It's unclear where the idea for a grotto came from. The younger Riley, in addition to his work selling newspapers, also wrote tourist guides for passengers on the Northern Pacific, so the great natural attractions of the West—caverns, geysers, grottos—weren't far from his mind. Maybe he was thinking of the newly discovered Carlsbad Caverns in New Mexico and their fantastically named rooms: the Bottomless Pit, Fairyland, Iceberg Rock. Maybe he was struck by the vivid accounts in the press of the day. "The colors were in a class by themselves," wrote an early explorer. "We saw all the colors of the rainbow, from pale pinks to deep maroons—from pale sky blue to dark purple." The Rileys weren't the only people thinking about the possibilities of grottos. About the same time, two hundred miles south of Union Depot on the Burlington, Cedar Rapids and Northern Railway, a

German-born Catholic priest in West Bend, Iowa, was building the world's largest man-made grotto, a shrine to the Virgin Mary. "What was once an unsightly place, a miry slough, bordered by bull rushes and inhabited by muskrats, was transformed into one of the most artistic beauty spots in the world as a memorial of love," they wrote of the West Bend grotto.

Maybe the Rileys had a similar idea. An artistic beauty spot, a memorial of, if not love, then at least leisure.

They tore out all the old retail fixtures that had held cigars and petticoats for the previous twenty years. They imported red, orange, and pink granite and marble from Italy and mixed barrels of Portland cement to fix agates and stones into billowing forms. They fashioned a row of nooks along the side wall, where a tired traveler could slip in and drink in peace. They lined the floor with brass spittoons. In the back, they hung an arrangement of American flags. To further the usefulness and profitability of the space, the Rileys added a third story to the brick building. Third Street between Jackson and Robert Streets would be a destination.

There don't seem to have been any grand public announcements when the bar opened, though. In retrospect, perhaps this was a sign that the enterprise wouldn't garner the attention the Rileys hoped. One more twenty-foot-wide saloon in a bleak, quarter-century-old commercial row, no matter how splendidly decorated the space or how wealthy the owners, wouldn't stand out. St. Paul was modernizing and leaving these types of saloons behind.

In 1913, Union Depot burned down, and a new one was built in its place. Sleek and modern, the new facility housed restaurants and coffee shops and other amenities for the middle-class traveler. There was little need for such travelers to traverse Third Street to the types of joints you'd find under the Maple Leaf Hotel, den of drunkenness and misery, when clean, well-lit options for food and drink could be found right in the depot itself. Even the Grotto, exotic and attractive though it may have been, was just too far afield to draw travelers away.

The postcards Cornelius had printed up ended up in the hands of hundreds and perhaps thousands of travelers. Maybe they came, maybe they didn't—it's impossible to know. It's difficult to say, too, what the Rileys made of their investment. The bar remained in their name for two years only, 1908 and 1909. The photo negatives were passed down, too, because subsequent owners would pay for a new batch of postcards every few years with that same picture of the empty space.

In the following years, between 1910 and Prohibition, it would have a new owner almost annually, some of whom retained the Grotto name, some of whom did not. The individuals associated with it were a colorful bunch, the sorts of people existing on the margins of civic life: strivers, immigrants, small-time operators looking for a break. The sort of people, in other words, you'd hope to meet saddled up at a bar like the Grotto.

A group of brothers named the Krutinas, Eastern European bootmakers, union agitators, and amateur baseball players, gave it a try for a year. Lena Kasel, a hotelier who also managed the restaurant on the corner, was around, too—two or three careers later, she'd end a long life at the age of ninety-nine on the West Coast as a Franciscan lay worker. (Perhaps she had a religious conversion in that grotto.) Fiorito and Farinnacci, two saloonkeepers who'd cut their teeth up the old Fort Road on the levee, the city's Little Italy, took over, maybe hoping to break into the more fashionable downtown district. They lasted all of a year. Following them was Angelo Goduto, a native of Puglia who was one of the city's best-connected Italian figures, the prosperous owner of a handful of saloons and the president of the Columbus Society to boot. Goduto seems to have had the idea to colorize the black-and-white postcards, distributing images of the Grotto in gaudy, full color, really showing off the pinks and yellows in the stone. Careful directions on the back nearly pleaded with travelers to stop by: "from the front entrance of Union Depot," it read, "half block to the right, then one block and four doors to the left, right-hand side of Third Street." Can't miss it!

Even Goduto, despite years of saloonkeeping experience and a wealth of connections in the Italian American community, couldn't make it work. A guy by the name of Diemert who'd been run out of Moorhead for selling booze to minors came in around 1916. He converted the place to a soft drink parlor when the Volstead Act passed in 1919—who knows what he was hiding behind those Portland cement fixtures. Not that it mattered. He was gone by 1921. A Greek immigrant named Karas came in next and also failed. He didn't need to go far, fortunately; he worked for the railroad when he wasn't pouring frosty mugs of soda pop.

All of them must have come in thinking it was a sure bet—a beautiful grotto! Near the train depot! And they all exited just as quickly. For whatever reason, the Grotto just never worked. Prohibition certainly didn't help. It soon closed, unmourned and mostly forgotten.

To the extent that the Grotto is remembered at all, it's not because it was closely covered by the city's writers or journalists (it was rarely written about) or passed down through oral histories of families that ran the space for decades (no family ran it for more than two years). None of those seem to exist. Instead, it's because of the thousands of postcards the Rileys had printed. Over the past century, they gradually circulated through the secondhand market and were noticed by those with an eye for the bizarre or the unusual. I found one in an antique mall in rural Minnesota, with an almost illegible message scrawled on the back to a woman in Pine Island, Minnesota, promising to be back Tuesday. *I think I may buy a . . .* something. Whatever the writer made of the surroundings, he didn't say directly on the rear of the postcard. He didn't need to. The image of the Grotto on the front, the image the Rileys were sure would make the place a legend, said it all.

Sometime in the mid-1920s, in the midst of Prohibition, the Rileys saw where business was heading: not in booze, but in cars. They tore out the chunk of the block that had housed the Grotto and the Maple Leaf Hotel and turned it into the Coleman Parking and Greasing Station, an expanse of asphalt where automobiles racing up and down Third Street—soon to be Kellogg Boulevard—could stop for gas and servicing. Those same automobiles would slowly kill off Union Depot over the next two or three decades, while the Coleman lot remained for many decades after.

The Grotto, most idiosyncratic of St. Paul's watering holes, met that most stereotypically Twin Citian fate, and much, much earlier than most. It became a parking lot.

"My pappa ran away and left my poor young mama."

LITTLE JAKE'S

1898–1918

44–46 SOUTH SIXTH STREET, MINNEAPOLIS

Minneapolis was in the throes of a brutal heat wave in August 1909. "A hot, humid, sweltering atmosphere," the *Sunday Tribune* reported, "was manufacturing grouches throughout the city." As a possible reprieve from the heat, the paper ran a wry blind item about the wettest parts of town, in terms of alcohol consumption—the sorts of places where all those grouches could soak for a few hours. Though Washington Avenue between Second and Third Avenues was home to eight saloons in a row, the wettest block might have been the one on Sixth Street between Hennepin and Nicollet Avenues, a few blocks south, in downtown Minneapolis. "More beer is sold here," the unnamed writer concluded, "than any other place in town, everything considered."

Walking east from Hennepin to Nicollet, you'd pass on your right-hand side the construction of the Hotel Dyckman, soon to be one of the premier luxury hotels in town when it opened the following spring. On your left, by contrast, you'd pass six very different saloons: Little Jake's, Isaac Weil's, Klein & Pauntz, the Cairo Cafe, Johnson's, and Wet Goods. The proprietors of these six establishments—sometime competitors, sometime colleagues—all had immigrated to Minneapolis, mostly from Europe, at the end of the nineteenth century to make their fortunes. At least a few of them died phenomenally wealthy. And for at least most of 1909, when all six saloons shared the block, they knew each other well.

As wealthy as some of his competitors became, Little Jake did just fine for himself, in terms of both his finances and his reputation. Decades after his bar had closed, the local paper still ran fond reminiscences of him and his establishment. "The roast beef was always prime," one old-timer said of Little Jake's in a 1943 *Tribune* story on the era of the free lunch in Minneapolis. "The finest of Western beef was lopped off," it was reported, "in great succulent hunks for the mere asking."

Jake Lingenfelder grew up in the saloon business. Born in Germany in 1864, he immigrated to California at age seventeen, became a citizen in 1891, and landed in Minneapolis a few years later. He worked his way through the bars of the Lower Loop, starting as a bartender at Shelley and Quark, a popular saloon on Hennepin Avenue, where he lived upstairs with his wife, Georgia. It was at Shelley and Quark that the diminutive Lingenfelder acquired his reputation as an amiable presence in the Loop, as well as the nickname that would follow him professionally for the rest of his life: "Little Jake."

This 1912 view down Sixth Street in Minneapolis shows the block where Little Jake's was located for two decades. *From George Odlum, "The Heart of Minneapolis," courtesy of the Hennepin County Library, James K. Hosmer Special Collections Library*

Little Jake bounced between a few other saloons in the Lower Loop until he saved enough to purchase his own. He bought a small bar and restaurant at 46 South Sixth Street called the Buffet, and Little Jake's opened for business on April 2, 1898. It was a block already crowded with saloons and restaurants, anchored by Alexander's, the oldest of them. Alexander's was remembered for having sawdust on the floors a foot deep; patrons apparently had to wade through dunes of it on their way to the bar.

Relations between the various saloonkeepers were not always warm. When Klein & Pauntz took over the Alexander's space in 1903, they shortly thereafter brought an unsuccessful lawsuit against a competitor on the same block to prevent them from obtaining a liquor license. The saloonkeepers banded together when they had to, though. They were on shaky ground. The entire block had an out-of-state landlord, New York representative John Andrus. An ardent prohibitionist, Andrus threatened on numerous occasions to buy up the leases of all the saloons on Sixth Street and raze the whole block to the ground. Andrus's ambitions were halfway realized in 1909, when several saloons were displaced for the construction of the Plymouth Building on the corner of Sixth and Hennepin.

If Andrus was hated by everyone on the block, so too was the Cairo Cafe, a "blind pig" run by a shady character named Jan Sakellarias that opened in 1909. Little Cairo was denounced in the press as a "cesspool of vice" and "rotten to the core"—not by moral crusaders or prohibitionists, but by the proprietors of the five other saloons on the block, who worried that the Cairo's grubby reputation was threatening their own positions in the community. Sakellarias was finally busted for selling booze after hours to minors in a front-page exposé by the local paper and was run out of town soon after. He sheepishly told the *Tribune* he was a reformed man and planned to reopen the space as a candy store, and then he promptly vanished from the historical record forever.

In this raucous environment, Little Jake carved out a niche for his saloon: not too fancy, not too grubby.

Little Jake's wasn't as high end as Isaac Weil's next door, a saloon and wine shop established in 1873 and presided over by its namesake, a "tall form . . . capped by a pompadour of snowy white," according to a contemporary account. "Dependability is accomplished through clear thinking" was the unlikely maxim found in his newspaper advertisements, but one Weil evidently took seriously in his own life. He sponsored word puzzles in the newspaper (you could bring in your answers for a free drink), ran the local saloonkeeper's league, and left an estate worth $250,000 when he died in 1925, an amount equivalent to $3.2 million today.

Nor could Little Jake's boast the same working-class bona fides as its neighbor two doors down, Klein & Pauntz. Despite their occasionally litigious nature, I. S. Klein and his wife, Rosa, and her brothers, Gabriel and Ignatz Pauntz, made their space available for meetings of the Structural Iron Workers Union, Painters Union, Upholsterers Union, and many others. They held union drives and information sessions. Moreover, the Hungarian-born family ran a separate bar on-site that was solely for women, an exceedingly unusual practice at a time when women were generally forbidden from drinking in public. (If anything, the Sixth Street strip was friendly to drinking women: Wet Goods, two doors down, actually had a daycare on-site until horrified Humane Society members stepped in to put a stop to it.)

One can get a sense for the sorts of wares Little Jake's had on offer from testimony he gave as an expert witness in a case before the Minnesota Supreme Court in 1905. "Are you familiar with the values of liquors and cigars and glassware?" Little Jake was asked by a justice. "I think I am: yes," he replied modestly, and then proceeded to rattle off, from memory, the contents and monetary value of a typical shipment of alcohol: claret, Scotch whiskey, Hennessy brandy, port wine, sweet Catawba, ¾ brand whiskey, Taylor, Old Crow, Anderson, Gukenheimer, sherry, Tom gin, New England rum, Jamaica rum.

Well known as he was for his brandy and scotch, Little Jake's most notable brush with notoriety came in a very different realm, in 1913. He and Georgia never had children. On March 18, 1913, while at home on Aldrich Avenue in Minneapolis, Little Jake's phone rang. The voice of a young woman on the other end told him to open his front door, and then she hung up.

Lying in a suitcase on his front stoop was a one-month-old baby boy with a note pinned to his clothing: "My good people! Please give me a place in your beautiful home. My pappa ran away and left my poor young mama before I was born, without any means of support. All I want is a home and someone to love me."

Also appended was a recipe for baby's milk.

Little Jake immediately called the police, who took the infant to the local hospital. The nurses named the suitcase baby George Washington.

Jake and Georgia were eager to adopt George. However, as a saloonkeeper—even a reputable one—Little Jake was not eligible under prevailing mores or laws to serve as a suitable guardian for an orphan. George was adopted by a Plymouth couple named Begin, and he lived the rest of his life as George Begin.

If this seems like the sort of incredible story you might hear in a bar like Little Jake's, one that seems to defy belief, well, you're not wrong. In some ways, it's the ultimate advertisement for Little Jake's saloon: a place owned by a man so reputable and so honest you would trust him to raise your own child. It's almost too good to believe.

Most likely, there was no suitcase or phone call. Certainly Little Jake, upstanding member of the community, was the intended recipient of this baby, but it's improbable that he came into the Lingenfelders' lives in that way. The evening of March 13, 1913, was not abnormally cold—a low of thirty-two degrees, just above freezing—but cold enough to make the prospect of leaving a baby on a doorstep unlikely. Either way, the police didn't seem to investigate the circumstances too carefully. Little Jake was a respected-enough citizen to be taken at his word. If Little Jake said a baby in a suitcase showed up on his doorstep one winter night, it must be true.

Janine Sherry, the daughter of George Begin, lives in Medicine Lake today and is the source of much of the information that lies outside the public record. Janine has a more credible theory. Little George was probably the son of one of Little Jake's employees or maybe the relative of a regular who trusted the owner. Most likely, baby George was given to Little Jake directly by the mother, and he fabricated an elaborate story to protect her identity.

Perhaps the mother was close to the family who took in baby George. Frank Begin, the man who adopted him, had a widowed sister who had four children before her first husband died and her second husband ran off. About this same time, she was quietly remitted to a woman's home to get back on her feet, and her children were temporarily put in state custody. Very likely she had a fifth child about this time, and very likely her family hatched a plan to keep the child in the Begin family. Little Jake must have been trustworthy enough to be the linchpin for the entire operation.

This is where we have to leave the written historical record and rely on family lore. George Begin died in 1961 without knowing the identity of his birth mother. However, Janine remembers that when he died, George's uncles, never particularly close to the family, showed up and wrote a very solemn remembrance in the guestbook. She got the impression there was something more going on.

Years later, Frank Begin's great-grandniece took a DNA test and compared it to Janine's. It was a perfect match.

The Begins didn't really keep in touch with the Lingenfelders. Little Jake's held on through the end of the 1910s, though World War I was a bad time to be a German-owned business in the United States, and on the eve of Prohibition, an even worse time to be in the liquor business.

Little Jake's didn't receive the same scrutiny as its neighbor Wet Goods, then operating as Gruenewald's and serving Jewish-German fare made to order by a cook from Chicago. The restaurant had its liquor license revoked in 1917. A month later, it was closed suddenly under the authority of War Order 7, an anti-saloon measure from the Minnesota Commission on Public Safety. The MCPS was a group of militantly moralistic civic leaders appointed by the governor who used World War I as an excuse to harass and disenfranchise German immigrants, saloon owners, political radicals, and other "disloyal" Minnesotans—essentially, a lot of the people you'd find hanging out at Little Jake's or Wet Goods. In 1918, the plot was razed, and in the ensuing years, the new structure operated under a few other names: the Colonial, Hankow Buffet, the Wind-Up Club. The restaurant was purchased for the last time in 1946 and rechristened Murray's Steakhouse. Though its old brick façade is now encased in glitzy postwar Art Deco claddings, it's the only building from that era remaining on the stretch of Sixth Street between Hennepin and Nicollet.

Little Jake's saloon closed around the end of World War I, also a victim of anti-German and anti-liquor sentiment. Jake got out of the service industry and went into oil speculation. The space that housed Little Jake's saloon became a liquor store, then a sauna, and finally an assortment of low-rent shops selling hearing aids, shoes, and eyeglasses through the 1970s. On the site now is the 50 South Sixth Street tower.

Little Jake wasn't there for any of that, though. He and Georgia sold their spacious home on Aldrich Avenue and retired to California, where they bought a little stucco cottage on Los Angeles' fashionable Westside. Georgia died in 1929, and Jake married her sister Lillian.

He died in Los Angeles in 1943 at the age of seventy-nine. A brief remembrance ran in the Minneapolis papers, and he was buried next to his first wife at Lakewood Cemetery. Lillian joined him at Lakewood later that year.

Whatever secret Little Jake might have carried with him about the suitcase baby who showed up on his doorstep in 1913, he took it to his grave. A month after his death, though, that fond remembrance of Little Jake's free meals of prime roast beef was printed in the *Tribune.*

"Mrs. Maurer will probably be the last woman to enter the liquor business in the city."

MAURER'S BAR AND CAFE

1898–1980

507 WASHINGTON AVENUE NORTH, MINNEAPOLIS

The women in the Maurer family did not choose to become saloonkeepers. It was forced upon them when their husbands died or were sent to prison. Like the women of that era—or any era—they had to step up when the men in their lives disappeared.

Louis and Elizabeth Maurer were German immigrants. His saloon was a Gluek's-affiliated bar on Washington Avenue North, a commercial stretch of Minneapolis. Washington Avenue was lined with factories and railroad warehouses, staffed with thousands of workers. Photographs of Washington from 1909, looking west from Fifth Avenue North, show an unbroken succession of cigar, beer, and whiskey advertisements lining the avenue, interspersed with ads for plows, oatmeal, and corn flakes. When the factory and warehouse steam whistles would blow at the end of the work shifts, men would stream out into the streets and then into the bars.

Maurer's Saloon was one of eighty-six similar establishments in

Maurer's Bar and Cafe was a "tied house" for Gluek Brewing Company for much of its early history. *Minnesota Historical Society Collections*

Minneapolis that year—saloons that were connected, or "tied," to Gluek. The so-called tied houses were propped up by Gluek, one of the largest brewers in the Middle West, which supplied them exclusively with Gluek's beer. Like most of these tied houses, Maurer's was a somewhat nondescript brick building with plate glass windows and a Gluek's sign overhead. Saloonkeepers come and go, but Gluek's remained. The address where Maurer's was located has hosted saloons since at least the middle of the 1880s, with most of the owners being German immigrants like Louis and Elizabeth. Many of the changeovers seemed marked by some sort of personal tragedy; the building had initially housed a tailor who was forced to sell because of his failing health. The saloon's first owner, an Emil Bader, turned it over to Anton Feilzer, who left the country after his wife committed suicide by drinking poison in the upstairs apartment. Louis took it over from him.

Louis managed the bar well, with the help of his son Frederic and his wife, Elizabeth. The saloon business made him a moderately wealthy man. In addition to the bar, he owned a home in south Minneapolis and a vacation cottage in Medicine Lake. It was at that lakeside cottage, on June 25, 1909, that Louis placed a shotgun to his head and pulled the trigger. Elizabeth, Frederic, and their other son, Charles, were in the next room.

June 25 was the anniversary of a severe stroke he'd suffered two years earlier. His doctor told him, in the days following, that in two years he'd be completely recovered. Louis had come a long way since then, but he was still severely weakened and didn't feel like he had much chance of recovering further. He was reported to be, at the time, "partially demented" and "temporarily insane" when he pulled the trigger. Louis was buried near Medicine Lake.

There was little time to mourn. Shortly thereafter, Elizabeth went down to city hall to apply for a liquor license. The liquor business was the only business she'd ever known and the only one that had kept her family fed. There were a few other women saloonkeepers in the city, and all of them worked alongside their husbands. Elizabeth's case was special. Perhaps the city councilmen took pity on her. In any case, it would be an exception. Elizabeth would be the only woman to own and operate a saloon in Minneapolis for at least two years.

Perhaps Elizabeth knew of Tillie Stockstad, who'd worked the Triangle Bar, on the other side of downtown on the hard-drinking West Bank. In 1910, the year after Louis's death, Tillie's husband, Hans, was gunned down in the saloon he owned over some petty grievance. She, too, had applied for her husband's license, but she was rebuffed by City Hall.

In discussions on the Stockstad matter, the city council decided there would be no more women in the liquor business in the city. They wouldn't force out any current license holders—Elizabeth, basically, though it's not clear if there were other women running saloons at the time—but they wouldn't make new ones available.

Elizabeth held on to the license until 1912, when she turned it over to her son Frederic. He was twenty-three years old at the time and ready to take over the family business. The transfer was approved by the city council. Elizabeth was faintly praised as the last and only woman saloonkeeper in Minneapolis. "Mrs. Maurer will probably be the last woman to enter the liquor business in the city," the *Tribune* reported. For years to come, that was true.

Frederic August Maurer was better known around Washington Avenue and the northside as Fritz. When he took over the family saloon, Fritz was only a few years removed from a successful career in high school football. He led the Blaine School football team in North Minneapolis, a multiethnic squad made up of Germans, Scandinavians, and Russian Jews. The team went undefeated in the independent city league in 1905, when Fritz was only sixteen years old. He was a natural front man for the family business: charming, outgoing, and well connected in the neighborhood. In 1917, he went overseas to fight in Europe. When he came back, he filed to run for alderman in the city's Third Ward. He won, joining some of the same aldermen who a few years earlier had voted against his mother receiving a liquor license. By that time, Prohibition was in effect, so the issue of who owned the liquor license at Maurer's Cafe was moot.

Fritz stayed closely connected to the restaurant business while serving as alderman. A little too close, it turns out. In 1929, Fritz was swept up in an anti-corruption effort led by Hennepin County prosecutor and future governor Floyd Olson that also involved a number of his fellow aldermen. He was arrested for accepting a thousand-dollar bribe from one of his colleagues on the city council, in exchange for clearing licensure for a northside club called the Stables. Fritz went to prison on a ten-year sentence and ended up serving through the mid-1930s.

His wife, Mabel, ran the store while he was away. And so, for the second time in two decades, a Maurer woman was in charge at 507 Washington Avenue North.

Born in Iowa in 1894, Mabel Cecilia Maurer had been married to Fritz since 1914. She was also personable and active in her community, serving as head of the auxiliary post of the Northside American Legion. While she was running the store, she hosted sewing meetings for the ladies of the post in the upstairs apartment. Of course, in 1929, when Prohibition was still in effect, Maurer's wasn't serving liquor—at least, not legally—but instead was serving meals, as well as soft drinks and cigarettes. After Prohibition was lifted in 1933, Mabel reapplied for a liquor license. Two decades after her mother-in-law transferred the license to her husband, Mabel was granted a license by the city council.

The Maurers ran the café throughout the 1930s, living sometimes in the upstairs apartment and sometimes in a house on the northside. The members of the family passed away in relatively quick succession: Elizabeth in 1941, Fred in 1943, and last of all Mabel in 1948.

Maurer's Bar outlasted its namesakes by at least a few decades. Over those years, the building seemed to collapse in on itself as the downtown core around it was hacked away by urban renewal: the 505 half of the building was demolished in 1963 and became a parking lot. The second story of 507 was removed in 1972.

Chester Tomcheck, a steelworker from the Northeast who had purchased a bar on the West Bank and renamed it the 400, bought Maurer's in the 1960s. He retained the name and ran it until 1977, when he retired from the barkeeping business. By this time, most of the old-timers who might have had a personal association with Elizabeth or Fritz had long departed the scene.

After Chester retired, the bar was known as Josie Jo's and then the Full Court. Since 1995, it's been Cuzzy's, a lone dive bar holdout on a tidy, revamped Washington Avenue better known for high-end eateries, condos, and gyms. The bar that stands on the site today is one-quarter the size of the original Maurer's and has been stuccoed and painted bright green, camouflaging the true age of the building. Though there are a handful of older bars in St. Paul, there aren't many existing bars on the Minneapolis side of the river that can claim an unbroken lineage stretching back to the 1880s.

Inside, Cuzzy's retains the shape of the classic turn-of-the-century saloon: a tile floor that may very well be left over from the Maurers' tenure, tables on one side and a wood-top bar on the other, nearly every wall surface barnacled with signed dollar bills from regulars.

One of Cuzzy's claims to fame is its resident ghost. The Cuzzy's menu mentions it, and the bar often appears in guides to haunted locations around the city, making it a popular destination for ghost hunters. Who knows how these stories get started, whether through hazy memories, coincidence, or some expression of the collective subconscious, but the ghost's name is said to be Betsy, for reasons no one can quite remember. According to the literature, Betsy was a woman of ill repute around the turn of the last century.

Certainly, the history of the bar has more than enough death and mayhem in it to play host to any number of spectral forces. The behavior of the ghost, though—moved drinks, switched-off lights, "enigmatic hugs"—doesn't suggest to me, anyway, a "woman of ill repute." It suggests, instead, the routines of a bar owner.

Perhaps the Betsy in question is actually Elizabeth "Betsy" Maurer, a hardworking woman keeping an eye on the family business a century later. She must have had quite a presence if she was able to maintain control of a barroom frequented almost entirely by hard-drinking men. If you do believe in ghosts, raise a toast to Betsy. Whether she's the spirit occupying the bar at Cuzzy's or not, she was a tough woman who ought to be remembered fondly.

Cuzzy's, a legendary Minneapolis dive bar, occupies the site of the old Maurer's Bar and Cafe on Washington Avenue. *Photo courtesy of T. J. Turner*

"Just keep drinking, and I'll have my fellas go to Wisconsin and get some frog legs."

HOLLYHOCKS CLUB

1929–1934

1590 MISSISSIPPI BOULEVARD SOUTH, ST. PAUL

First of all: there was no secret tunnel at the Hollyhocks Club. Not then, and not now.

If every tunnel said to be built under the various bars and saloons of the Twin Cities in the past hundred and fifty years really existed, the layer of earth stretching between the Chain of Lakes and the St. Croix River would collapse on itself, the supporting layer of limestone beneath hopelessly compromised by miles of hidden passageways filled with moldering barrels of whiskey and skeletons.

It's true that gangsters did their drinking, dancing, and gambling at the Hollyhocks Club during the latter years of Prohibition and the Depression, up to and possibly including John Dillinger himself. It's true they had large quantities of money and booze moving through the back door. But they didn't need to hide it in tunnels or even be particularly secretive about it. St. Paul was a protected city. It's not like the cops were going to raid Hollyhocks. The proprietor, Jack Peifer, went down to St. Paul City Hall every week with an actual envelope full of money to pay off the police. In 1929, Peifer's predecessor, a former boxer who turned the mansion on

Mississippi Boulevard into a casino, had been given clear instructions by the county attorney to set aside 20 percent of the house's winnings for bribing politicians and cops. It was as easy as that.

The Hollyhocks Club had the reputation around St. Paul as the place to go to see prominent gangsters do their business. The reputation was well earned, but it wasn't just the gangsters who frequented the joint. Middle- and upper-class professionals in St. Paul and the surrounding areas also came to Hollyhocks—gambling and drinking and enjoying steaks in the first-floor dining room. At a time when any drinking in public had to be undertaken at great personal risk, Hollyhocks gave moderately well-to-do St. Paulites a way to do so with a sense of glamour and danger, and with a tacit guarantee they would be well taken care of by Peifer and his staff. The staff were discreet to a fault. In Paul Maccabee's indispensable guide to St. Paul's gangland years, *John Dillinger Slept Here,* he recounts a tale told by Martin Rohring, the Hollyhocks doorman. Early one morning, a man came to the door and demanded to enter. Rohring turned him away. "I'm the mayor of St. Paul! Let me in here!" he yelled. He was indeed the mayor, it turned out, but no luck. Rohring turned him away.

At the time, Hollyhocks seemed a little bit more like a country estate than it does today as a private residence; infill has surrounded it on both sides, and after a renovation in the 1990s, it looks very much like the other large private residences around it. No pictures of the interior seem to have survived, but the exterior shots make the establishment look dark and slightly forbidding, an austere Victorian three-story with some outbuildings on a lonely expanse of open land. It was named for the colorful pink and yellow hollyhock flowers that bloomed around the house. It's about as far outside the primary commercial districts of St. Paul as you can get without leaving St. Paul proper. It faces the Mississippi River from atop the bluff, set back from the road, south of Montreal Avenue in what was still fairly undeveloped land in the 1930s. When the FBI wiretapped one of the club's phones in the early 1930s, the agents casing the building painted it as a sylvan retreat, describing it "opposite a park which is at the bottom of a hill in St. Paul territory." A roundabout off Mississippi River Boulevard led right to the front door. "Valet parkers met Cadillac limousines at the door," is how author Steve Thayer describes it in his St. Paul crime novel *Saint Mudd,* which features as one character a fictionalized prostitute who works out of the third-floor master bedroom. "Tuxedos and evening dresses were mandatory."

It was the perfect location for a technically but not functionally illegal private club: somewhat tucked away and fairly discriminating, but not exactly hidden or exclusive. "Insurance Firm Dinner Held," went a 1929

Tribune headline about just such a function at Hollyhocks. Not exactly Al Capone and the Green Mill.

Peifer seems to have made up his staff exclusively of middle-aged men from the cities' Japanese American community. The head waiter was a man named Sam Tanaka, born Shigematsu Yukimura in Hiroshima in 1888. Tanaka emigrated to the West Coast in 1906, settled in San Francisco, and came to St. Paul with his Minnesota-born wife. He was an experienced hand in the service industry, and he recruited men like Ben Doi and Roy Watanabe as his colleagues to run Hollyhocks. All of them had served in cafés or managed restaurants in Minneapolis and St. Paul, in most cases for decades. Doi had been at the Sochu Inn, a chic, Chinese-owned café on South Fifth Street throughout the teens and twenties. Watanabe was among the first Japanese nationals to immigrate to Minnesota in the early 1900s, and he had worked his way up from a bellboy at the Merchant's Hotel in St. Paul, eventually owning a series of cafés in Minneapolis. Tanaka, Doi, Watanabe, and their colleagues brought with them an expertise in running high-end restaurants catering to diverse clientele, as well as a sense of discretion.

The first floor was for dining, with booths lining the room, and a kitchen run by Tanaka in the back. It was glamorous, but Rohring doesn't recall much eating. "The food they gave away," he later recalled. "You could get a Porterhouse steak for $1.50." People weren't there to eat, he clarified: "They came to *gamble*." Other memories of the food are more effusive. Maccabee recounts a story of a group of gamblers being seized with a desire for frog legs late one night. Peifer told them, "Just keep drinking, and I'll have my fellas go to Wisconsin and get some frog legs." Two hours later, everyone was drinking gin rickeys and eating deep-fried frog legs pulled off of amphibians that had been croaking away in a marsh near New Richmond just hours before.

Gambling took place on the second floor, with roulette tables and booze flowing. Elsewhere, there were high-priced call girls. Jack Peifer sat upstairs on the third floor by himself with a German shepherd and his piles of money hidden away throughout.

Peifer was a reasonably smart guy, but his business associations caught up with him. He became embroiled in the kidnapping of beer baron William Hamm with the Barker-Karpis gang, who were regular guests of Hollyhocks. The kidnappers got their ransom money, but Peifer was identified via a fingerprint on the ransom note, and he was tried and convicted. He committed suicide in 1936 by taking a cyanide pill that someone had slipped him at some point between the trial and imprisonment. His wife, Violet, sold Hollyhocks in 1941. The owners since have searched in vain for those hidden passageways.

The Hollyhocks Club on Mississippi Boulevard in St. Paul, 1920s. *Ramsey County Historical Society*

But again, Hollyhocks didn't need tunnels to smuggle in booze, or smuggle out bodies. It was easy enough to bring it all through the back door. If you were in a certain station in society, you didn't need to bother with speakeasies or homemade bathtub gin. If you were a reasonably well-off couple who owned some formalwear and were looking for some drinks and maybe the thrill of fraternizing with gangsters, you could find your way into Hollyhocks. Beyond the right connections and accessories, all you really needed was the smug, easygoing sense that you'd be taken care of.

It didn't work out that way for Jack Peifer, of course. Years later, though, a friend of Peifer's, Mock Larson, remembered the breezy illegality of the Hollyhocks Club in this way: "That's the way St. Paul was in those days. All friendly."

"People asked you your opinion and you got to know what to tell them."

CASSIUS BAR

1949–1980

207 SOUTH THIRD STREET (1949–1958);
318 SOUTH THIRD STREET (1958–1980), MINNEAPOLIS

For most of the history of Minneapolis, the granting of liquor licenses was the decision of the men who sat on the Health and Hospitals subcommittee of the city council. If you wanted to run a bar in Minneapolis that sold hard liquor, you had to go in person to city hall, walk past the marble *Father of Waters* sculpture reclining indolently in the rotunda, and head up to the hearing room to make your case. After hearing you out, the committee members would make a final decision that was fair, equitable, and in the best interests of the people of Minneapolis.

Well, ideally.

In reality, the process went like this: There were a set number of liquor licenses that could be granted around the city, and if a license was vacated or revoked, another person could apply for it. The application had to clear the public health committee, as well as secure support from the two aldermen from the ward where the business would be located. The process for how those licenses were doled out was about as clean and transparent as one might imagine for a potentially lucrative business decision based on personal relationships, business interests (licit and illicit), prejudices, and financial considerations—and *especially* when these decision makers could cover for their own conflicts of interest or business deals by grandstanding on morality when it was convenient for them to do so.

Anthony B. Cassius found himself wrapped around these systems for eighteen months in the late 1940s.

Cassius had arrived from Oklahoma in the 1920s as a young teenager, the third youngest of twenty-three children. His parents sent him north with one of his brothers after two young boys he grew up with were lynched. After studying at Macalester College, Cassius became involved in politics and union organizing. He worked at the Curtis Hotel in Minneapolis, where he organized the staff and successfully struck for a pay raise. He ultimately founded the Black Cooks and Waiters Union Local 614 in the early 1930s. In 1935, he opened a restaurant in south Minneapolis called Dreamland Cafe, later recalled by the *Twin Cities Courier* as "the first decent place for Blacks in the city" and located at the heart of the city's African American community at East Thirty-Eighth Street and Fourth Avenue South. Cassius sold Dreamland to his nephew in 1946 and turned his attention to downtown, where he had long wanted to open a similarly classy destination for the city's African Americans.

Anthony B. Cassius, circa 1949. *Photo by John F. Glanton; courtesy of Hennepin County Library and the children of John Glanton*

Cassius purchased a dingy, mobbed-up 3.2 beer joint near Washington Avenue, and once he turned out the numbers runners and drug peddlers, he went looking for an opportunity to begin selling strong beer and liquor to complement the other offerings. When a bar at 408 Cedar Avenue on the West Bank had its license revoked for selling on a Sunday, Cassius put forth an application. If granted, he would be the first African American in the city's history to hold a liquor license.

Cassius's application went before the council in the summer of 1947, and it was met immediately with opposition from the conservative faction of the council. It also was met with overt hostility from the gangsters who controlled the liquor trade in Minneapolis; depending on the version of the story, either Kid Cann or one of the aldermen in his pocket was said to have indignantly stated that the liquor business was a white man's business.

The aldermen were less overt, but no less determined, in their opposition. They found numerous reasons to oppose Cassius's application, none of which mentioned his race. Each of the following reasons was offered: For one, there were already too many liquor bars around Washington Avenue. Two, Dreamland had been a nuisance in its neighborhood (something the police record did not bear out—in fact, it had a reputation as the sort of high-end place where celebrities like Lena Horne would frequent while in town). Three, although Cassius had sold the bar to his nephew a few years earlier, the nephew most likely was just a front and Cassius was still secretly running it, and at the time a person was permitted to have only one license. Four, Cassius was taking advantage of another man's misfortune by not buying him out of his tens of thousands of dollars' worth of bar fixtures, as was the custom—never mind that the unfortunate man whose license was being evacuated also happened to be a client of the alderman's business partner, an attorney. Five, there was a nice cop named Rickman who wanted the license, too. And beside all of this, wasn't it well known that Cassius was a committed Communist? (Besides the fact that the cop wanted the license, none of these reasons for opposing Cassius's license were true.)

In years to come, Cassius's bar would be one of the first stops for newly arrived African Americans from the South looking for advice on navigating the transition from what one writer called "Southern prejudice to Northern prejudice."

"This is Minneapolis," he'd advise. "But don't be fooled by appearances."

Cassius had the support of the local black community as well as the labor community. "We blow hot for the rights of people in Greece, in China,

Interior of the original Cassius Bar at 207 South Third Street, circa 1949. *Photo by John F. Glanton; courtesy of Hennepin County Library and the children of John Glanton*

in Poland, but are as cold as ice when it comes to the rights of 15 million colored people right here at home," Cassius wrote in a letter to the *Minneapolis Star* in September 1947. "What stand will the people of Minneapolis take on these issues right here at home?"

The license was denied. It would be a year before another opportunity opened up, and in November 1948, Cassius tried again. "I didn't get a very good deal the first time I applied," he noted wryly.

"There are only two places in the city where a Negro can buy a drink now and not be grossly insulted," he said at the time. He didn't think much of the other two, and his place would be professional, clean, and safe for everyone.

Cassius Bar at 318 South Third Street in Minneapolis, 1960. *Hennepin County Library*

In December 1948, the license was finally approved. In the end, it was framed as a civil rights issue. There were no other African American license holders in Minneapolis, and it was right that there be, at the very least, one. One alderman quoted Cassius's letter directly, noting that there were only two establishments in town where a black man could get a drink without being insulted. Cassius's bar began serving liquor shortly thereafter.

For at least thirty years, Cassius Bar was one of the city's great institutions and one of the few places in a segregated city where blacks and whites intermingled. The bar was originally located at 207 South Third Street, until 1958, when the block was condemned by the state legislature to make way for a state job office—presaging the wave of redevelopment that would soon lead to the eviction of most of Cassius's nearby colleagues in the liquor trade. There was a sense that some of the city's white merchants had been unusually eager to work with the state to condemn the block in question and be rid of Cassius. Although eminent domain enacted by the state was not subject to judicial review, Cassius appealed the relatively meager buyout offer, and he won. He used the proceeds to open a second location a block away, at 318 South Third Street. The Cassius Bar remained there for more than two decades.

Both locations had their admirers. The 207 location was remembered for having a slightly more integrated crowd, and for appealing to a higher-end clientele. Photographs from the early days of the bar bear that out: men in tuxedos and women in evening dresses, in front of a well-stocked bar with a galaxy of shiny glassware behind them. Cassius had been an early booster of the DFL when the state Democratic Party and Farmer-Labor Party merged in the 1940s, and visits from local politicians, including Hubert Humphrey, were common. The menu offered expertly mixed cocktails in

Bartenders at Cassius Bar, circa 1949. *Photo by John F. Glanton; courtesy of Hennepin County Library and the children of John Glanton*

"a dozen different types of glasses," Cassius recalled later, as well as soul food: barbecued chicken, fried shrimp, pork chops.

The 318 space was gorgeous, too. The building had long been owned by the On Leong Chinese Merchants Association, which retained a clubhouse upstairs on the second floor. The first floor featured a bar with a mirror behind it, red vinyl booths, and more space for live performances. Cassius commissioned a number of local artists to create four wall-size murals depicting great moments in sports; two of them were painted by Mel "The Rondo Street Jinx" Brown, himself a boxer. They depicted boxing matches with Joe Louis, Muhammad Ali, and Sugar Ray Robinson as well as Jackie Robinson's dramatic slide into home in the 1955 World Series. Ali, Sugar Ray, and Jackie Robinson visited the Cassius Bar while in town, and they befriended the owner and his staff. Mel Brown painted Cassius's face into the crowd in the Sugar Ray Robinson mural, which depicted his spectacularly bloody 1951 St. Valentine's Day fight against the Raging Bull, Jake LaMotta. It wasn't just artistic license; Cassius had actually been ringside at that fight, and he recalled the first three rows being covered in blood.

Patrons at Cassius Bar, circa 1949. *Photo by John F. Glanton; courtesy of Hennepin County Library and the children of John Glanton*

The crowd at Cassius Bar was more predominantly black in the second iteration, at least in part because of the city's shifting demographics. Cassius had noted early on that a black-run bar in the 1950s couldn't make it solely on black trade; that was less true starting around 1970, when the African American population in Minneapolis grew significantly, from a little under twelve thousand in 1960 to nearly nineteen thousand by the end of the decade. This was during a period when the city's white population was in decline. The Cassius Bar remained a hangout, social club, and important first point of contact for newly arrived African Americans. Cassius dispensed wisdom, advice, suggestions for professional contacts, and anything else that was needed of him; he later recalled spending "a third of my time helping people fill out job applications."

Being behind the bar, "people asked you your opinion," he said, "and you got to know what to tell them."

"I always tried to see that people got along and one of my criteria was that you had to respect the person next to you."

The way people talked about the bar changed over time, too. It's telling that the first iteration of the bar was remembered as "integrated," though Cassius himself put the figures for the clientele at about 35 percent black and 65 percent white. A bar is typically thought by white patrons to have a "mixed crowd," rather than being considered a "black bar," as long as the total number of black patrons stays well under half. In the second iteration of Cassius Bar, the clientele was majority black—a 90–10 split by Cassius's own estimation. He pointed out how there was a feeling at this point in the African American community that the bar should prioritize black clients. Not for nothing: a black police officer brought a high-profile suit against two white cops who had arrested a black patron at Cassius's using extreme force. The bar gained a reputation with white patrons for being somewhat dangerous, though the Cassius Bar didn't necessarily seem rougher than any other downtown bar in the 1970s, a time when an undercurrent of potential violence permeated most of the downtown drinking establishments. Occasionally there would be violence—when Cassius moved out and the next owner moved in, he found an arsenal of tire irons and a pistol under one of the booths—but most often, you'd walk in and find the usual crowd drinking whiskey and beer. The bar attracted a mix of longtime regulars and the newly arrived, with a stream of Cassius's well-known friends from the world of sports. Cassius, it was agreed by all, ran a clean house and welcomed everyone—his regulars "lived and died for me," he recalled later. His staff, too, was noteworthy for their good humor, hospitality, and longtime service. Joseph Lewis Jr., a southside native, managed the bar for years and was said to be one of the most popular bartenders in town.

The bar closed in 1980 when Cassius retired at the age of seventy-three. Business had dropped off, and, according to Cassius, the major culprit was a generational shift. Marijuana, he complained, was the recreant of choice, and it made younger people less likely to come in and spend money on elaborate cocktails like sidecars and martinis.

When Cassius died in 1983, he was remembered as one of the pillars of the community, a generous man who'd devoted his life to "serving humanity and loving every minute of it." That service took many forms, not the least of which was an expertly mixed whiskey sour in a highball glass on a Saturday night in downtown Minneapolis.

“The oom-pa band there in the corner, three fellas playing, and they’d be four deep at the bar on a Friday or Saturday.”

HEXAGON BAR

1934–present

2600 TWENTY-SEVENTH AVENUE SOUTH, MINNEAPOLIS

When the infamous liquor patrol limits of 1884 were drawn up, they scratched clean lines around downtown, the West Bank, Northeast, and Near North Minneapolis. The boozy areas were confined to the working-class neighborhoods within a mile or so of downtown, and they did not extend south of Franklin Avenue, east of Northeast Fourth Avenue, or into any of the park-laden bourgeois neighborhoods of respectable Minneapolis. From that moment on, once the limits were in place, it was hard to find whiskey anywhere in south Minneapolis. (Though it must be said, a few old bars were grandfathered in, and in ways that were quite lucrative for the holders of the exceptional liquor licenses.)

There was one glaring exception to the neatly drawn liquor limits: south of Franklin Avenue, the city officials carved out a square area, two blocks on each side, centered on the intersection of Twenty-Sixth Avenue and Twenty-Sixth Street, smack in the middle of the zone of factories and warehouses

The Hexagon Bar, in the "Hub of Hell," 1965. *Hennepin County Library*

that hugged the rail yards of the Seward neighborhood. In this four-block zone, bars were crammed together so thickly that the area warranted its own dark name: the Hub of Hell.

As one alderman described it, surveying the area in 1905: "There was practically no police protection, and the big factories brought hundreds of strangers into the neighborhood, many of them pretty tough characters. There was every opportunity for carousing of all kinds, and stabbing and shooting affrays sometimes occurred."

The Hub of Hell, also known as Hell's Half-Acre, was its own special place, where the Puffer-Hubbard gang (from the nearby foundry) was just as likely to police social norms as the actual Minneapolis police.

At least that's what was said during the early decades of the twentieth century. To hear Auralea Hupp tell it, though, by the end of the 1940s, the old bars of Seward were almost peaceful. Along with Duffy's, Mr. Nib's, the Magic Bar, and a handful of others, the Hexagon was one of the bars that

popped back up into the gap in the patrol limits following the end of Prohibition. The place was named for its hexagonal bar (sadly, no longer extant), which dominated the center of the room. Hupp's husband's stepfather restarted the bar in the 1930s in a spot that had once been owned by the Schlitz brewery to make beer and, before that, had housed a shop that manufactured milking machines.

In an interview for a neighborhood history project, Hupp recalled the bar scene of the 1950s, when she and her husband, Claude, kept the peace in the neighborhood: "It was mostly truck drivers. . . . There would be fights in the bar, because we had a hexagon-shaped bar and there only was the one room. We had the oom-pa band there in the corner, three fellas playing, and they'd be four deep at the bar on a Friday or Saturday. The fellas would be arguing, you know, and my husband, who was a friendly guy, he and Jack Reilly would have to stop these fights."

The Hexagon Bar sat on the seam that separated the factories and warehouses of Seward from the working-class homes to the north and east. In those days, there were a lot of industrial facilities in the area, like the Milwaukee Road rail yards, which employed hundreds of working stiffs; Minneapolis-Moline, a farm implement factory; or Flour City Ornamental Iron Works Company, a foundry that crafted large, decorative railings, gates, and doorways. The railroad tracks through the neighborhood were lined with smokestacks and the streets full of men roving around and looking for work and fun.

Auralea Hupp herself only drank scotch and soda, a trick she learned from her brother. Because she didn't particularly like scotch, she sipped it slowly, which allowed her to keep a clear eye on the customers.

The relationship between Minneapolis's bars and its police force had always been a contentious and corrupting one, and during the 1950s the "liquor patrol" had become a routine world of low-stakes grift. A few times a year, the neighborhood patrolman would stop by each establishment and be gifted a pint or two of the best whiskey in the place.

Hupp recounts one such visit by a beat cop out of his element:

> *They used to take a case to the Police Department at Christmas, but once this policeman came in. He was not in our district, he had already moved to some other district, but he came in anyway for his liquor, he wanted his fifth. My husband got disgusted, and says you're not even in our district, what are you doing here? And the cop says, don't worry; next time you need me, I'll just sit back and watch, and you'll be sorry.*
>
> *And then some customers said, "We heard that Claude, we'll back you up."*

According to reports from the 1970s, the morals squad evolved through time to annual envelopes stuffed with cash, as was alleged by one police reform advocate during Mayor Al Hofstede's terms in office. (See also: the King of Clubs, page 164.)

Sometimes, the area bars really needed their police protection, as places like the Hexagon or the Magic Bar got robbed on the regular every few years. Most of the newspaper accounts of mid-century Minneapolis bars were confined to these robberies, and Claude Hupp had no shortage of stories of being burgled at gunpoint. There was the time when a guy in a car pulled Claude off the sidewalk with a sawed-off shotgun, or the time when a pair of robbers entered the bar late one night and duct-taped everyone's mouths shut as they ransacked the till.

But most of the time, as Hupp says, despite the fights and the burglaries, the Hexagon was a fun place to hang out.

These days, the Hexagon is one of the last two original remnants of the Hub of Hell, which once had ten different bars and saloons within just a few blocks. The old hexagonal bar is now a rectangle, and some pool tables have been tucked into the main room on the "bar side" of the building. The other side of the one-story structure houses one of the city's most intimate punk venues, where all kinds of local rock bands play short sets under low ceilings every weekend night. Without the factories and the cluster of bars and the parking lots full of rowdy drunken workers, it's hard to imagine the old world, when the Hub of Hell struck fear in the hearts of the city's middle-class living rooms. But with its mix of punks and locals, old and young, the patio of the Hexagon is the closest you might come to resurrecting the previous era of crowds, music, and beer.

“Its glittering lights seem to dominate the scene by night much more than by day.”

PERSIAN PALMS

1942–1961

111 SOUTH WASHINGTON AVENUE, MINNEAPOLIS

In Minneapolis's Gateway, the streets teemed with drunks, tourists, rubes, scores of working men from the rail yards or the mills, cops on the beat, and always winos popping in and out of the alleys that ran behind the old brick buildings. There, from 1942 until 1961, when it was razed in the massive downtown Gateway demolition, the name “Persian Palms” was on men's lips as the most exciting bar in Minneapolis. A titillating nightclub in the heart of the skid row district, the Palms was a place people went to escape from banal Minneapolis routines. Nearly synonymous with Dionysian revelry, the Palms was the flagship for the whole culture of nightlife and seedy excess that lurked in the heart of downtown Minneapolis.

The Persian Palms occupied the first floor of a large three-story building on the south side of Washington Avenue, within a few blocks of the two large railroad terminals that gave the Gateway its name. Typically, the Palms' two doors would be wide open, propped like welcome mats and providing glimpses of the pulse and rhythms of the bar inside. A large red marquee was mounted on the wall of the building beneath the fire escapes, bearing the name THE PALMS outlined in neon. Two rows of bright white bulbs lit up

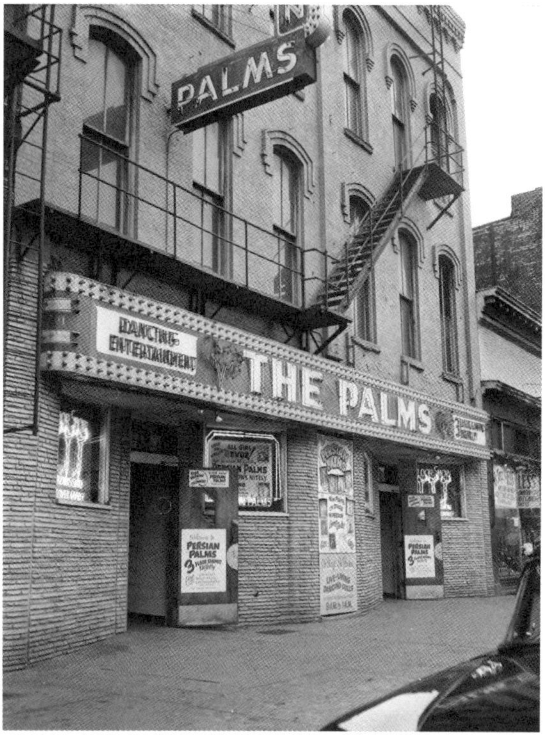

the pavement below, and the club would glow and beckon from sundown to late into the night, attracting the curious and the weak like flies to honey, until the last drunks were kicked to the curb, sometimes quite literally.

The Palms was a place you went to lose yourself and, quite often, to lose other things, too. Newspaper want ads from the Palms's heyday were sprinkled with Palms-related regret, requests for things lost inside the bar, such as one man's persistent plea for the return of a gold diamond ring, lost somewhere in the Palms in 1953. An article from 1959 tells of a bitter Palms patron who sued the bar after he lost consciousness on account of (he claimed) "a deleterious substance known as knock-out drops." Another man lost a knuckle when he scraped his hand on the doorframe after a particularly forceful Palms bouncer removed him from the premises.

The Persian Palms, in Minneapolis's Gateway District, shown in 1959. *Minnesota Historical Society Collections*

While many locals looking for a good time wound up there, the Persian Palms especially catered to rubes from the sticks, eagerly welcoming the curious, fresh-off-the-train tourist or groups of men in town for a convention—a cornucopia of opportunity for the Palms bartenders and their minions. For example, the bar was always well stocked with so-called B-girls, young women encouraged to approach single men with fluttering eyelids and requests to buy them drinks in exchange for flirtation. The bar served the girls watered-down "champagne" at an inflated price tag, the rube footed the bill, and the girl and the bar would split the proceeds. This is not to mention actual prostitution, which was certainly part of the Palms experience if you wanted it. In 1955, the Palms was named alongside a handful of other Gateway bars as part of a police-assisted prostitution ring.

For most people who went to the Persian Palms, though, it wasn't the B-girls who were the main attraction—it was the girls on the stage. The club was famous for its tantalizing floor shows, and in the late 1940s, they were at their peak. Before the rise of television and at the end of the vaudeville era, the Palms in the 1940s hosted all kinds of bizarre performances. For example: the Klassic Komedy [*sic*] of Lou Streeter, EmCee; the trick cycling show of Europe's famous "Two Winslows"; a group of female impersonators presenting the "Gay Time Review," a "rib tickling" evening's entertainment; an underwater titillation act involving a woman in a massive tank of water; and, most famously, Betty Vester's Beef Trust, a burlesque show featuring scantily clad obese women.

A typical night at the Palms, August 1945. *Minnesota Historical Society Collections*

The Beef Trust, "that rollicking gang of five hilarious hefty gals," was a particular pleasure for the Minneapolis faithful of the Palms, and one of the bar's most famous attractions. Vester got a lot of press attention for defying stereotypes, and the newspapers made a regular meal of stories of Vester fending off marriage proposals from lonely truckers or defeating columnists in eating contests. She and her crew were legends, and the Palms' tradition of having large women of the Klondike Kate variety serve as the emcee for the night's activities continued for years, even after the Beef Trust ceased being a reliable draw.

The Beef Trust and other acts make it rather easy in retrospect to brush off the vaudeville nature of the Persian Palms as a constant parade of sideshows, but in practice, the varied slate of Palms performers was full of legitimate, if now-forgotten, talent.

Take Delsey McKay, an African American singer and pianist who performed at the Palms. She grew up in the Hill District of Pittsburgh surrounded by early jazz musicians, and she studied briefly at Juilliard, starting out as a singer. At some point, she persuaded the band to allow her to play piano as well, and she was good at that, too. Famous for her thin stature and her flexibility, she also had a contortionist act and could put her entire body through a coat hanger. Later in life McKay had a brief career recording funk and disco tracks, including an obscure hit named "I Have Never Been to California."

The Palms was like that, a seemingly random mix of the amazing and the irrelevant. You never quite knew who would appear on stage any given night, how scintillating, embarrassing, or jaw dropping it might be. That's why you had to be there.

The Palms walked the thin, red-lit line of respectability, and that meant that it was always on the edge of castigation, disaster, and scandal. In the early 1940s, the bar was the center of a well-publicized trial over whether it had served liquor to a teenage boy, who was found by the police stumbling drunk around downtown Minneapolis. Asked where he got the booze, he could only say "the Palms," and that might not have been a big deal except that people working at the bar tried to bribe and threaten him into staying silent. The whole affair was a front-page scandal throughout 1942, and it set the tone for the Palms' later fights with the city's forces of moral hygiene. The concern over respectability was one reason why the Palms (allegedly) greased the palms of local cops and annually sent fancy monogrammed calendars to all the pertinent local officials—judges, police captains, aldermen, and the like—depicting the various features, and women, of the bar.

Such tactics became more important as the club evolved away from old-fashioned vaudeville shows and toward even more old-fashioned straightforward striptease in the early 1950s. By that point, the Gateway had become best known for its red-light acts and girlie shows, and the Persian Palms offered one of the grandest stages on Washington Avenue.

Matchbook advertising "Minneapolis' Most Popular Night Club," the Persian Palms. *Author Collection*

In a column for the *Minneapolis Morning Tribune,* nightlife correspondent Will Jones offered a rough taxonomy of some of the Palms' performers. There were the "gimmick girls," who used a simple song-and-dance routine combined with soft-edged flirtation. There were the contortionists, like Delsey McKay or Ann "Bang-Bang" Arbor, who used folding fans as a prop. There were professional striptease experts like Princess LaRaye, who, according to Jones, "had the added distinction of ending her act with less covering than any of the other girls in town this week. Since she's a big girl, too, the high flesh-to-clothing ratio is even more apparent. Finally," Jones concluded, "there were the serious seductresses, like Suez, a sultry brunette who looks like a well-fed Ava Gardner, and the only one of this type in town at the moment. She's at the Persian Palms. She fiddles coyly with each article of clothing before she takes it off. Her movements are slow and sensuous."

With the tides of sin and smut rising quickly in the 1950s, the inevitable backlash from city hall and the police department headquarters ensued. The "morals squad" announced a crackdown on exposed skin, though in one 1951 announcement, the morals squad chief offered the following fig leaf to the Palms management: "I'm not a censor, but the show at Persian Palms seemed cooler than the dancing act at Vic's [another girlie-show bar in the Gateway]. It's a hard thing to draw a line on."

Reading the descriptions of the Palms' various acts from the 1950s, one gets the sense that the owners of the bar were always on the lookout for a new gimmick to attract male customers. In 1953, they even installed a few mechanical-bull-style rides, which bar patrons were encouraged to try. Girls employed by the Palms were supposed to catch the men as they flew off the contraption, and they often ended up being knocked to their elbows or knees as the drunks flew at them.

By the mid-1950s, it was clear in the minds of civic boosters that the Gateway District was not long for this world; ample federal urban-renewal dollars had seen to that. It did not help that a few high-profile incidents reinforced the reputation of the Persian Palms as a place to be shunned. In 1958, an ex-con saxophone player, upset about an impending divorce from Palms dancer Ms. LaCount (the famous "black cat"), came in and shot her four times while she was sitting on a barstool in her black negligée.

In another incident, an African American ex-con stabbed a bartender on the sidewalk outside the bar, allegedly in response to a racial insult hurled his way from a passerby.

In a 1953 ode to the disappearing Gateway, a journalist for the *Minneapolis Star* described the Washington Avenue scene: "There, the Persian Palms, with its glittering lights, seems to dominate the scene by night much more than it does by day. It gets a constant flow of men and women, often together, but not always. Music wafts out into the warm air of the street from its two sets of open doors."

The Gateway's glory days were nearing their end. When the Palms was finally torn down in 1961, it was replaced with a blank, antiseptic modernist office building. The *Minneapolis Star* described the demise of the legendary club:

> *Gone are the bar stools that stood at the two bars in the club's front room and the exotic dancers who used to sing on these tall pedestals with their short skirts hoisted above their knees.*
>
> *The musician's stand is crushed. The traditional "bump and grind" band, which specialized in such dancers' songs as "Night Train" and "Tangerine," has moved out.*
>
> *The cash registers are hushed. The clink of ice and glass and the spew of beer is absent. The swinging doors that used to "whump" to and fro are sagging silently on their hinges.*

On that day, Minneapolis took a turn for the boring from which, for better and for worse, it has hardly recovered.

“The noisiest joint in town.”

THE GREAT LAKES BAR AND FUN HOUSE

1949–1960

101 NICOLLET AVENUE, MINNEAPOLIS

There had been a bar at 101 Nicollet Avenue for at least fifty years before John Suback purchased it from his aunt in the late 1940s. At the time, the Great Lakes Bar and Cafe shared a block with a few hotels, bars, and missions, including the Gateway Gospel Missions next door. After World War II, the Gateway District was the most enthusiastically patronized and, in some circles, most loathed section of the city. It was where, for ten years, Suback ran a bar and fun house.

John Martin Suback was born in January 1915 in Radošić, Croatia, a remote village in the mountainous region on Croatia's southern coast—so remote, in fact, that the village wouldn't have electricity until the 1970s. (Suback would never take electrification for granted again, as you will see.) Remote though it was, Radošić was not insulated from the worldwide calamities of the time. Like a lot of his generation, John was orphaned in the worldwide flu epidemic of 1918. The only professional opportunities available to a young man in rural Croatia were horse trading and cattle herding, both of which he tried his hand at. He decided he could do better in America, and so John left Croatia at the age of twenty-five to join family in Minnesota. He spoke English with a Croatian accent for the rest of his life.

For the first few years, the Great Lakes Bar was very much like its skid row neighbors at Nicollet and Washington, such as the Sourdough, Silver Dollar, and Pastime bars. It was maybe a little less rough and tumble than those places—John was a driven businessman, but also a kindhearted guy, a devoted Catholic, and a socially conscious Roosevelt Democrat. His daughter, Helen, remembers people would come in, "give him a sob story, he'd lend them five or ten dollars, and he'd never see them again." For those who did return and pay him back, though, a community built up around the bar. Helen also has stories of post office workers coming in on Fridays. The post office was right across the street, and the Great Lakes was a popular destination for its employees starting their weekends. Occasionally, some of them would get drunk and want to cash their paychecks to keep the party going. In these cases, Helen says, John would scoop up the money, put it in his pocket, and send for a cab or call the intoxicated worker's wife "before he spent his family's money."

Things were humming along just fine, but nothing about the bar quite distinguished it from what was a very saturated market. John Suback was a friendly guy, and one with an aggressively corny sense of humor that fit right in with the sensibilities of the Upper Midwest. In 1953, he decided to change the direction of the bar somewhat. He decided to add a fun house, complete with distorting mirrors and everything.

There was a precedent here, and one Suback may have been aware of when he began making crucial remodels to the Great Lakes Bar. John's Bar

The Great Lakes Bar attracted a diverse crowd throughout its history. *Photo courtesy of Helen Forster*

Interior of the Great Lakes Bar in December 1952, shortly before the owner converted it into a "fun house." *Minnesota Historical Society Collections*

and Funhouse, located at 2500 Marshall Avenue Northeast, was a wacky joint, the sort of place known for gags like spiders suspended from the ceiling and rubber worms in the drinks (both signatures of the Great Lakes in years to come). As it happens, those zany gags were cover for something much more dire going on at the fun house. In early 1953, the FBI, working with police in Minneapolis and Chicago, uncovered what was said to be the largest prostitution ring in the United States, operated out of the second floor of John's Bar and Funhouse. An employee of the bar, John Gawron, worked in concert with two women, Dee Wheeler and Frances Elliott, recruiting girls in Minnesota and sending them back and forth to Chicago. Gawron went to prison, and John's was shut down.

Suback may or may not have consciously taken up the torch after seeing the opening for a new fun house–themed blue-collar bar in Minneapolis. The timing suggests it's certainly a possibility. At the end of May 1953, John Suback spent $300 (about $2,800 in 2018) on remodeling the back room of the bar, installing a drop ceiling and new floors, and he soon reopened with a fully operational fun house in the rear. One early newspaper sniffed about its similarity to John's, but Suback would take the concept much, much further. If Gawron used the fun house motif as cover for something else, Suback was fully and totally committed to it.

"COME WITH YOUR FRIENDS for a real good time," requested an advertisement in the *Tribune*. John was a little less restrained with his advertisements in a bowling journal directed to a more working-class customer. "NO PRUDES ALLOWED! BROAD MINDED PEOPLE ONLY! The noisiest joint in town," it proudly proclaimed. The sign on the side of the building said the same thing. The Great Lakes Bar anchored the intersection of First and Nicollet, and one side was taken up by that building-long painted sign. The sign featured, among other things, a number of zany tableaus: a monkey swinging from a vine, a clown beating a drum, a man ice fishing.

On a typical Friday night, you'd be greeted by the bartender, or maybe even Suback himself. "Hey, congratulations!" he'd say. "You're the one-thousandth person to enter this room." He'd hand you a gift-wrapped package. You'd take it and receive a light electrical shock. Electrical currents were a standard feature: each of the barstools was also rigged up with an electrical current described by contemporaries as "mild but emphatic," to be delivered at the bartender's discretion.

At the bar, you'd probably receive a drink with a plastic spider or rubber worm in it. Your ashtray would be emptied into a bedpan by a waitress, cracking wise with a running banter that may or may not have been rehearsed in advance.

You might see the floor show, which was a riff on the popular floor show at Vic's, a few blocks away on Hennepin. Vic's featured Big Jay McNeely, a Los Angeles–based saxophone player, whose honking style of saxophone became a sensation around the Lower Loop, and whose set culminated in a wild, sweaty sojourn through the bar, serenading individual tables. At the Great Lakes, one of John's guys would put on a McNeely record and also go table to table, but with a giant salami in place of a saxophone. Another guy would trail him with a mop.

Once you'd loosened up a bit—and maybe hit the head, where you'd be greeted by a dummy of the opposite sex on a fake toilet, posed in some outrageous position—you'd be ready for the "tunnel of horrors." The back of the room was a series of fun house mirrors that you'd pass through. Puffs of air would blast out at you unexpectedly. As the centerpiece, Suback had at least one person on his payroll whose job on Friday and Saturday nights was to dress in a gorilla costume. This employee would, at some point, jump out at you.

People loved it. Beyond all reason, in some cases. One night in 1956, after a fire in the back room emptied out the bar, a forty-five-year-old Northeast Minneapolis man was so perturbed that his night had been interrupted and was so keen to get back inside to the fun room that he punched a firefighter in the face when he was stopped at the door, while the fire was still going, and then clocked another one before he could be restrained. ("He just had too much to drink," one of the firefighters later explained.)

What had been the bar's strengths—its central location in Minneapolis's liquor district and its regular community of customers—became a liability in the early 1960s. In the late 1950s, the city, in conjunction with business leaders, devised a plan to clear, for good, the Gateway District of the bars, single-occupancy hotels, flophouses, and small businesses that defined it in the public imagination, along with the one thousand or so itinerant men who inhabited the area. The plan was three-pronged: "(1) Attack blight. (2) Attract new enterprise. (3) Development of business in the loop." Attacking blight was step number one, and blight included bars like the Great Lakes.

It wasn't just the Great Lakes. In all, two hundred buildings and twenty city blocks were wiped out between 1959 and 1963, taking out dozens of

Matchbook for the "New Fun House" at the Great Lakes Bar. *Author Collection*

bars, saloons, and nightclubs, including Schiek's and the Persian Palms, among others.

Suback was devastated. He wasn't compensated by the city for the loss of the business, and the business was his only asset. It was then that the bar's greatest strength, its community of regulars, once again came into play.

Though the Gateway had a reputation for being the playground for hard-core drinkers living in skid row hotels, in reality the clientele was much more diverse. "From noon to six," according to a contemporary report by students from the University of Minnesota, "the neighborhood's bars and liquor stores were filled with typical skid row residents. They were replaced at the end of the workday with an influx of men and women who lived in other neighborhoods." The bars, it continued, were "largely patronized by outsiders." So while you might have been sitting at the Great Lakes' bar enjoying a whiskey on the rocks with a fake spider in it next to a skid row resident, there was also a good chance the person on your other side was a businessman from southwest Minneapolis dropping in after work.

One such outsider approached Suback in the last days of the Great Lakes, a wealthy man whose name Helen can't recall. "John," he said, "I will make you an interest-free loan to get you started again. I know you're a man of honor, and I know you'll pay me back." They shook hands, and the man made a loan to John Suback to open a new restaurant. It was the 5-8 Club, a truck stop down on the outskirts of town on Cedar Avenue that had the first color TV in its neighborhood, and that claimed at another time to be the inventor of the Juicy Lucy. Suback did indeed pay back every cent of the loan to the family's benefactor.

"No more tricks," he promised in 1964 when the 5-8 Club opened. "Just treats." Suback ran the restaurant along with a supper club in Shakopee until he retired in the early 1970s. He died in 1987 at the age of seventy-two.

Many of the proprietors of the Gateway bars slipped into obscurity. Suback was one of the few whose career had a second act. The bar owners of the Gateway and their clientele had a bad reputation, and some of them undoubtedly deserved it. But the Gateway was also a place where different types of people rubbed elbows, and where you never knew whom you might meet. John Suback certainly had no idea that, at some point in the 1950s, he poured a drink over a rubber gag worm for a man who years later would write him a lifesaving check, in gratitude for the noisy, close-knit bar and fun house Suback had created.

"Unless we give them something different, they'll drink at home and watch *I Love Lucy.*"

SADDLE BAR

1950–1975

415 HENNEPIN AVENUE, MINNEAPOLIS

Eddie Holman, already a figure with some notoriety, strode purposefully into the public imagination of the Twin Cities in the late 1940s. "Former airline pilot, pinball and nightclub figure" is how he was described in 1949, when it was noted he was interested in purchasing the Red Feather bar at 415 Hennepin Avenue, right across the street from the Brass Rail and Gay 90's. His name had appeared in the papers a few years earlier in connection with his involvement in the pinball racket, which was not the wholesome recreational enterprise you might imagine. It was a racket controlled by the mob, and Holman fronted a pinball machine distribution company in the late 1940s that was partially owned with Minneapolis gangland kingpin Kid Cann.

Holman and Cann had a falling out, and Cann punched Holman in the face. This in and of itself wasn't an uncommon occurrence. What made it notable was that Eddie punched Kid Cann back. Each of them sported a black eye for weeks.

The Red Feather was originally a café on Fourth Street, owned in part by two former Golden Gopher football stars. It was already serving hard liquor, and the owners wanted to move the establishment around the corner, to Hennepin Avenue, and operate it as a bar. The city council was nervous about allowing more liquor licenses into a block already saturated with them, but since it was a short move, they allowed it ("I could practically spit from the old location to the new one," shrugged one councilman). In December 1949, the bar moved into a vacant cigar shop around the corner. The Red Feather had been around since 1935 and had some name recognition, but the owners went all in on a western theme at the new location. When Eddie Holman purchased the bar in 1950, he doubled down on it.

The bar was lined with saddle-shaped stools. A bronze saddle was bolted to the front of the building. (It would be stolen a year later and apparently never recovered.) All the bartenders, Holman decreed, would wear western outfits. Not cheesy knockoffs from some Hennepin Avenue junk shop, but the real thing. He wrote Rex Bell, the former cowboy actor and husband of actress Clara Bow, who owned a western-wear shop in Nevada, and placed an order. Bell shipped everything with the exception of some western-style shirts, which he had to have special ordered from a supplier in the Midwest. In Minneapolis, in fact, a hundred yards from the Saddle Bar. Someone walked them over.

Rex Bell would later pay a visit to the Saddle Bar while passing through town on his way to Chicago to serve as a Nevada delegate at the 1952 Republican Convention. He presented Holman with a life-size silver saddle to replace the one that had been stolen the previous year.

As of 1950, the Saddle Bar was open for business. What would go on there for the next quarter century would be well known to Twin Cities residents, even those who never frequented Hennepin Avenue bars.

The stretch of lower Hennepin around the Saddle Bar—which also included the Brass Rail and Gay 90's, as well as the Copper Squirrel and Augie's—was right in the heart of the noisiest, most active, more colorful part of downtown Minneapolis. It was the kind of place writers loved to visit; the *Tribune* and *Star* columnists would file slice-of-life-on-the-Avenue columns profiling strippers and barflies with clockwork regularity. On the outskirts of the liquor patrol limits, neighborhood bartenders could ply their trade in relative peace, limping along with the support of the regulars and *maybe* getting a sketch written about them at some point by George Grim, Barbara Flanagan, Will Jones, or Jim Klobuchar. Bartenders working on Hennepin, though, were always the object of scrutiny, for better or for worse.

Something about Holman in particular attracted publicity. Probably it was his colorful background and his eye for promotions, but some of his peers seemed to have it in for him. A few months into his tenure, an article in the *Tribune* stated that he was attempting to open a private "key club" in

Interior of the Saddle Bar, April 1950. *Minnesota Historical Society Collections*

the rear of the shop. The piece, which seemed to have been written entirely from unsourced gossip, was nevertheless complete with some strangely specific details, possibly provided by Holman's competitors: the club would issue "gold-plated keys" to members, who would drink, smoke, and listen to football returns in luxury, sitting in the plush easy chairs and davenports someone saw being loaded into the back of the building one afternoon. All of which sounds nice, but running a private club would have been grounds for having his license revoked.

Oh no no no, Holman told the paper. He never intended to run such an establishment. That would be *illegal*! The photo of him that accompanied the story appears to have been snapped five inches from his face, and not necessarily with his permission.

When Holman wed—and a few months later, divorced—a professional golfer named Moonie Devereaux, the sordid details were splashed across the pages of the local paper as well.

This intense interest in the goings-on in the Lower Loop coincided with a crisis of sorts for the city's bars. In the years after World War II, the population of the city core was heading for the suburbs. Where you might have gone out to your neighborhood saloon for a drink twenty years earlier, by the mid-1950s you might simply choose to enjoy the comforts of your own air-conditioned home, with a wet bar in the basement and a color television in the living room to keep you entertained. Stories appeared over and over again in the papers about the emptying of the city's bars. Holman and his peers were a little panicked. "Unless we give them something different, they'll drink at home and watch *I Love Lucy,*" complained one Hennepin Avenue saloonkeeper in 1953.

Holman had at last two ideas for that *something different.* In an oversaturated market, the Saddle Bar provided the sort of live-action performances that customers couldn't get on their TVs at home: striptease artists and jazz musicians.

The Saddle Bar became one of the best places to see live jazz in the Twin Cities in the 1950s. It offered a reliable paycheck for many musicians, even if their repertoire was a bit limited in this particular venue. Pianist Jim Trost was born in Minnesota and spent his career playing in combos across the United States. At 9 PM a few nights a week, he performed at the Saddle Bar accompanying the dancers. "The routine was simple and invariable," he wrote in his memoir. "One slow tune followed by a medium-tempo song and finally one fast-tempo number to close each dancer's set. Since the strippers had little appreciation or concern for the music, we played 'straight ahead' jazz while the drummer would 'catch' (emphasize) an occasional bump or grind with a rim shot or drum roll." He recalled such strippers as Miss Dairy Queen, known also as Miss Milky Way (less a tribute to the state's dairy industry than to her ample bust), and Athena the Grecian Goddess, described as "a young attractive lesbian from rural Georgia."

Another of these dancers was Darlene LaBette Varallo, a native of Toledo, Ohio.

At the time, stripteases were common in the bars along Hennepin. Most of the performers were referred to as "exotic dancers." Holman and his dancers had the novel idea to identify them as "esoteric dancers"—something about the word seemed less nakedly sexy and more rarified, almost mystical. Or, maybe it merely skirted the local regulation governing "exotic" dance.

Nonetheless, at about 10 PM on a Friday night in 1953, Varallo was picked up by the vice squad and booked in the city jail. The charge was "disorderly conduct," though Neal Karlen asserted much later in his roundup of those years, *Augie's Secrets,* that the real violation was Holman's failure to pay off the cops with the customary fifty-dollar bribe. Varallo

Saddle Bar dancer Raven Roland occupies her time with some knitting during the city's ban on dancing, June 1953. *Photo from the* Star Tribune, *Minnesota Historical Society Collections*

was bailed out, pleaded innocent, and was fined a hundred dollars after a humiliating trial that culminated in her modeling in court the pasties she wore that night. Varallo, whose reasons for coming to the Twin Cities to pursue exotic dance are unclear, certainly had no reason to stick around after the spectacle of the trial, and she appears to have returned to Ohio shortly thereafter.

The city went on a morality rampage in the wake of Varallo's arrest, instituting a ban on dancing—exotic, esoteric, or otherwise. An article checking in on the Saddle Bar after the ban featured the indelible image of dancer Raven Roland sitting at the Saddle Bar and knitting, drawing her salary but legally unable to perform. Moreover, the city council unearthed a much older and previously unenforced ban on serving liquor to women sitting up at the bar. "The women are mad," Holman said at the time. "They want to know why men can drink at a bar and they can't."

Eventually, the city eased the bans, on both drinking and dancing. Striptease continued along Hennepin for the next twenty years, even as the demolition of the Gateway District got underway. Over time, as Hennepin Avenue became more and more seedy, and pasty-clad dancers were being edged out by private viewing booths for pornos, old-fashioned va-va-voom striptease began to seem almost wholesome by comparison.

This culminated, perhaps, with a glowing 1968 profile in the *Tribune* of Mrs. Lynda Beckner of Spring Lake Park, Minnesota, headlined "Mom's Stripping Act Shakes Up Suburbia." A middle-age mother of five daughters, Beckner had been a dancer in her youth, and after some hard economic times in the 1960s, she took up dancing once again. She drove down from Anoka County to the Saddle Bar every weekend to do a comic striptease routine—where she made a lot more money, she pointed out, than she did waitressing. Not only that, but the male patrons were a lot less handsy when she was dancing and not waitressing. Describing her work, she cut a playful, matter-of-fact and strangely conservative figure: "It's funny when the girls get together and they try to be sophisticated and call themselves 'exotic,'" she reported. As for sex itself: "I think it's downtown where it belongs, instead of in school, where they're preaching sex to the kids a lot worse than anything downtown."

Holman wasn't around for any of that. He seems to have tired of the saloon business after a few years. Having racked up some major debts over the four years he ran the bar, he transferred the license for the Saddle Bar to Oscar Rubinsky in 1954. From there, Holman moved into businesses that were both lower profile and higher grossing: he founded the Holman Oil and Gas Company in the late 1950s and devoted himself to the oil business for the rest of his career until his death in 1991. Devoted it to oil, that is, with the exception of the year he spent in the late 1960s serving as general manager of the Minnesota Muskies professional basketball team. That single season, the team lost $400,000 but also made it to the American Basketball Association semifinals before the franchise moved to Florida.

The Saddle Bar hobbled along with its contemporaries on Hennepin through the 1970s. Liquor licenses at the time were like ghosts, moving from one host body to another; the Saddle Bar's license, originally from the Red Feather, was transferred to Howie's Bar on West Broadway, and then to a pizza place, before it vanished into the bureaucratic mists of city hall's licensing division.

The Copper Squirrel, a sort of sister bar to the Saddle Bar located next door, which also featured live dancing, was graced by an enormous wooden sculpture of a can-can dancer on the exterior. Though the buildings were eventually demolished, the can-can dancer managed to make her way out of the Lower Loop. She's now hanging behind the bar at Whitey's Saloon, just a mile over the bridge on East Hennepin Avenue. You can't say the same for the silver saddle at the Saddle Bar.

"Federal agents raided the place and seized several bottles of allegedly altered liquor."

THE TOWN PUMP

1940s to 1980s

801 MARSHALL STREET NORTHEAST, MINNEAPOLIS

Marshall Street parallels the Mississippi River through the heart of Minneapolis's industrial Northeast neighborhoods, and it's long been one of the centers of the city's bar scene. Two massive breweries—Grain Belt and Gluek's—towered over the area like grainy castles, while all along the riverfront the bars lined up like dominoes among the neighborhood's train tracks, unadorned duplexes, and warehouses. The concentration of bars was largely the result of the liquor patrol limits instituted in the 1880s that sought to restrict the consumption of booze into just a few neighborhoods, but it meant that over time, Minneapolis bars became more and more concentrated in a few limited areas.

In Northeast's Sheridan neighborhood, the bar issue became a recurring concern for locals, especially as the Gateway demolition began increasing demand for booze elsewhere. One letter to the editor of a neighborhood paper put the problem on full display: "Is the Third Ward to become the dumping ground for Skid Row and Lower Loop liquor licenses? Already a move has been made to slip another liquor place into Northeast Minneapolis at 2420 Marshall N.E. under the guise of a restaurant. This was the unanimous approval given by the City Council on October 30th to the transfer of the Casanova Bar license to the Northeast address."

As Northeast became the place to be, the Town Pump Bar was in the thick of it. On the corner of Marshall and Plymouth, the bar guarded the key bridge that linked the two sides of the city over the Mississippi. The bar sat on the bottom floor of a solid two-story 1900s brick building with an apartment on the top floor. (Today the building has only one story, its top floor lost in a fire; a bunch of old bars in Northeast were similarly decapitated, such as Jimmy's Bar on nearby Fourth Avenue.)

As with many of the bars that survived Prohibition, rumors persisted about secret bootlegging tunnels underneath the Town Pump. Here, the idea of a booze tunnel seems more believable than in other cases — and the tunnel is still there in the basement, a low brick archway leading under Marshall Street. With the close proximity of the river and the way the banks gently slope up from the water's edge, a secret whiskey chamber extending from the river to the bowels of the bar is plausible.

Booze wasn't the only thing in high demand during the early years of the Town Pump. As the name suggests, a literal water pump stood in front of the bar, and it was surely well used. In this working-class neighborhood, for much of the early twentieth century, not every home had indoor plumbing, and it's easy to picture old women carrying water from the corner up the rickety back steps of a rudimentary apartment in the middle of winter.

As Frank Rog's Northeast memoir describes, the river was not always pleasant to be around in those days. He writes, "The river was really dirty then, with nasty things such as human waste floating downriver all the time. The carp fed on that. I think that's why we never ate carp." The state of the river being as it was, one can imagine the appeal of having access to good drinking water. And even better than drinking water, the Town Pump had plenty of liquid alternatives, guaranteed uncontaminated, on hand as well.

Inside the Town Pump, a long wooden bar was tucked along the wall underneath the second-floor staircase, the whole thing framed by a large mirror, rows of liquor bottles, and the requisite barstools—similar to how it looks today, as the Northeast Yacht Club. There was probably a small grill at one end of the bar with a small menu of food. On the wall opposite the bar, booths and tables were positioned below a few windows offering views looking west toward North Minneapolis and the Mississippi.

While whiskey at the Town Pump was uncontaminated by pollution from the river, for a time in the 1950s the whiskey was not necessarily devoid of Minneapolis water. In 1954, the Town Pump was one of a handful of Minneapolis bars that were caught in a crackdown by federal prosecutors on whiskey tampering, the long-standing and frowned-upon practice of

Above: Interior of the Town Pump, circa 1930s. *Photo courtesy of the Northeast Yacht Club*

Left: The Town Pump, at the corner of Marshall and Plymouth. *Photo courtesy of the Northeast Yacht Club*

watering down or swapping out cheap for expensive brands of whiskey.

Throughout the late 1940s and into the mid-1950s, the feds in Minneapolis made a show of cracking down on small bars for things like minor sports gambling, pinball machines (!), and other petty misdeeds that were often ignored by local law enforcement. In 1954, Minneapolis's US district attorney, George MacKinnon, joined the trend and boosted his career with a widespread sting operation meant to make public examples of barkeepers caught up in the mendacious practice of whiskey tampering. The sting at the Town Pump took place in January, and the owner of the bar, Theodore Wisniewski, was charged with two counts of switching whiskey brands. The following newspaper account described the events at the trial in the federal court:

> *[Bartender] Andrew Dordan testified that he was employed at the Town Pump when federal agents raided the place and seized several bottles of allegedly altered liquor in January 1954.*
>
> *Only a few minutes before the raid, Dordan testified, he had finished refilling several bottles labeled Seagram's Seven Crown or Lord Calvert with liquor from bottles bearing the Kinsey label. Currently a fifth of Lord Calvert sells at an average of $5.20, Seagram's Seven Crown at $5.55, and Kinsey Silver label for $4.25.*
>
> *Dordan testified under direct examination that he was under continuing instructions from Wisniewski to make such switches, but under cross-examination he testified that the proprietor had countermanded the order about a week before the raid.*
>
> *On the day of the raid, Dordan testified, he was acting on "my own volition."*

In a surprising move, the charges were thrown out, based on the argument that swapping one tax-paid whiskey for another tax-paid whiskey was not in violation of federal tax laws.

Despite the successful defense of Wisniewski and the Town Pump, there was never any doubt that cheap whiskey was being poured into the expensive bottles. The legal question on which the fate of Andrew Dordan and the others rested was whether or not tax had been paid. The final appeal went all the way to the US Supreme Court, where the initial judgment was reversed.

Regardless, the case was a shot across the bow for the old-school corruption of the Twin Cities saloonkeepers. It was one of many crackdowns that would be waged in subsequent years over things like gambling, vice, and evasion of city liquor laws.

The folks at the Town Pump did not necessarily learn their lesson, as a few years later, bartender Anthony Mancino would be charged with making a false report of a robbery with the Minneapolis Police Department, and two years after that, he got in trouble with the city again for having firearms in the bar.

(The Mancinos were among the many Minneapolis saloon owners of the time who skirted rules about single-bar ownership. Seeking to get around the restriction, tavern owners would buy additional bars and put them under the names of spouses or close family members.)

Regardless, Joe Mancino ran the Town Pump with a steady hand for many years afterward. The bar offered bus service to Vikings games in Bloomington or shuttles to events downtown. Mancino always had a Crock-Pot of spaghetti sauce cooking all day long, offering a free meal of pasta and red sauce for folks popping into the Town Pump for a pint of Grain Belt.

Eventually, the bar was sold and renamed the Northeast Yacht Club, an inside joke that fit nicely with the Polish sense of humor that pervades Northeast Minneapolis. To this day, the Yacht Club remains a proper Northeast dive, with a pool table, old-school clientele, and menus that fit onto an index card.

The Town Pump, after the building was converted from two stories to one story. *Hennepin County Library*

"If it weren't for the Jucy Lucy, I'd be out of business."

MATT'S BAR

1955–present

3500 CEDAR AVENUE, MINNEAPOLIS

In the first week of August 1955, a few men from the Naegele Outdoor Advertising Company were up on ladders at the corner of Thirty-Fifth Street and Cedar Avenue in south Minneapolis, removing the sign for Nib's Tavern, which had hung there for the past eight years, and installing one that read "Matt's." Other than the new sign, very little had been changed, inside or out—the new Matt's sign even used a similar typeface to the old one. (It may be the same *S* at the end.) People hanging out at the wooden bar, drinking and chatting—that was what went on at Nib's, and that's what would go on at Matt's. The transition from the one to the other was virtually undetectable. Very likely, the regulars barely noticed.

What masses of regulars and irregulars alike would soon take notice of was the culinary novelty that had been developed in the final three months of the bar's life as Nib's. The guys at the grill had been messing with grilling cheese *inside* a hamburger patty. The new namesake had no intention of putting an end to this kind of innovation.

Today, more than sixty years later, Matt's is a Minneapolis institution.

Matt Bristol, the namesake of Matt's Bar, mentioned numerous times in newspaper profiles of his bar that the fruit of those experiments, the Jucy Lucy, was the only thing that saved him from financial oblivion. The burger that made Matt's Bar famous and, by the early twenty-first century, was

Minneapolis's primary contribution to American vernacular food—two patties pressed over a molten core of American cheese—saved the 3.2 bar from the same fate as its many neighbors on Cedar Avenue. "If it weren't for the Jucy Lucy, I'd be out of business," he told the *Star Tribune* in 1984. A year earlier, he'd said something similar to *City Pages*.

Nib's Tavern and its successor, Matt's, didn't seem a lot different than Bob's, or the Pink Elephant, or the Red Feather, or any of the other now-forgotten neighborhood bars in south Minneapolis that had vanished by the middle of the 1970s. Indeed, most references to these bars in print are found in later profiles of Matt's, used as points of comparison, names that some readers may have dimly recalled from driving down Cedar Avenue in the 1940s or '50s.

"Vinyl booths and baseball trophies," read a 1978 profile of Matt's, "a jukebox and a small bar and grill." The décor was described as "Late Beer Hype," with lampshades, glasses, and calendars all bearing the names

Nib's Tavern at Cedar Avenue and Thirty-Fifth Street, in April 1953, bears a striking similarity to the corner's current inhabitant, Matt's Bar. *Minnesota Historical Society Collections*

of national and local beer brands. In fact, the building permits filed for Nib's and Matt's between 1947 and 1960 read like a roll call of popular beer brands: permits for neon or plastic wall signage for Pabst, Hamm's, Budweiser, and the Minneapolis Brewing Company, the predecessor of Grain Belt. Indeed, the scene described in 1978 could just as easily describe Matt's in 1958 and in 2018.

It's tempting to argue that Matt's would still be a special place even without its marquee menu item, a little time capsule of the 3.2 era. But it's hard to imagine, as Matt himself pointed out many times, that the bar would have survived at all without the Jucy. So closely associated is the bar with the burger that it's miraculous that the name of the bar didn't become "Jucy Lucy's" at some point.

While some may contend that Matt's is, in 2019, mostly a tourist attraction—a sort of south Minneapolis Katz's Deli—that assessment doesn't recognize the extent of Matt's pull on the psyche of the neighborhood. It's one of the few places that manages to be both a tourist attraction and a genuine neighborhood bar. In the years since the rise of cable TV food shows and the accompanying hunger for telegenic regional novelty foods, the lines for a table at Matt's have increased. But it's still fundamentally a hangout for people in the neighborhood, embracing a wide demographic cross section. As with any neighborhood bar, if you show up regularly, the servers will get to know you by name. You'll see other people you know from the neighborhood, often with their kids or their parents. The old-school charm that Matt's retains—the gold vinyl wallpaper, the wood paneling, the cash-only service—are all things that the Jucy Lucy made possible.

One wonders how Norbert Lowell Martin would have felt about all of this. Nib or Nibs, as he was variously known, was a Minneapolis native who owned a few establishments around the Twin Cities—Matt's immediate predecessor, but also a bar and nightclub variously known as the Magic Bar, Nib's Magic Bar, and Mr. Nib's, located at Twenty-Sixth and Twenty-Sixth in the so-called Hub of Hell.

Nib, a semi-notable bowler in the local amateur leagues, served in World War II—a photo of him somewhere in Italy using his helmet to scoop water out of a muddy river to shave with appeared in a December 1944 issue of the hometown paper and was undoubtedly clipped and placed over bars around the city. In 1947, he bought a building at Cedar and Thirty-Fifth that had housed a number of grocery stores since before World War I, and he opened a 3.2 bar. The building was shared with a dentist's office upstairs.

The bar wasn't, as previously noted, a lot different than most of its neighbors. It was a typical stucco neighborhood joint, maybe a little on the rowdy side—the neighbors complained to the public health commission about the noise in 1953—but otherwise the kind of cozy place you'd pop into for a drink or three after work. They served beer and fries and sandwiches.

Nib didn't invent the Jucy Lucy, but he was close by when it was invented. It was created at Nib's Tavern in 1955, three months before ownership turned over to Matt Bristol. It was Bristol who developed and promoted the burger, building a faithful clientele. In the early years of the bar, he purchased a meat press to more effectively envelop the cheese in the patty. Twenty years passed before the Jucy Lucy was first mentioned in the local paper. It's a blind item from an unnamed reader in the nightlife column that suggests the burger's status was already an open secret around town—not the stuff of feature profiles or restaurant reviews, but something people knew about.

The Lucy itself was given its first and fullest origin story in a 1983 profile of Matt Bristol in *City Pages*. The story is fairly well known around the Twin Cities, but in short, a neighborhood bachelor comes into the bar regularly and experiments with combinations of meat and cheese, dictating grilling orders to the cook and telling him to improvise with the meat patties. Cheese goes between meat, a spontaneous exclamation is made, and a misspelled transcription is preserved on the menu for decades to come. This is something that could only happen in a neighborhood bar by a guy who had ingratiated himself with the staff or, at the very least, whose presence the staff had come to tolerate. Though his name is lost to time, Bristol describes seeing the bachelor for years afterward, in his later years brought into the bar in a wheelchair.

In contrast to the longevity of Nib's/Matt's, places like the Pink Elephant are almost entirely erased from the historical record, and a trip through the city directories shows ownership of other neighborhood bars turning over constantly. A few blocks away, for example, at 3744 Cedar Avenue, starting in the mid-1940s, a place called Nelson's became Conrad's became the Blew Inn, and no iteration survived into the 1970s. The Cedar Inn, six blocks south of Matt's, actually predates Matt's by some time, having opened in the mid-1930s, and it still serves beer and burgers with little attention from the local or national press. Its orange and black exterior identifies it as a biker bar, bikers being a particularly loyal clientele who have adopted many a foundering neighborhood beer joint over the years across the United States. But for the most part, these types of neighborhood dives turned over fast.

The difference between Matt's and the others, of course, is the Jucy Lucy. Not just the burger itself, but the reinforcements that came with it: a flow of media coverage bringing fame and a steady stream of customers. For years, the only press clipping on the wall was a piece from the 1980s by Dick

Youngblood, former columnist for the *Star* and *Tribune*. It has been joined by a flurry of other profiles and reviews, from local and national magazines alike. The surest evidence of the bar's fame is a framed photo of President Barack Obama with the staff, from his visit in 2015—the same day, in a cosmic twist, that Matt Bristol died.

If Bristol had thrown out Nib's old menu and shooed away the regulars in 1955, there would probably be a Subway restaurant at 3500 Cedar Avenue today. He was smart enough to recognize not only an interesting competitive edge when he saw it but also that it was in his best interests not to disrupt the continuity of the place.

Maybe Nib had a sense of what he'd walked away from. The first print mention of the Juicy Lucy—with an i—was in the *Tribune* in 1969, in an ad for Mr. Nib's, his bar and nightclub at the Hub of Hell. "Nib's Famous 'Juicy Lucy' Is Back!" it cries. Until it burned down in the late 1980s, Mr. Nib's was known as a rock club, a wrestling venue, and a comedy club. It was never known as a place to get a Ju(i)cy Lucy, though.

At some point, John Suback's post–Great Lakes Bar venture, the 5-8 Club, farther south on Cedar, issued a claim on the origin of the "Juicy" Lucy. By the 2000s, dozens of other Minneapolis and St. Paul restaurants and bars began to add Juicy Lucys to their menus. It's the sort of thing periodically discussed when parsing the specifics of the regional identity: in a city that often finds it difficult to break free from rural *Prairie Home Companion*–isms, the Juicy Lucy has been adopted as Minneapolis's version of Philadelphia's cheesesteak or Massachusetts's lobster roll.

Matt's version, though, is generally regarded to be the first and the best. Any anonymous guy at a bar can come up with a good idea. But it takes something extra to hold on to that idea, and keep holding on to it for five decades.

"I think we better go to church next Sunday."

THE NICKEL JOINT

1935–present

501 WEST BLAIR STREET, ST. PAUL

Uniform jersey for the Nickle Joint-sponsored baseball team. *Minnesota Historical Society Collections*

"Attention gentlemen, the official meeting of the Old Timers Baseball Association is now in session."

With the announcement and a firm *thunk*—I imagine the sound coming from a baseball bat–shaped gavel—the men gathered before a small metal statue of a hot stove that had been placed ceremonially on the table at the front of the room. The tables were filled with men and their hats, pretzels, and pitchers of beer, and thus did the city's foremost off-season baseball society kick off its monthly meeting in the back room of the Nickel Joint, as they had since 1939. The Old Timers group was a testament to the link between fraternity, bars, and baseball, formed long before the Twins came to town. This group of bored minor league ballplayers who were part of the New York Yankees organization were trying to make it through the long, cold off-season and decided to keep hanging out even when winter had covered the ball fields with snow and ice.

Meetings were a mix of formality and jokes, and the reading of the minutes or the report from the treasurer was usually laced with barbs, nicknames, back slapping, and the like. A typical meeting might feature plans for upcoming ball games, tributes to old players or old teams, shout-outs to rivalries between different parts of St. Paul, and gossip about the managers, teams, and chances of the upcoming year.

"It started with guys who would stay in town," one regular explained. "It was like a bowling night, the third Wednesday, and guys would get together and play cards and talk baseball and whatever they wanted to talk about. It ran from September to May, and then ball started and they were gone. That's how it started, 1929, the Saints and the Millers and the guys who played for them."

It appears that nobody from the early days of the Old Timers ever played in the major leagues except for one guy: Larry Rosenthal. He was born in 1910 to Polish immigrants in Frogtown, just a baseball's throw from the Nickel Joint, and he played for the Chicago White Sox for six seasons before going off to the war. He came back and played a few more years with the Yankees and Connie Mack's Philadelphia Athletics before retiring in 1945. It's a sure bet that Rosenthal hung around the Nickel Joint in the off-season, sharing stories of the bigs with the boys in the back room.

For years after that, Rosenthal was at every one of the Old Timers' annual banquets, the premier event of the off-season, where the men gathered as many friends and baseball fans as they could in places like the Deutches Hall/American House on Rice Street to give awards and tributes to members of the club. Over the years, no fewer than three St. Paul natives have been inducted into the Baseball Hall of Fame, and no fewer than three members of the Old Timers have gone on to be mayor of St. Paul.

The walls of the back room have accumulated the documentation of the club's meetings and traditions, most notably a massive collection of framed photographs of old St. Paul amateur ball clubs. Nostalgic and old even in the 1950s, the photos depicted such teams as the nine from Lindeke Warner & Sons Dry Goods, huddled around their trophy; the Unique Theater Base Ball Team, St. Paul amateur league champions in 1909; the Alain Johnson team of 1907; Holm & Olson Landscaping, Capital City champions of 1915; and the 1910 American Hoist & Derrick squad.

There were dozens of photos of small groups of men representing bars, factories, city departments, companies, and neighborhoods, each one identified with small typewritten labels, some with nothing but "?????," if a name was forgotten.

The Nickel Joint nine became one of the many teams to have its photos mounted on the walls of the bar. The Nickel Joints won the city league championship in 1950, defeating the Harding Boosters 9–3.

The Old Timers were just one of the many clubs that used the back room of the Nickel Joint for meetings, tributes, and schemes. Large and located right off the back parking lot, the bar was the perfect place to hatch a jolly conspiracy and smoke cigars. The Nickel Joint sat in a two-story brick building built in 1903 on the corner of Mackubin and Blair. At least through the 1950s, the surrounding area was a mostly white, working-class community of old homes and quiet streets between University Avenue and the Burlington Northern railroad tracks. The

The Nickle Joint Tavern, with a police car parked outside, November 1957. *Minnesota Historical Society Collections*

Nickel Joint is just far enough from the massive St. Agnes Catholic parish and school that the shadow of the church spire—the distinctive two-hundred-foot-tall clock tower that serves as a landmark for the whole neighborhood—brushes across its doorway.

That church cast its shadow in more ways than one, as in those days it was still illegal for bars to be open on Sundays. For example, in the fall of 1954, the following incident took place at the Nickel Joint. Under the *Minneapolis Morning Tribune* headline, "Gloomy day ended for a small band of tipplers," came the following account:

> *Detective lieutenant Joseph Schmitz parked his police car, noticed a number of men going in and out of the tavern. More going in than out. They did not appear downhearted. One man walked in carrying an 18-month old child in his arms. But their gayness left them when Schmitz and two morals squad officers walked into the tavern and upstairs to the clubrooms. . . . Police said they found 19 men in the clubrooms, drinking strong beer and whisky.*
>
> *They ordered the men into a patrol wagon and an emergency vehicle in full view of some of their neighbors leaving a nearby church. That, some of the men admitted, is where they should have been. . . .*
>
> *They were in the habit of telling their wives they were going to church Sunday mornings, but went to the tavern instead. This was not news to the police. A suspicious wife had given them the tip.*
>
> *Most admitted buying the liquor in the tavern and taking it upstairs for a drink. Police charged Maurice O'Connor, 58, proprietor of the tavern, with selling liquor on Sunday.*
>
> *One said he didn't want to go home because he had given his wife and two grandchildren a ride to church, let them out and said he would park the car and join them. "We've got to get together," he was heard to say. "Look, a couple of you guys come home with me. And then I'll go home with you so we won't have to face them alone."*
>
> *Another shook his head.*
>
> *"I think we better go to church next Sunday," he said.*

Such were the scandals of Frogtown in the 1950s.

The Nickel Joint bar is still there, and the Old Timers still meet once a month during the off-season. They are always looking for new members and will have you know that they have been admitting women for years.

Today the bar is owned by Ethiopian Americans who use the back room in very similar ways as their predecessors did a hundred years prior, hosting important meetings, events, and celebrations where St. Paul dreams are hatched. Some of the old baseball photos still hang on the wall, and it's even open on Sundays.

"These are the guys that can help you out when the car breaks down."

CARIOCA CANTINA

1950s

124 STATE STREET, ST. PAUL

St. Paul's West Side flats was a tight-knit community set within a few square miles of streets gridded out just south of downtown, in the low land between the flood-prone Mississippi River and the train tracks that edged the bluffs to the south. A large swath of land hosting some of the oldest parts of the city, the West Side offered a dense and vibrant mix of industry, simple homes, and lots of different kinds of people. Immigrants from Mexico, Lebanon, Russia, Switzerland, and Jewish communities from all over Eastern Europe and many other groups landed there because it offered the best shelter of last resort, apartments and houses near to the blue-collar and merchant jobs that were the lifeblood of newcomers. Homes butted right up against the river—which by the twentieth century did not smell that great—and neighborhood kids would jump in on a regular basis to cool off from the summer heat, hoping not to cut their feet on any broken glass. One thing was sure: the West Side flats was a place where people knew each other, for better and for worse.

Today the area comprises an industrial park and vacant lots, all protected by a levee that keeps the river from flooding over the land. But back in the 1950s the flats hosted an active working-class and immigrant community, full of characters, families, strivers, grifters, businessmen, and bums. Of course, bars were at the center of the mixing and give-and-take between the different parts of the neighborhood. The bars themselves reflected a diverse mix as much as the people did, with places like the Jalisco, a Mexican bar, or the Tap-a-Keg, frequented by Native Americans. All around the West Side there were old bars like these: the Monterey, Blair's Bar, the Silver Dollar, the Coronado, the Riverview. They are all gone now, but back then, they all had stories to tell.

"They were socializing places; bars meant culture, friendship," one longtime flats denizen explained. "At the bars, you could depend on one another, though it does not happen all the time. These are the guys that can help you out when the car breaks down, when the sidewalk is shoveled. The camaraderie, you build that."

The Carioca Cantina was one among the crowd, a small bar in the midst of the shops and apartments on State Street, next to Skolnik's grocery store, a barbershop, and, on the corner, a pool hall. Known for its Mexican clientele and often featuring music and dancing, the bar was fairly simple.

The Carioca Cantina was a West St. Paul neighborhood bar offering nightly "Mexican Dancing." *Minnesota Historical Society Collections*

The doorway and façade were covered in signs that read "Pepsi-Cola" and "Carioca Cantina: Mexican Dancing Nightly." Inside, the narrow, dark room had a simple bar on the left and a few tables on the right. Behind the bar leaned a one-legged bartender who hopped around on one foot and a pair of crutches, often to the amazement of the local kids, all the while serving 3.2 beer to an ever-changing crowd.

The name *Carioca* comes from the Brazilian slang term for someone from the area near Rio de Janeiro, but here the name stood in for a broader sense of Latin American music and culture. The Carioca Cantina was primarily a Mexican hangout, and new Mexican Americans who had come to St. Paul would gather there daily to drink Hamm's beer. Like at most of the city's 3.2 bars, if folks wanted anything stronger, they'd bring it in themselves, slipping bottles out of their pockets to knock back something with more punch.

The Carioca had a small stage and an open space in front that was perfect for a night of dancing, and by the 1950s, the Cantina was well known for its scene. The stage regularly featured local musical acts on the weekends, bands like the Blues Jays, a group of guys from around Selby Avenue who set up shop and rocked the joint, to the delight of the West Siders.

On other nights, the Amazers would show up. They were a Motown-inspired soul band who would arrive looking sharp in slick suits and slicker hair. Their presence created some conflicts, too. As West Side historian Gilbert de la O remembers it: "These guys came down on Sunday afternoon in [their] three-piece suits. . . . Then they'd start hitting on the ladies, and eventually they'd talk to the wrong one. And soon enough, there'd be a fight. It still goes on today."

On an average night, though, the Carioca Cantina was just a place to chat with the one-legged bartender and other folks from the neighborhood, a place to make connections and friends who would have your back on the flats.

The Carioca did not last long, however. As part of its widespread urban-renewal plans, the City of St. Paul declared in the early 1960s that the flats were slums. The greater good would be served by bulldozing the old neighborhood, removing the street grid, and creating a blank slate to bring industry to the riverfront. Nowadays, State Street, from the river down to the railroad tracks, is lined with drab industrial buildings and warehouses. There's no sign of the old bar, the old neighborhood, or the culture that once thrived here, in the shadow of downtown.

“Oasis for the proven and untested.”

GALLIVAN'S

1941–2003

354 WABASHA STREET NORTH, ST. PAUL

Gallivan's, an Irish bar named for its owner, was a hive of influence in downtown St. Paul for generations, but it did not truly hit its stride until the mid-1960s. Gallivan's original bar was torn down in 1967, when the large brick building that had housed it since 1941 met the wrecking ball. In those days, St. Paul's Capital Centre project was in full swing, funded by the city's Housing and Redevelopment Authority, the agency central to the postwar rebuilding movement and the city's modernist ambitions. Many of the old brick buildings in the central blocks of downtown, including Gallivan's, on the southeast corner of Wabasha and Fifth, were marked for progress and demolished in favor of new, superblock office buildings.

"Leading the Way to the New St. Paul" read the big sign on the corner as the wrecking ball swung and the three-story building tumbled into the vacant lot waiting for its brick remains. (The former Ecolab building, now named Osborn370, stands there today.)

This "New St. Paul" was not a big setback for Bob Gallivan, a White Bear Lake farm boy who had run his first bar on Selby Avenue in the 1930s. The demolition was an opportunity to remodel and get some new digs, and he soon moved into the first floor of the new Victory Parking Ramp building, one block down on Wabasha Street and even closer to the city hall and county courthouse. The location proved a boon to the new bar, and it quickly became a landmark in downtown St. Paul's booze landscape. For the next several decades, it was in the cozy confines of Gallivan's that the city's finest plots were hatched, and over the years the corner booth became a symbol for scheming, for good and ill, successful and otherwise.

Gallivan's was dark, cozy, and full of wood hues, as any good Irish bar should be. A curving bar ran along the left side of the room, a wide space where patrons bellied up and exchanged stories. When you walked in, chances are that one of the Gallivans, either Bob or his sons, Tim and Pat, greeted you at the entrance with a handshake and a smile, especially if you were a regular. All along the back and right-hand walls were booths of various sizes, trimmed with more wood and dark red upholstery. The low ceiling featured thick wood beams (purely decorative) and large hexagonal light fixtures.

Pioneer Press sports journalist and Gallivan's regular Don Riley described the conspiratorial atmosphere of the bar in his loose, exaggerated half novel/half memoir, *Gallivan's Gang*. "Most of the machinations took place at the large round table or in the back corner booths, which were lodged in the deeper recesses of Gallivan's, isolated from prying eyes and inquisitive ears. They liked to beat the lunch hour rush and slip quietly into the tavern's shadows around 11:30 AM. The mahogany beams, long bar and cardinal carpet of the restaurant, located in the heart of the St. Paul loop, was an

Interior of Gallivan's on Wabasha Street in downtown St. Paul. *Courtesy of Tim Gallivan*

oasis for the proven and untested. Those who had made it bought rounds for those still trying."

As Riley describes it, the social scene was well sorted: "The young gray and blue clad attorneys huddled at small tables on another side of the establishment. The loud sports talkers permeated the bar. This arrangement left the front of the place open to shoppers, newcomers and the downtown workforce."

The rest of Riley's book describes a series of failed get-rich-quick schemes hatched in the back of Gallivan's, many of them based on true stories. The most bizarre is surely the effort to create a new state fair food: a "burger on a stick." Sometime amid the many rounds of drinks, Bob Gallivan and his buddies came up with the so-called Moonburger. Unlike most of the Gallivan's schemes, they actually followed through with this one, and the Moonburger debuted at the Minnesota State Fair in 1962, a "cooked hamburger baked inside of a bun, each warmed up in a microwave oven borrowed from NSP." (At the time, microwaves were quite rare.)

Alas, the Gallivan's Moonburger was not a lasting success. It was too expensive, and fairgoers did not "get it."

Despite the culinary failure, the bar's proximity to city hall and the courthouse made Gallivan's a hub of influence in the 1960s and '70s. Here is where you found your most intense backslapping, dealmaking, rumor trading, brownnosing, promise breaking, cajoling, and all manner of lobbying. According to one retired official, during lunch on a workday and again in the early evening, entire city council quorums and courthouse benches were gathered in the different nooks and crannies of the place.

"At the council, there was a morning meeting and an afternoon meeting," he reminisced. "You always wanted to be on the morning agenda, because people would drink their lunch at Gallivan's. The whole city council would be there, judges, lawyers from opposing sides. You never wanted to be on an afternoon agenda, because by then everyone would be sloshed."

The political and social ties between Gallivan's and city hall reached a zenith in 1970 with the election of Charlie McCarty Jr. to the mayor's office. McCarty was an unorthodox Irish American politician who ran as an independent and got elected on a platform of commonsense deregulation and cracking down on crime. He famously had a massive Lincoln Town Car that he was driven around in by a young police sergeant. McCarty had the car modified with a police scanner and (allegedly) a device that could switch traffic lights from red to green. The car was frequently parked in front of the striped awning of Gallivan's bar, an iconic image of St. Paul in the early 1970s.

The house band at Gallivan's was called the Gallivanters, led by an Irish musician named Bob Conlon. Along with Gallivan's regular Andy Roberts, they wrote songs about local politics and devoted a set to McCarty that they played frequently during his two-year reign in office. The lyrics, dedicated to his reputation for fighting crime, did as much as anything to burnish McCarty's standing throughout the city:

Psychedelic lights a flashin'
See that super car go dashing
Someone's called for help
Super mayor's on his way

From his super car he can control
Control the stop and go signs
As he races through the night
To stop some villain on his way

Kids adore him
Bad men scorn him
He's brought sunshine to this town

With his faithful driver Dan
They roll the streets at night
You can sleep tight tonight
Cause super mayor's
watching over you.

The Gallivanters played for decades on Friday and Saturday nights from a stage in the corner. The quartet of two guitars, banjo, and mandolin performed an assortment of Irish, folk, and country tunes in three-part harmony, often laced with jokes, ribaldry, and political commentary.

Even after McCarty's fall from power (he died in 1974 while living in the Commodore Hotel), Gallivan's carried on for nearly two more decades as a place where politics, whiskey, and St. Paul traditions met. Its largest legacy might be the resurrection of the city's St. Patrick's Day parade, a tradition that teetotaling Archbishop John Ireland had put a stop to in 1915, alleging "midnight orgies."

According to the Saint Patrick's Association, the decision to revive the tradition was made one bitterly cold day in 1967 during St. Paul's Winter Carnival, when some of Gallivan's pals stopped into the bar to get out of the cold. As they enjoyed their drinks, Gallivan simply said, "Let's have a St. Patrick's Day parade, before we get too old."

Thus, the modern-era St. Paul St. Patrick's Day parade was born. The first parade was a small-scale, high-key success, and it revolved around Gallivan's bar on Wabasha Street. The parade continues to this day, though Gallivan's no longer graces the streets of downtown St. Paul. One of its big round booths, however, was preserved and sits in an Irish pub on Grand Avenue named Emmett's, where you can still bring an entourage and scheme about the future of St. Paul.

Bob Gallivan, at the second annual St. Patrick's Day parade in St. Paul, 1968. *Courtesy of Tim Gallivan*

“Mini skirts and Nehru shirts.”

COZY BAR

1961–1977

522 PLYMOUTH AVENUE NORTH, MINNEAPOLIS

The Cozy Bar was the kind of place that, if you were a young person from the northside, you'd have to avoid during the day. Not because it was too rough—though it could be—but because it's probably where your dad and uncles and older cousins hung out. “What're you doing in here?” they might yell at you from the bar. “I told you to go do the dishes.”

That is, if you even got in. The bouncers at the Cozy were no joke. More than one neighborhood kid under the drinking age who tried to bluff his way in found himself tossed out like a rag doll onto Plymouth Avenue.

But what you might have glimpsed inside the doors in that split second before being sent airborne was unlike anyplace else you had ever seen. Most dive bars in the Twin Cities—or anywhere in the Midwest, really—were four walls of dark wood paneling, enlivened maybe by a neon sign or an electronic advertisement for Hamm's depicting a woodland scene. Not the Cozy, though. You would have seen a room saturated with color on top and bottom: red, white, and black linoleum tile floors below; mustard, aqua, red, and white drop-ceiling tiles above; and a polished wooden bar lined with red vinyl barstools opposite green or red vinyl booths. No one could decorate a bar quite like James Fuller Sr.

Fuller was born in Virginia in 1910 and arrived in Minneapolis via Ohio. He'd studied at Wilberforce College, an HBCU halfway between Cincinnati and Columbus, and worked in Columbus hotels as a young man. After arriving on the northside in the 1950s, he worked in the machine shop at the Onan Corporation, manufacturing handsaws and auto repair tools.

The interior of the Cozy Bar featured brightly colored stools, booths, and ceiling tiles. *Minnesota Historical Society Collections*

A lifelong singer, Fuller wanted most of all to entertain people. He'd get plenty of practice. Beginning in the late 1950s, Fuller owned a series of bars on the northside with his wife, Margaret, each a step up from the last. The Northside Inn on Olson Memorial Highway was his entrée into the saloon business. It was a pretty rough place; it lost its license after a fatal shooting there in 1959 and reportedly received a "second chance" the following year. Fuller's next stop was the Regal Tavern on Sixth Avenue North, which also developed a somewhat tough reputation, as evidenced by its nickname: the Bucket of Blood. To this day, there are older northsiders who never knew the bar's official name; it was always just the Bucket of Blood. The Regal, though, was the first to feature live music by local R & B acts, who appeared on the bar's small stage.

The Cozy was Fuller's bar from the early 1960s until he was forced out in 1977. The space had been an old polka bar, and Fuller added a liquor license and expanded the live music offerings.

The Cozy Bar became well known as a music venue, both at the time and in popular memory today. In the 1960s, a jazz and R & B scene was burgeoning on the northside, refined in basement rehearsal spaces, churches, and community centers and presented at black-owned clubs like the Cozy, Blue Note, and Peacock Alley; this was the scene that John Lewis Nelson was moving through in the 1950s and the scene his son, Prince Rogers Nelson, would come out of at the end of the 1970s. For black musicians, it was both a crucial place to get your start and a frustrating dead end in a segregated city where white promoters rarely booked black groups.

Journalist and librarian Barbara Sybil Cyrus, however, remembered a scene that was exciting in part because the community felt a keen sense of ownership of it. The Cozy Bar always had a somewhat racially mixed crowd, but the majority of patrons and performers were black. "An over-amplified Muddy Waters at the Guthrie is not the same as Muddy Waters at the Cozy Bar . . . where his style is most appreciated," she remarked in 1968's *Minneapolis Negro Profile,* a pictorial celebration of prominent members of the Twin Cities' black community, written and published by Walter R. Scott. "There is something to being 'at home' and knowing that there won't be 'too many of them.'"

This was the main room. In the side room, with the orange booths and multicolored ceiling, the Cozy Bar was a neighborhood hangout, one of only two to four black-owned bars in Minneapolis, depending on the year. It was where northsiders would come to drink, hang out, and meet one another. "Meet the gang at Minneapolis' newest and most exciting," said the advertisements in the *Spokesman* newspaper. "The friendliest place in town." (These ads often appeared right above ads for Cassius's bar, which *also* billed itself as "Minneapolis Friendliest.") During the day the Cozy hosted an older crowd of neighborhood residents and regulars, the kind of place where your dad might have hung out after work. And if your dad happened to work a third-shift factory job, well, there was a spot at the bar for him, too: those ads in the *Spokesman* in the middle and late 1960s invited readers to "join the eye opener club every day, 8 a.m. to noon."

Matchbook for the Cozy Bar, advertising "choice wines and liquors." *Author Collection*

At night, the scene shifted from the regulars and middle-aged guys to one of impeccably dressed young men and women, most of them there to dance to the live music, but also just to hang out in the lounge. "Mini skirts and Nehru shirts," according to a contemporary account. Images of the crowds at the Cozy from that time show double-breasted blazers with gold buttons, elaborately patterned shirts, white go-go boots. Another *Spokesman* ad from the early 1970s gives you a taste of the place: a young woman smiling broadly, with chic coiffed hair and a modish collared jacket.

The Cozy was located on Plymouth Avenue, just on the North Minneapolis side of downtown, a sort of interstitial zone between the two. When musician John Arredondo complained to the paper in 1968 about the segregation of Minneapolis nightlife, saying that "at night . . . blacks are supposed to stay in the black bars on the outskirts of downtown or on the northside," he was referring to the Cozy. Fuller himself made a geographic distinction in 1968, the year of the black uprisings on Plymouth, noting that the Cozy was somewhat removed from the center of the Near North neighborhood, too. "That stuff you're reading about is on down the avenue," he told a reporter. "Things aren't like that on this end of the avenue."

It was the Cozy's location on that end of the avenue that doomed it, though. In 1977, the Department of Transportation was completing plans for the path of Interstate 94, and the favored route ran along the edge of downtown, between Lyndale and Washington Avenues—and right through the Cozy Bar. The building was condemned and demolished. Today, if you're exiting I-94 eastbound on the Seventh Street North exit, you're more or less driving over the site of the Cozy.

Relocation presented an opportunity, though. For years, Fuller had wanted to open a club that was less a neighborhood tavern and more a full-service community hub, with a banquet room, event space, professional stage, and high-end menu. He found a site for such an endeavor at 2300

The Cozy Bar on Plymouth Avenue, early 1970s. *Minnesota Historical Society Collections*

West River Road, along the long-neglected waterfront on the northside, across the Mississippi River from the Grain Belt Brewery and with a view of the downtown skyline. The Riverview Supper Club would inherit the Cozy's liquor license. Fuller and his son James Jr. raised $750,000 to build it. All it needed was the approval of the city council.

In some ways, his experience was a repeat of Anthony B. Cassius's ordeal thirty years earlier. The council denied the request by a 9–4 vote. Again, it was chalked up to "aldermanic courtesy," opaque and behind-the-scenes dealmaking, and a hemming and hawing from the council that never quite came out and *said* anything racist, but instead raised concerns about the location not being "proper," the license transfer not being "in the interest of public health," and the fact there were "adequate and sufficient" liquor bars already in the area. Fuller was even more direct than Cassius had been in calling out the council. "It's purely prejudice," he told the *Recorder*. "They just want to stop a black man from getting into a white location."

An election in the Riverview's home ward eventually changed the aldermanic seat. When the proposal went back to a vote three years later, it was approved. Fuller, then seventy years old, ran the View, as it was called, for nearly twenty years until his death in 1999 at age eighty-nine. The club shut down a year later.

Upon his death, the *Spokesman* ran a front-page obituary, noting that "many of the talents Minnesota has produced got their start from Fuller's clubs." The Riverview was mentioned in the headline, but it was the Cozy where a lot of those talents had started.

James Fuller Sr. opened the Riverview Supper Club, on West River Road in North Minneapolis, after his Cozy Bar was demolished to make way for Interstate 94. *Photo by Charles Chamblis, Minnesota Historical Society Collections*

"A martini shaker in her left hand and a court summons in her right."

THE RED BARON

1966–1969

217 SOUTH SIXTH STREET, MINNEAPOLIS

The overwhelmingly masculine clubbiness that defined drinking establishments in the downtown central business district in the middle of the twentieth century is tidily summed up by the name and business plan of a bar at Second Avenue and Sixth Street in 1962: the Office. You know this stupid joke: The wife asks her husband why he's going to be late after work, and he truthfully tells her, "Oh, don't wait up, I'll be working late at the Office."

The Office was a result of the series of demolitions that radically reshaped downtown in the early 1960s. The bar opened in the small turn-of-the-century building that had housed the Minneapolis Public Library's Business Branch since 1946, a satellite library stocked with city directories, phone books, and trade publications. The branch closed when the library demolished its old, main location on Tenth Street and consolidated all its holdings at a new location in 1961.

The Office's owners, George Schaumberg and George Flynn, had acquired the liquor license of the infamous Sourdough Bar after it, too, was torn down in the demolition of the Gateway District that same year. The two Georges had no intention of continuing the Sourdough's tradition as skid row's premier destination for destitute single men. The Office's clientele was no less male than skid row's residents, but it consisted nearly entirely of downtown businessmen on expense accounts. The intimate, wood-paneled atmosphere of the old library translated well into this new cocktail lounge format. Apparently, the Georges had plans to install a sound-effects machine near the bar's telephone that would provide the clatter of typewriters in the background while tipsy businessmen called their wives.

In January 1966, a five-alarm fire gutted the building, along with the improbably named Vincent Van Gogh-Go nightclub next door. Later that year, the city council declined to renew the Office's license at the same location, and instead granted the license to three ambitious young men who'd organized a corporation called Page, Inc.: a salesman named Ted Doman and two former Vincent Van Gogh-Go employees named Tom Grey and Ronnie Berglund.

Their new bar, the Red Baron, opened in the summer of 1966, the same year as the publication of St. Paul native Charles Schulz's best-selling anthology of *Peanuts* comic strips depicting Snoopy's battles against the Red Baron. A drawing of Snoopy and the Red Baron hung in a place of honor at the bar.

The Page, Inc., team removed all fire-damaged traces of the Office and completely refurbished the interior. The new space had a World War I theme, a variation on the nostalgic bric-a-brac décor favored in the mid-1960s: aviation maps of Europe under a layer of varnish on the tables, model airplanes hanging from the ceiling, and military medals and photos of mustachioed airmen on the walls. Rock bands played there several nights a week. It was a reasonably chic, lightly countercultural hangout, with much more gender parity in its clientele than its immediate predecessor. It didn't attract an overwhelmingly young crowd, but it was a fairly popular evening spot for college students and downtown workers in their twenties and early thirties.

Liquor laws in the city had not kept up with the times, however. Since 1948, women had been legally forbidden to tend bar in the Twin Cities, and in practice much, much earlier than that. The few exceptions before then tended to be situations in which a woman was the wife of the license holder or a widow who'd taken over a liquor license from her deceased husband. Typically, if you encountered a woman working at a bar in the mid-1960s, she wasn't behind the bar; she would be a cocktail waitress.

Judy Jarosak was such a cocktail waitress in 1969. She was twenty-eight years old, was recently divorced, and had gone back to school at the University of Minnesota to earn a sociology degree. She supported herself

Bartender Judy Jarosak, mixing drinks at the Red Baron, March 19, 1969. *Photo from the* Star Tribune, *Minnesota Historical Society Collections*

and her nine-year-old daughter by working tables in the downtown lounges. She'd been a waitress for eight years at that point and had picked up a lot of knowledge about tending bar and mixing drinks along the way.

Sometime in early 1969, Jarosak, with backing from the Minnesota Civil Liberties Union, approached Berglund at the Red Baron about hiring her as a bartender. St. Paul's city council had just rejected a measure to overturn its city's ban on female bartenders earlier that year, and the MCLU was looking for a test case. The Red Baron seemed to be the right venue—a "clean action place," with no go-go dancers or striptease artists—and Jarosak was the right bartender. She'd left the waitresses union and applied for membership in Bartenders Union Local 152, and she was accepted after taking the required entry test. Reportedly she achieved one of the highest scores in the chapter's history. The Red Baron owners seemed favorably disposed to take on the cause, whether because they were social progressives at heart or because it seemed like a great promotional opportunity for their club. Maybe it was a little of both. "I look on it as a kind of civic duty," Berglund asserted, adding, "I'll admit, we may get a few nonregulars in here to view civics in action."

If anything, it was the union and its entirely male membership that seemed most opposed to the idea. "I still don't like the idea of women behind bars," Faye Frawley of the union was quoted as saying at the time. "This one's okay," he hastily added.

And so, for four hours on the night of Wednesday, March 19, 1969, while a band called Zarathustra played upstairs, Judy Jarosak donned a starched white shirt and paisley scarf while mixing pink squirrels, horse's necks, and gin and tonics in the Bomb Shelter, the basement bar at the Red Baron. Photographers from the dailies were on hand to snap photos of her in action, in case anything went down. "It's only part protest," she told a reporter. "I passed my bartender's test and now I want a dependable income."

"A martini shaker in her left hand and a court summons in her right," was the *Tribune*'s prediction the day before.

The evening came and went without incident. Compared to the guy upstairs, "she makes a better Manhattan," one customer commented. Two men from the city's morals squad stopped in to look around, but no arrests were made. There would appear to be no test case.

Later that week, however, the Red Baron was served with papers. The city had decided to avoid the publicity that would come with arresting Jarosak and instead went after the bar itself. The Red Baron's owners were taken to court, and they lost. They signed a stipulation that they wouldn't violate the ordinance and wouldn't work with Jarosak again. Indeed, she would never work another shift behind the bar at the Red Baron.

Jarosak and the MCLU went back to court, filing a brief with the Minnesota Department of Human Rights. The city ordinance, they argued, conflicted with the state civil rights legislation that stated that people must be hired based on their qualifications, not based on "stereotyped generalizations." There was no evidence, they argued, that there was any more disorder in bars in cities where women could bartend. Judge Tom Bergin struck down the Minneapolis law in November. Jarosak, and any woman, was free to tend bar anywhere in the city.

There would be no more bartenders of any kind at the Red Baron by the time Judge Bergin made his ruling. The building fell victim to another fire in late 1969—the fourth in ten years. That seemed to be the final nail in the coffin. In 1970, the building was demolished. Ten years later, Pillsbury Center, now US Bank Plaza, would rise on the site. The three principals from Page, Inc., drifted into other related areas: liquor wholesaling or managing other downtown bars.

Judy Jarosak married again in 1970, and then she vanished from the historical record. Pictures of Jarosak from the one night she tended bar at the Red Baron, pouring drinks and smiling broadly, ran regularly in the daily papers through the middle of 1969—not just in Minnesota but in newspapers all over the country after the story was picked up by the Associated Press. Perhaps she simply wearied of the attention—some of which was positive, but much of which was quite patronizing and outright sexist. "Pretty Judy Jarosak" is how the AP wire piece began. Perhaps she had no interest in being a high-profile symbol. For all the attention she received at the time, there was no follow-up in any of the local papers after the trial concluded, and she dropped out of the city directories around then as well.

Wherever she is, Judy Jarosak would be about eighty years old today. Hopefully she has been comfortably retired from bartending for a long time.

"The boys have been crying into their boilermakers and brandy with water so long about our present troubles."

THE SPOT BAR

1887–present

859 RANDOLPH AVENUE, ST. PAUL

The Spot Bar sits on its quiet Randolph Avenue street corner like a statue of a forgotten pioneer. For more than a century, it's been the neighborhood bar for folks wandering up from St. Paul's West End—working men, a few guys wearing ties, retired soldiers, and the like, all sidling into the small rooms of the Spot to tip back a beer and reminisce.

Located at the intersection of Randolph Avenue and Victoria Street, the bar occupied a spot in "Little Bohemia" along the strip of businesses on Randolph that connected the rich neighborhoods up the hill with the Schmidt Brewery on West Seventh, the complex of brick buildings that had been churning out beer since 1855 and literally towered over the working-class neighborhood.

In the 1970s, the Spot Bar was run by a guy named Bob Koehnen, who purchased it after his previous bar burned down. He had owned a place called the Tropics in the Frederic Hotel, a stately but aging four-story building on the corner of Cedar and Fifth Streets, in the heart of downtown. The Tropics had an equatorial theme, with a few fish tanks and a slide projector that displayed photos of beaches and rainforests. One of the tanks even had a piranha, and if you were lucky and a good tipper, Bob would drop a minnow in there and everyone would watch what happened next.

The hotel and its bar burned down in January 1961 in a dramatic three-alarm fire that had firefighters dousing everything in sight with water hoses in the freezing cold. Entire cars and streetlamps were encased in ice, and by the end of the day, nothing was left of the old building. Soon after, Bob set his sights on the small joint called the Spot Saloon, about three miles away on Randolph Avenue.

By the 1970s, the Spot Bar was like a living room for the neighborhood, and Bob held court on a daily basis. In the evenings, music took over as Marion Dusterhoft, a young woman who lived a few blocks away, sat at the organ in the back room. A piano bar was one of Bob's tricks from the old Tropics, and he brought it with him to the Spot. Oliver Towne, a columnist who chronicled St. Paul life for the *Dispatch*, once described the scene of the Spot's piano bar:

The Spot Bar has been a fixture at Randolph Avenue and Victoria Street in St. Paul since the 1880s. *Photo by Anna Botz*

> *"Marion at the organ" is all the sign says.*
>
> *The sign has been there for 15 years. And so has Marion Dusterhoft. Four, sometimes more nights a week, Marion is at the organ.*
>
> *There's a thick book of song titles in front of her, maybe 1,000, who knows. No music. Just titles. She knows them all and she learns the new ones.*
>
> *The customers sit at the long bar and they sit around the organ. They sing along, tap their feet.*
>
> *"Hey Marion . . . can you play . . . ?"*
>
> *"How does it go?" she says, never stopping to take her hands off the keys, never breaking the rhythm.*
>
> *"Hum it," she says.*
>
> *"Let me just hear that a second . . . okay."*
>
> *And she plays it as if the music were on the rack and she'd been repeating the song for ten years.*
>
> *I sat around that night, testing her, challenging her and she never missed. She played French songs, Italian songs, German songs, old favorites, and she did it like Shearing, Oscar Peterson, and anybody else of fame at a keyboard.*
>
> *"For me, it's great . . . I live near here . . . I know everybody . . . this is my neighborhood and my recreation," said Marion.*

The weekends, especially, were "family nights," and the back room filled with neighborhood women, otherwise a rare sight in the Spot. And it had probably been that way since 1885, when a bar first opened at the site. The address first appears in a want ad in the *St. Paul Globe,* something to do with a lost horse: "Horse strayed—white Mexican pony, blind in left eye, letter J on left shoulder. Finder leave at city hall or 859 Randolph St."

Most of the bars that survived the nineteenth century were made of brick or stone, and for a wooden structure (as most of the old saloons were) to have survived that long is a sign that it was well cared for. By the time Koehnen took over, the Spot retained its frontier look and spirit, with spare wood walls on a limestone foundation, just like a stable from which a white pony may have strayed. Inside, the place felt almost like a cabin, and you could imagine what it might have been in the days when it was heated by a woodstove and had an outhouse. The wooden walls, the small back room full of implements, the spartan bathrooms with only curtains for doors, the creaking, tilted floor, and a dozen other details worked together to create a vague frontier atmosphere.

To plant one's rear on a stool at the Spot was to make a pact of solidarity, a nod toward togetherness and conversation. Entering the bar and joining the row of stools or, if lucky, nabbing one of the booths along the far wall was like coming home for dinner with family and friends, as Bob served up some roast beef sandwiches or maybe a polish sausage on a roll.

Another time-honored Spot Bar tradition was paging through the newspaper and providing real-time commentary. Towne described another visit to the Spot in 1974, when he was struck by the incongruity of the newspaper scuttlebutt:

> *Along about noon if you drop into Bob Koehnen's Spot Tavern . . . the boys at the bar will be in feverish discussion and often dispute about the headline of the day.*
>
> *But wait, they are talking about the British evacuation at Dunkirk, the bombing of Paris, the fall of France. Every now and then someone will parody Hitler or Mussolini. . . .*
>
> *"Hey, read the grocery ad from Schoch's (long gone) on the back of the page," suggests a regular.*
>
> *"Pork chops 15 cents a pound; coffee 29 cents a pound; freshly ground beef 18 cents a pound," he intones.*
>
> *Another groan ripples down the mahogany.*
>
> *"Pardon me," you say to Bob Koehnen, the "Dutch Burgher" for the Spot, "but isn't this 1974? I seem to have stepped back about 30 years in time."*

Interior of the Spot Bar.
Photo by Anna Botz

"Well, I'll tell you," says Burgher Bob "the boys have been crying into their boilermakers and brandy with water so long about our present troubles—inflation, Watergate, the income tax, gasoline shortages, the Middle East and streaking—that Carl here suggested they needed a little cheering up."

"So what I did," says Carl, who is retired from Brown & Bigelow, "is start bringing down Dispatch *front pages from my collection of about a hundred during World War II and hanging up the headline of the day."*

"And it boosted morale and brought laughs and joie de vivre and gemutlichkeit and old Scotch Ballads?" I ask.

"It did at first," says Carl. "I mean everybody figured things couldn't have been worse than they are now. And they read these and figure things have been worse."

"Then a strange thing happened," says Burgher Bob.

"They begin to relate. They got what is called empathy. They begin to believe they really are sitting here 35 years ago and it's 1939 or '40 or '41 or '42. All except when they pay for a beer—30 cents a glass now and a nickel then."

It's not hard to imagine people getting confused about what decade it was inside the Spot Bar, as the place retained so much of its spirit through

A painting of a night at the Spot Bar in 1982 still hangs on the wall of the establishment. *Photo by Anna Botz*

the decades. Even today, a painting hangs on the wall depicting it as it was in 1982, a decent folk-art stab at capturing the spirit of the Spot.

The painting was done by one of the bar's regulars. It depicts two bartenders, both with mustaches and well dressed, holding court. They are surrounded by men leaning on the bar—drinks, ashtrays, coasters, and other pocket paraphernalia (including dice) arranged before them like ritual relics. At the back of the room, a couple examines a pull tab vending booth, fingers poised decisively over a button. In the mid-ground, a woman in a red skirt leans over the jukebox, knowing full well that her decision will cause a ripple effect of culture, nostalgia, or dissonance to wash over the bar. In the foreground, another woman in a stylish brown trench coat is walking into the frame, her face turned away from the viewer.

Today, the atmosphere inside the Spot Bar is little changed. Perhaps the Spot has a Dorian Gray arrangement with the picture. Perhaps the bar, dating back more than 130 years, is one place in the city where, while the people might age, the bar itself remains forever young.

"I can remember the day when you could walk into a Cedar-Riverside bar and get a schooner of beer for a dime."

PALMER'S BAR

1906–present

500 CEDAR AVENUE SOUTH, MINNEAPOLIS

If, in the early 1970s, you had put odds on Palmer's Bar surviving the decade, they would have been long indeed. It was almost a given that Palmer's was not long for this world. Not only was business down and the neighborhood changing, but the seventy-year-old building that housed the dusty bar was in the crosshairs of a huge government housing project slated to revolutionize both urban planning and the West Bank of Minneapolis for generations to come. In the first years of the decade, entire blocks next to Palmer's Bar were leveled and replaced with a complex of towering concrete, hundreds of new housing units rising twenty stories over the back of the Palmer's building.

The Riverside Plaza development, originally known as Cedar Square West, was part of an ambitious Nixon-era Housing and Urban Development program called the "New Town in Town." The officials and developers sought to take advantage of the brand-new surrounding freeways to shoehorn

The front façade of Palmer's Bar on Cedar Avenue, showing the gap in the second story where a pedestrian bridge passed through for a brief time. *Photo by Anna Botz*

a huge complex of residential towers into the neighborhood. The new buildings behind Palmer's Bar represented the first in what was planned to be many phases of demolition and reconstruction that would transform nearly the entire urban fabric along Cedar and Riverside Avenues. Ten apartment complexes were to be built in all, housing thirty thousand people at a cost of $1 billion (in 1970s money). The old buildings that had lined the thriving main street of the city's industrial working class would be erased. It seemed a foregone conclusion that Palmer's Bar would come down, too.

Walter Heller, a professor at the University of Minnesota and the main developer on the project, foresaw the seemingly inevitable demise of the dive. In a 1973 *Minneapolis Tribune* article Heller stated that the planners and engineers would "ultimately" insist on widening Cedar Avenue by ten feet, which, the article explained, "might be taken off the west side where Palmer's and Caesar's and the Cedar Villager Theater now reside." (Today, the theater is the Cedar Cultural Center.)

Even in the first stage of the development, Palmer's took a hit. The new housing projects were intended to transcend the old neighborhood, and not just figuratively; in tandem with a network of plazas, parking ramps, and concrete walls, a series of skyways and second-level bridges (and possibly, someday, a "people mover" based on the one in Disney World) were planned to transport pedestrians over the cars speeding on Cedar Avenue between the freeways. To build the pedestrian bridge, planners cut a chunk out of the second floor of the Palmer's building and ran a wide concrete walkway through its right side.

For decades before that, and still to this day, Cedar Avenue served as the neighborhood's main street, offering an incredible diversity of shops, languages, and street life among the modest homes and apartments of Cedar-Riverside. In the early 1970s, the neighborhood had everything: the Electric Fetus and Circus Maximus record shops, the cooperatively owned Riverside Café, a tailor, the Depth of Field yarn store, Phil Richter's drugstore, Smith's leather shop, a noodle factory, a newspaper office, a bookstore, a deli, and a burgeoning community radio station. Across the street from Palmer's, on the corner of Cedar and Fifth, the huge building called Dania Hall stood tall, albeit largely dilapidated by that time. Decades before, the turreted building had housed a vaudeville stage and had been a thriving concert venue.

And there were plenty of bars, too: the Triangle Bar, Caesar's, the Five Corners Saloon, and a dozen others that ran up and down Cedar, Washington, and Riverside Avenues, the result of the concentration from the liquor patrol limits. A *Tribune* article in December 1973 quoted longtime neighborhood denizen Margie Shafsky, then sixty-two, recalling the old days hopping from one bar to the next: "We'd drink and dance, we'd go from one bar to another. I can remember the day when you could walk into a Cedar-Riverside bar and get a schooner of beer for a dime."

But by the early 1970s, the neighborhood was on the precipice of change, and nobody knew which way it would fall.

In that same issue of the *Tribune,* another account laid out the thoughts of people on the street, including the owner of Palmer's Bar:

> *Business is not so good at Palmer's Bar, Don Carmichael, 67, will tell you: "I let the bartender go. Who do I need? A bartender? I can drink as much as he can."*
>
> *As a younger man, Carmichael used to roam around Cedar and Riverside Avs., distributing bootleg liquor (three gallons for $10). He was what he calls "a young conglomerator" in the old days, with his low-overhead, high-proof business, interest in a bakery and coin machines and a speakeasy that he rented at 1001 Park Av.*

Carmichael had bought Palmer's from the son of the bar's longtime proprietor, a Slovak immigrant named Adam Folta. Folta had come to Minneapolis after World War II and worked his way up bartending at the

The distinctive, wooden "Palmer's man" sculpture leans on the short side of the Palmer's building. *Photo by Anna Botz*

various establishments on Cedar Avenue. In the early 1950s, he bought the bar and named it Palmer's. He and his wife, Maria, ran it for twenty-seven years. Folta claimed he "never drank too much," which was one of the reasons why he had a long life.

Palmer's had the distinctive tile flooring of an old Grain Belt Brewery (Minnesota Brewing Company) "tied house." And like many of the parcels located where the different Minneapolis street grids clash and come together, the plot of land on which Palmer's is located is not rectangular. As a result, the building narrows as you walk inside, and the bar room culminates at a small stage raised a few feet above the red tile floor. The bar was and is an intimate space that seems somehow to grow larger on the inside as it fills with people.

In the mid-seventies, a variety of factors combined to save Palmer's from the wrecking ball. First was the neighborhood pushback, as the music, arts, and working-class community looked skeptically at Heller's top-down plans for the neighborhood. The second factor was trouble at the federal level, where large-scale public housing projects were being viewed with increasing skepticism while urban poverty entrenched itself in many US cities (Minneapolis included).

The first phase of the Cedar-Riverside "New Town in Town" project ended up being the last, and Cedar Avenue never did get widened. The massive Cedar Avenue pedestrian bridge that blotted out the sun over half of Palmer's eventually came down. Even more surprising, in 2014 wider

Mural on the concrete support structure next to the Palmer's patio. *Photo by Anna Botz*

sidewalks were put in place in front of Palmer's as Cedar Avenue was narrowed, and a regulated crossing was restored at Fifth Street. Below where the concrete walkway once loomed, a sprawling patio for Palmer's Bar was born sometime in the 1990s. Today, the patio is regularly filled with artists, hippies, students, punks, musicians, and new immigrants—all drinking, bumming cigarettes, and swapping stories around a regular campfire.

At some point, someone painted a mural on the side of the walkway's concrete support structure that abuts the patio. The mural features the words "Sorry, We're Open" and bears a painted depiction of the wooden, sculpted "Palmer's man" that leans on the odd-angled edge of the building. In the mural, the nineteenth-century boulevardier in a bowler cap and waistcoat is checking his watch, an actual timepiece embedded within the concrete wall.

The painting and stopwatch marks the spot where one strain of Minneapolis's large-scale, modernist urbanism ended, where the top-down reforms of the Great Society were swapped out for a bottom-up approach to preservation and incremental change. Somehow at Palmer's Bar, the prewar spirit of the West Bank survived and even thrived through the visions of mid-century reform and redevelopment. In the midst of the concrete towers, freeways, and ever-changing demographics, Palmer's remained relatively unmarked by time.

Big John the bouncer has manned the door and kept the peace at Palmer's for decades. Behind the bar, there remains a catalog of the shifting cast of characters, regulars, and West Bank wanderers, as names are continually added to and subtracted from a small and overstuffed message board. The notes bear the names of customers who have been 86'd—kicked out—from the joint, according to the whims of the bartenders and bouncers. Examples of messages from the collection: "Chi Town is 86'd." "Phyllis is 86'd. Period." "Little white guy w/ flat top likes to touch female customers. Is 86'd. Low talks." "All of the women at Palmer's have 86'd Spencer. Let him in and die." "Crackhead Christine. White woman, shoulder length. Lives on a farm. Is 86'd for pills."

The concert calendar at Palmer's also remains consistently vibrant, maintaining the bar's place at the heart of the West Bank music scene. It is one of the last venues where you'll regularly find local blues legend Spider John Koerner performing when the annual Palm Fest celebration is held on the patio every July. On Wednesday afternoons, the "Hippienanny" takes place at the round wooden table near the entrance. It's a scene straight from the 1970s: longhaired, aging hippies with guitars, wooden flutes, tambourines, bongos, and any other instrument they can find sing protest songs, Dylan covers, and other lefty folk tunes together while the life of the bar hums along behind them. On other nights, punk bands, hip-hop artists, or DJs take the stage, and the place fills with clientele ranging in age from twenty-one to eighty-one.

The stubbornness of Palmer's Bar was even strong enough to survive the dreaded national nod. The bar appeared on the *Wall Street Journal*'s 2013 list of key spots for the "ultimate long weekend" in Minneapolis, citing its "authenticity." Palmer's was named one of *Esquire* magazine's "best bars in America" a year later. Unlike other bars from the list (see: Nye's Polonaise, page 213), not even New York acclaim could change the vibe at Palmer's.

In 2018, a regular named Tony Zaccardi bought the place from the widow of the old owner. Though the bar now accepts credit cards, Zaccardi has pledged to keep Palmer's just as it has always been, a place where all manner of Minneapolis life comes together like a peerless cocktail, seamlessly blending the past and the future in delightful harmony.

“If you can’t make it at the Guard, you can’t make it anywhere.”

THE LEFT GUARD

1972–1977

7717 NICOLLET AVENUE SOUTH, RICHFIELD

"*Time* magazine said we have a drink called the 'Thigh Opener,'" Left Guard general manager Dick Smith complained to the *Tribune* in 1974, sounding extremely annoyed. "That's never been true and still isn't."

We just call them vodka gimlets, he clarified.

The sexual revolution had arrived in the Minneapolis suburbs by 1974. A sports bar and steakhouse owned by two former Green Bay Packers and located in a warehouse-like former supermarket on the Bloomington strip, far from the countercultural environs of the West Bank, was that sexual revolution's suburban epicenter. The revolution had slowly worked its way up from the college kids to the professional class. The Left Guard was pointedly not a hangout for the young and hip. It was a place frequented by, as *Tribune* columnist Richard T. Jones noted with a mix of bemusement and faint horror, "singles between 25 and 35 years old."

"Most of the girls are older," explained Smith, the general manager, "so the young guys, those guys 18 or 19, come in, have a beer and turn around and leave."

"It is known as a place," Jones continued in that *wink-wink* tone of middle-aged postwar newspaper columnists, "where you can meet somebody if you're lonely. Or if you're not."

Across twenty-seven hundred square feet, the club housed three bars, the

Men and women regularly filled the bar at the Left Guard in suburban Minneapolis, as depicted in this 1974 photo. *Photo from the* Star Tribune, *Minnesota Historical Society Collections*

longest of them ninety feet and often packed a dozen deep. The Swinger's Lounge was for dining, and the Other Room was for the thirty-five-plus set. On an above-average night in 1974, the Left Guard hosted fifteen hundred patrons, all buying several drinks ranging in price from a dollar to a dollar-fifty. On a particularly good night, more than three thousand people might be packed in there, dancing to a live band and drinking.

The Left Guard was said to have, at the time, the largest gross revenue of any singles bar in the entire United States. Not just in Minnesota or the Midwest, but anywhere in the United States. So well known was it that a 1974 classified ad for an otherwise unremarkable suburban office park a block away boasted to potential tenants in the first line that you could "walk to the Left Guard from your new 600 square foot office." Perhaps this description caught the eye of the lonely, bored office managers and secretaries who made up a significant portion of the bar's clientele.

"If you can't make it at the Guard," it was commonly said, "you can't make it anywhere."

The Left Guard site on Nicollet Avenue, just on the north side of the Richfield-Bloomington border at I-494, is now a Menards. You can stand near the entrance of the building and get a sense for its most noteworthy feature, then as now, one that distinguishes it from every establishment that's appeared in this book so far: an enormous parking lot, stretching for what seems like miles.

On a typical Friday night in mid-1974, the six-hundred-space lot would be filled with hundreds of Valiants, Hornets, Fury IIs, and Rivieras driven by white, middle-class professionals coming in from Minneapolis and St. Paul, but also from Edina, Burnsville, Eden Prairie, Eagan, Minnetonka, and other first- and second-ring suburbs whose populations had exploded in the three decades since World War II. These were the baby boomers raised in the suburbs who thought of a "downtown," according to a 1976 profile of the Strip, as "a shopping center with lots of free parking."

The sorts of numbers the bar supported were possible because of the easy access to 494, then only fifteen years old and responsible for what was becoming known as "the Bloomington Strip," a stretch of highway terminating at Metropolitan Stadium that seemed poised to become a third center of gravity in the binary system of the Twin Cities. "Downtown Bloomington" was something of a running joke in the area for years. Its imprecise location was even the subject of a local, sixties-era novelty hit by Dale Menten called "Downtown Bloomington," in which a lovelorn country boy meets a girl who tells him to meet her in downtown Bloomington. "Where is downtown Bloomington?" he wails. "Nobody seems to know." By the end of the 1960s, though, the joke had a clear answer: it was the 494 strip. The head of the city's convention bureau at this time enthusiastically called it the "Anaheim of the North"—a suburban nowhere that had quickly become a vibrant somewhere.

The Left Guard and the Bloomington Strip were also close to the airport and to the thousands of hotel rooms along 494, which brought an influx of traveling salesmen and off-duty stewardesses into the mix. In the many profiles that appeared in the media about the Twin Cities singles scene in the 1970s, the simple utility of the Left Guard and its successors came up. One patron commented at the conclusion of a 1976 profile that, "when you come right down to it, I think most people, guys and girls, don't really like the bars. But what else is there to do?"

Despite all that, the Left Guard was an unlikely place to have a reputation as the nation's premier swinging singles bar. There was nothing particularly sexy or alluring about the space itself. It was not chic, nor was it cosmopolitan. It had aspirations to class, in a meat-and-potatoes sort of way: the logo was a shield and banderole, with a crested football helmet and martini glass. After being a Kroger and then a Piggly Wiggly, the building retained the wide-open feel of a suburban supermarket, even after an $875,000 renovation. In addition to its steakhouse, the Left Guard also housed a red-sauce Italian restaurant called Martine's, and

The Left Guard logo, featuring the uniform number (63) of Fuzzy Thurston, who played the left guard position for the Green Bay Packers in the 1960s. *Author Collection*

Pro-Central, a pro shop where people could buy football uniforms and memorabilia. The walls of the steakhouse were brick and dark wood, and covered with photos of Vikings football players. The menu was divided into sections like "Super Bowl Specials" and "Central Division Luncheons" and offered specialty items like the "House of Murphy," which consisted in part of a "Volcano of Fresh Ground Sirloin." The bartenders—male and female—wore football jerseys.

It looked and felt, in other words, like the sort of establishment you might expect from two reasonably wealthy former Green Bay Packers in their mid-forties (left guard Max McGee was born in 1932, and his colleague Fuzzy Thurston was born in 1933). The Richfield location was one of a few supper clubs of the same name the duo owned around the Upper Midwest, and all of them were modestly successful, frequented by local businessmen, families, and traveling salesmen. Before 6 PM, the Left Guard in Richfield was where old folks could get a blue plate special, or where the local chapter of the Shriners might meet. ("I'm so old I go to the Left Guard for the food" went one popular dad joke of the day.) The front door was covered by an oversized photomontage of the Minnesota Vikings in action. After dark, a dress code was strictly enforced: denim, tank tops, and cutoffs were all out. Even a pair of three-hundred-dollar designer jeans wouldn't pass muster. Double-knits, blazers, medallions, and pattern skirts were preferred. The combination of over-the-top tackiness and male energy led regulars to dub it "the Bronze Jockstrap."

Not the sort of place you'd necessarily consider if you were a free-spirited, relatively young single guy or girl looking to get lucky.

And yet, it was.

Time magazine filed a short piece entitled "The Body Shop" in a January 1974 issue ("What may well be the nation's ultimate singles bar is not on Sunset Strip or Manhattan's Upper East Side but in Bloomington, Minn."). What was already a regional phenomenon became a national one. The piece was full of the sort of reportage that is still familiar today when a national publication turns its sights to the Midwest: describing wide-eyed provincials, getting a taste of the big city. The best quote is from one Cindy Barton, visiting from Estherville, Iowa: "I've never seen anything like this. There is nothing in Sioux City to measure up to it."

The piece did seem to catch a moment when a cultural tide was turning in Middle America, however. Though the Left Guard had a definite vibe of utilitarian manliness, men and women were on somewhat even footing there, at least as far as taking advantages to find a one-night stand. "I get ten offers a night," reported a beautician from Minneapolis. "The body friction is enough to get everyone going."

This perhaps wasn't what McGee and Thurston had in mind when they opened the restaurant in 1972. McGee was a hard-partying, fun-loving guy—he scored the first touchdown in Super Bowl history in 1967 while hungover—but he was emphatically not a liberated baby boomer, and he seemed to find the sexual free-for-all on the floor every night somewhat distasteful. In 1977, McGee and Thurston shut down their flagship store and tried something else that they hoped would be equally profitable.

In a newspaper article with the headline "Classy disco replaces Left Guard," McGee explained his thinking: he "didn't like the bar's widespread reputation as a pick-up joint—or meat rack, as others have called it." So McGee and Thurston conspired to change the image.

Out went the football memorabilia, well-done steaks, and dark wood paneling. "We practically brought a bulldozer through here," said McGee. In its place was the "classy disco" in question: a chic, velvet-shrouded, high-end club called Maximillian's of Mexico. It charged a five-dollar cover and catered to the sorts of young, upwardly mobile professionals that would soon be known as "yuppies." Within a year, McGee was boasting that the new disco had completely erased the Left Guard's sleazier public image. The other singles clubs that now dotted the Bloomington Strip—Steak and Ale, La Cantina, Spectators—were happy to pick up the business that the Left Guard had left behind.

Adjoining Maximillian's in the old Left Guard space was another attempt to keep up with the times: a Mexican-style restaurant called Chi-Chi's, begun in partnership with a Minneapolis businessman who'd opened the first "Tex-Mex" restaurants in the state.

Within two years, Chi-Chi's had absorbed the Maximillian's space. As bottomless a desire as there might have been for singles bars operating on a nearly industrial scale in the 1970s, it had cooled off by the more conservative sexual revolutionary backlash of the early 1980s. America's desire for bland, fast casual Mexican food, on the other hand, was entering a golden age. In part, it was built on capital reaped from the thousands of vodka gimlets the Left Guard had sold in its heyday.

MOBY DICK'S
A WHALE OF A DRINK
BAR
DICK'S
OF A DRINK
MOBY DICK'S
WHALE OF A DRINK
MOBY DICK'S

"A Whale of a Drink"

MOBY DICK'S

1972–1988

620 HENNEPIN AVENUE, MINNEAPOLIS

For better or for worse, Moby Dick's on Hennepin Avenue was a bar whose reputation preceded it. Moby's was a constant subject of tall tales and watercooler reports, a bar that folks visited just to say they'd been there. At Moby Dick's, you didn't need a band or floor show; the bar itself was the entertainment. Inside the big doors, behind the blue whale, was the center of Hennepin Avenue, a bar that thrust you into downtown's vital, jostling dance.

Moby Dick's was smack in the middle of Block E, the most well-known example of the antiquated nineteenth-century naming convention whereby every block in downtown Minneapolis received its own letter of the alphabet. In the 1970s, as Hennepin Avenue was the heart of Minneapolis's theater scene, Block E was the heart of Hennepin Avenue's edgy arts community. As the Minneapolis poet Roy McBride put it:

It's the main line
It's the drag strip
It's the edge
Down on Hennepin

Or as Tom Waits put it:

Well, it's 9th and Hennepin
All the donuts have
Names that sound like prostitutes
And the moon's teeth marks are
On the sky like a tarp thrown over all this
And the broken umbrellas like

Opposite: Moby Dick's sat at the heart of downtown Minneapolis's notorious Block E. *Photo from the* Star Tribune, *Minnesota Historical Society Collections*

Dead birds and the steam
Comes out of the grill like
The whole goddamned town is ready to blow
And the bricks are all scarred with jailhouse tattoos
And everyone is behaving like dogs.

The Hennepin Strip was the center of an entire world within downtown Minneapolis, a kaleidoscopic jumble of businesses, people, and flotsam that defined the city's grittiest hang. Hennepin housed some of the best Minneapolis street life, boasting art galleries, theaters, the last remaining flop hotels, all-night diners, bowling alleys, arcades, music clubs, low-end restaurants, and newsstands offering magazines, newspapers, and porn from around the world. On Block E, everything and everyone was pressed together, jostling and bumping elbows to get closer to the action. And, of course, there were plenty of bars on this stretch of Hennepin—Mousey's, Brady's, and more—but, befitting its name, Moby Dick's was the biggest and most fearsome of them all.

Whether Moby Dick's deserved its reputation was a topic of heated debate for decades. To many, Moby's was the poster child for vice in downtown Minneapolis, a symbol of the area's crime, disorder, and immorality. In the eyes of certain people in the Minneapolis Police Department, Moby's was the most wretched hive of scum and villainy the city had ever known; one MPD sergeant once claimed, "It is our estimation that if you go into Moby Dick's bar you have a one in four chance of being assaulted." Headlines routinely pilloried Moby's, and the bar served as a convenient scapegoat for larger anxieties about crime and the future of downtown.

To other observers, Moby Dick's was a force of stability, even a civic pillar, of sorts. When asked about Moby's dubious reputation, one Hennepin beat cop in the mid-seventies said: "Moby Dick's, the worst bar in town? That's a bunch of baloney! I can't name a bar that doesn't have drugs and fights; there must be something wrong at Moby's though, because you can get in on the weekend nights now. It used to be packed to the rafters."

Moby Dick's was an easy stand-in for the conflicting views on downtown Minneapolis. One's reaction to mere mention of the bar's name was a quick tell about whether that person thought downtown should be a placid bourgeois office haven or a diverse, edgy mix of pell-mell nightlife.

From the outside, the bar was large and iconic. Its slogan, "a whale of a drink," was mounted on a sign over the front façade, one among dozens of signs that hung above the wide Hennepin Avenue sidewalks. Moby's was distinct: the blue whale, spouting, gleeful, a twinkle in its eye.

During the daytime, Moby Dick's was relatively tranquil, but never boring.

Patrons playing foosball and pinball at Moby Dick's, July 1978. *Photo from the* Star Tribune, *Minnesota Historical Society Collections*

As one observer described it, "Daytime sounds are some friendly haranguing among the players and muttered commentary from the old men watching along the wall. . . . It's got a good racial balance and some of the best drinks in town." You might even find, as one regular admitted, the occasional kid stopping in on his or her way home from school for a free pop from the bartender.

At night, it had a different vibe. The "whale of a drink" slogan referred to the potent pours you'd get at the bar. At Moby's, shots of liquor went for a dollar, for which you got almost two ounces of rail booze, well below the prices at other bars. As a result, Moby's was the best place to get drunk on a budget, which was why it attracted almost every type of boozehound in the city: black and white, rich and poor, office stiffs and bums, men and women, hustlers and rubes, tourists and locals, conventioneers and pool sharks, drunks and more drunks, and "swarms of pool players and pinheads."

"It was a place you'd meet your friends before you went to a concert or out to eat. Or you'd just wait at Moby's because it was great for people watching," remembered one Block E regular. "They did a lot of things you couldn't do today. If you turned in your AA medallion to the bar, they'd hang it up on the wall and you could drink free for the rest of the night. That used to happen every night."

Years before, the bar had originated in a classier vein, when it was known as the 620 Club and was famous for its turkey sandwiches. The 620 was a massive place owned by boxing promoter Ernie Fliegel and future Minneapolis Lakers and Minnesota Vikings owner Max Winter, and the downtown movers and shakers would hang out there every night. (According to legend, the deal that sent the Lakers to L.A. was made at a back table in the 620.) In 1971, a new owner rechristened it Moby Dick's, and for a while, Moby's operated as a disco.

A *Minneapolis Star* reporter described Moby Dick's whirlwind of excitement during a 1978 visit:

Moby Dick's originated as the 620 Club in the 1930s, following the end of Prohibition. *Minnesota Historical Society Collections*

Pudgy matrons in dashikis, flirtatious girls in ruffled dresses, bearded youths with shoulder length hair, old men in pork pies and pulled coats, hot shots posing in white summer suits and hats next to bankers in stolid grey mingle in the low-ceilinged main room. Flamboyant glitter-rockers and sinister-looking super flies, everyday folks in jeans and sport shirts . . . By mid evening, the air in Moby's windowless rooms is as dense as 800 smoking guests can make it. It is sodden with cigarettes, women's heavy perfumes, patchouli from a smattering of long-haired youths, and whiffs of marijuana from the men's room.

Another regular recalled, "I've never seen a bar before or after with such a mixed group of people. Businessmen, pimps, prostitutes, neighborhood people, and people from all walks of life and they all got along. And you really didn't have to worry too much."

The bouncers at Moby's were big and tough and perhaps as legendary as the place itself. The most famous was named Clarence; if he didn't like you, that was the end of your night there. The Moby Dick's bouncers also may have done more policing than some of the cops who patrolled Block E. They did not always handle things properly, however. The record is scattered with various lawsuits charged against Moby's bouncers for being excessively rough with unruly customers in the 1970s. In fact, watching people get bounced from Moby's was almost its own form of entertainment, and provided the source of some of the best stories about the place.

"If someone was giving you a hard time, you'd just tell the bartender and the bartender or the bouncer would just throw the person out," one regular patron said. "I remember one day I was walking along Hennepin Avenue with a friend on Block E. We were a few yards away from Moby's, and this guy came flying out of the front door in the air, just like a cartoon, and landed on his butt."

The flying exit from Moby Dick's was a Hennepin Avenue staple, right up there with swingers strolling like Travolta down the wide sidewalks, or beat cops nudging a bum along his way.

"There were two methods of being bounced," recalled another customer. "If they throw you out the front door, you didn't do anything too bad, just enough to be thrown out. But if you went out the back door, you did something real bad. There was a dark alley back there, and they got in a little bit of trouble for beating people up back there. Anyway, you wanted to stay in line at Moby's."

By the 1980s, the police department and the downtown business interests had Block E in their sights. The dingy art galleries, porn theaters, and bar scene were viewed as the cause of downtown's slipping business and retail culture. Following a misguided plan to transform the block into an urban mall, by the early 1980s the city evicted and bulldozed almost all the businesses on the block.

"Moby's is the perfect example of the type of cesspool that breeds crime; you've got to attack it," declared the police chief at the time, and attack they did.

When the last closing time hit the bar, and the final crowd passed through the big door with the whale on the front, the bulldozers came for the old brick building. One city council member was so elated with the demolition of Block E that he composed a song for the occasion, to the tune of "Bye Bye Blackbird," and sang it onstage at the ceremony for the new surface parking lot that would occupy the block:

Pack up all your rime and porn, Block or scorn, be reborn.
Bye-bye Block E!
Moby Dick's is beached at last, problems vast, now are past,
Bye-bye Block E!
No one here can stop and aggravate us,
No more hard-luck stories will deflate us.
Say good-bye to urban blight, now we'll light up the night,
Bye-bye Block E.

Like much of the old downtown core, the site of Moby Dick's, and all the other establishments that filled Block E, was just another parking lot for the next twenty years. Then, in the early 2000s, the city turned the block into the long-envisioned urban mall. Christened Block E, the new retail building opened to great fanfare in 2002. It even boasted a bar (Applebee's) in the skyway level next to a multiscreen movie theater. Within less than a decade, most of the shops of the new Block E had failed, and the entire structure was eventually remodeled and rechristened Mayo Clinic Square in 2014. Somewhere underneath the new gray façade lies the grave of Moby Dick's bar, and every once in a while, someone walking down Hennepin Avenue will invoke its name—a legend that has stood the test of time.

“A limousine, a blonde, and a hundred-dollar bottle of 1976 Rothschild’s Burgundy.”

COMMODORE HOTEL BAR

1936–1980; 2015–present

79 WESTERN AVENUE, ST. PAUL

Of the many compelling things about St. Paul’s Commodore Hotel bar, the most notable is that it survived the 1970s. Tucked in the dusty network of Victorian mansions, elegant apartments, and carriage houses that cluster around the intersection of Summit and Western Avenues, the large, brick, U-shaped hotel occupies an awkward position in the thicket of prestige. Even F. Scott Fitzgerald had mixed feelings about the place; he mentioned its “faded rose corridors” in a short memoir, referring to the brief time he lived there in 1921, after he and Zelda had been kicked out of their cabin in White Bear Lake for excessive goings-on.

Naturally, every history of the Commodore Bar that has since been written makes mention of Fitzgerald. Typically they describe Scott and Zelda drinking there, though according to Fitzgerald biographer John Koblas, those stories are “all hogwash.” Koblas points out that Prohibition was in place at the time, and the bar did not yet exist. One instead imagines Fitzgerald drinking alone in his hotel room, looking pensively down at the sidewalks of Holly Avenue. In his memoir, he described his months at the

Commodore Hotel: "In the fall we got to the Commodore in St. Paul, and while leaves blew up the streets we waited for our child to be born."

Despite his feelings or intentions, Fitzgerald may have granted immortality to the bar at the Commodore. At the very least, the bar that was eventually installed in the first floor of the building became the saving grace of the stately hotel. When Prohibition ended, the owner launched a grand remodeling of its old lounges, hiring no less a personage than Werner Wittkamp, a Hollywood set designer who was making a name for himself as an interior designer specializing in Art Deco. (In St. Paul, Wittkamp was also responsible for the Art Deco elaboration of the Town House bar on University Avenue and the Lexington on Grand Avenue.) Wittkamp's style was gaudy and camp, and no Art Deco remodel was more flamboyant than the bar at the Commodore. Its backlit trim, gold lamé touches, and wedding cake ceilings seem today like they came out of a spirited *Great Gatsby* remake, although at the time, Fitzgerald's now-famous book was a forgotten dud.

Throughout the mid-twentieth century, the stately flamboyance of the Commodore Bar was unmistakable: a classy room lit by fanciful lighting, trimmed with curving deco lines, and full of mirrors. But by the 1970s, the Commodore was showing its age. The two-hundred-room hotel, like many of the homes in the Cathedral Hill neighborhood, had an air of fading aristocracy.

That said, the Commodore remained famous for its Sunday brunch—the menu might have included scalloped oysters, chicken livers, bacon, or pancakes—and a half-elegant prix fixe service of cold sandwiches, crepes, and homemade potato chips, served alfresco in summertime.

At the center of the action was the Art Deco bar, manned daily by its bow-tied tender, Ralph Setley, who had been serving martinis and daiquiris there for decades.

An account in the *Minneapolis Tribune* describes the scene:

> *After a couple of late afternoon martinis, bizarre things may begin to happen to a patron at the bar in the old Commodore Hotel. . . .*
>
> *It is the sense of time that fogs.*
>
> *There is no country western juke box and no color TV soap operas breaking the blackness. Nothing to tell that it is 1977, not 1938.*
>
> *Ralph Setley won't tell you either. He's been mixing drinks at the bar since 1938 when the place was filled with talk of hard times getting better mingled with talk of Europe going to war again.*
>
> *Setley's biggest fear wasn't a European war. It was an order for a drink called a "mousse cafe." Seven layers of different liqueurs, he said, floating atop a bit of brandy. "It took 15 minutes to make and 15 seconds to drink."*

By 1977, the bar was thriving again. A big band, the Wolverines, played jazz there on weekends, and the classic songs filled the place with nostalgic dancers to the tune of two dollars a head. The owners hired a new manager with big ideas for progress, a flamboyant character named Bradley DuVall, who arrived each night in a bronze Porsche 911 and a fancy suit.

The Commodore Hotel, following a fire in February 1978. *Photo from the* Star Tribune, *Minnesota Historical Society Collections*

The relationship between DuVall and the Commodore did not end well, however, as described by Ron Bacigalupo, the editor of St. Paul's cantankerous weekly rag the *Downtowner:* "[DuVall] had a deformed hand, from polio, he said, and it was hardly big enough to hold a hundred thousand dollars, but that's what they claim it held when he went AWOL on November 6th. . . . Because of his lifestyle I nicknamed him 'the Count' . . . a big deal just around the corner, a limousine, a blonde and a hundred dollar bottle of 1976 Rothschild's Burgundy. . . . He liked money, and all of the things money could buy—or charge, or lease."

After remodeling one of the dining rooms, installing an expensive squash court in the hotel (still there today), and repaving the parking lot, DuVall absconded with tens of thousands of dollars of Commodore management funds. (He was caught a few months later in North Carolina, trying to buy another old hotel.)

Coming on the heels of the downfall of the Count was the Commodore's most famous event. At 3:30 PM on February 15, 1978, a small twenty-year-old compression coupling that connected the hotel's massive furnace to the pipes broke off. Natural gas began filling the bottom floors of the hotel.

An architect who had an office in the basement heard a "wooshing" noise and smelled the distinctive odor. He called the fire department and the front desk to urge an immediate evacuation. Within minutes, a handyman named Larry Liebe began knocking on doors, getting people out of their rooms, and likely saving a few lives.

The first explosion was small, but it blew out all the windows of apartment 101. The loud noise and subsequent flames put a charge into the evacuation, and folks began scrambling from hotel rooms and squash courts as firefighters ran toward the Commodore.

That's when the big explosion hit. The whole side of the building shuddered and all the windows blew out, along with windows in nearby buildings, some blocks away. Shards of glass and other debris peppered the huddled groups of firemen and evacuees, injuring more than sixty people. By one account, "plaster was falling like a ticker tape parade."

One of the few people who didn't leave the building was Ralph, the bartender, who "refused to leave his post because there was money in the till."

Somehow, neither the explosion nor the embezzlement did in the Commodore. The building was so solidly built that—despite a massive fire that left it charred and uninhabitable—it remained structurally sound and wasn't torn down. By the early 1980s, the preservation movement had emerged in the Twin Cities, and the Cathedral Hill neighborhood was being revived as folks began fixing up the old homes.

Soon after the explosion and fire, a new owner purchased the old hotel and began fixing it up before converting it to condominiums. Though the bar did not reopen to the public for another few decades, it remained a venue for occasional weddings, conferences, meetings, and other rental events. For example, in the 1990s, the hotel bar hosted French philosopher Jean Baudrillard, who wrote about it in his collection of travel musings from America.

> *All around is Indian summer, its mildness presaging snow. But where are the ten thousand lakes, the utopian dream of a hellenistic city on the edge of the Rockies? Minneapolis, Minneapolis! After the patrician elegance and feminine gentleness of the Indian summer in Wisconsin, Minneapolis is merely a rural agglomeration, simply waiting in darkness amid its silos and hunting grounds for the winter and the cold on which it prides itself. But in the depths of this real America, there is the Commodore bar, with the finest art deco in the world, where Fitzgerald, they say, drank every evening. I drink there too.*

If anyone would be okay with the eclipsing of truth with a false façade of narration and image, it is Baudrillard, who not only got his cities wrong but repeated the false legends of the Commodore Bar. After all, as he argued, the simulation often eclipses reality.

Today, the Commodore Bar & Restaurant is open to the public, serving a full dining and beverage menu. It fully embraces the Fitzgerald-era "roaring twenties" theme and offers among its specialty cocktails drinks named after the power couple.

"You can thank Rosalie Butler for that!"

PAYNE RELIEVER

1966–2000

899 PAYNE AVENUE, ST. PAUL

In his youth, Marv Frejlach, the founder of the Payne Reliever, was an excellent kegler. He grew up running bowling alleys in the 1950s and '60s, places like Bloomington's Stadium Bowl and St. Paul's Ran-Ham Lanes. Years later, the hand-eye coordination came in handy when Marv displayed uncanny precision and velocity as he flicked bottle caps at patrons who got too friendly with his go-go dancers—preserving what Marv claimed was a first-class culture at the Payne Reliever, his infamous East Side bar.

Owner Marv Frejlach backstage at the Payne Reliever, 1978. *Photo from the* Star Tribune, *Minnesota Historical Society Collections*

"Bouncers, we don't have here. We don't need 'em," Frejlach once bragged to the *Minneapolis Tribune*. "In the first place, we have an image that we've created here. It's known that we handle our problems very expertly, and physically, too, if we have to. We don't get the so-called bar flies in here because we don't have 60-cent shots. That's when you get the trouble."

(The Payne Reliever did have bouncers, at least in its later years. And by all accounts they had a lot of work to do.)

In the late 1960s, Frejlach converted a bowling alley on Payne Avenue into something new that would epitomize the East Side's fighting spirit for decades to come. Marv bought three separate businesses on Payne Avenue (a fact that would come in handy when the city later declared war on his bar) and, in 1966, launched a new enterprise. It was called the Payne Rec "Go Go," a risqué dance bar on the corner of Payne Avenue and York Street, about a half mile north of the Hamm's Brewery.

The first thing you noticed, walking into the "go go" joint, was the darkness. As in any good gentlemen's club, little was well lit except for the dancers. Depending on the year, there might have been one stage or three. The bar itself was on the left when you entered, and the main dancing stage was straight ahead, centered in a large, high-ceilinged room with booths around the walls and small tables scattered about, each surrounded by orange molded plastic chairs.

According to one regular, the "place was always filled with a broad cross-section of the East Side working class. You never saw a suit in it, except maybe during the so-called lunch hour." In the 1970s, the East Side was still a neighborhood full of working-class men with some money to burn on a good time. This was the twilight of St. Paul's factory era, when the massive 3M complex of buildings on the other side of the train tracks, the Whirlpool refrigerator plant on Arcade Street, the Hamm's Brewery farther down Payne Avenue, and a dozen smaller places kept guys working around the clock in cramped quarters, getting ready to burn off steam.

In the early years, the "go go" stage was fueled by Marv's back-page ads in the city's newspapers, which featured an ever-present call for auditions. (For example: "Les Femmes, Oui Oui! Must be 21 or over, good figure and personality.") In fact, the auditions were a regular part of the afternoon

The Payne Reliever on Payne Avenue on St. Paul's East Side, February 1978. *Photo from the* Star Tribune, *Minnesota Historical Society Collections*

show, with new talent trying their hands (or whatever) before a live audience. As the night went on, the Payne Reliever professionals took over. They were all kinds of, what Marv would call, "first-class acts," from the "Lovelee Loveable" Renée London (aka "The original Cat Girl!") to Chesty Morgan to the Swedish Blue Angel to Ginger, well known for her purple G-string, or Ms. Heaven Lee "in all her gorgeous splendor."

But nobody made more of an impression than Billy Anderson, "The Ladies Centerfold Come To Life." Anderson was a staple of the Payne Reliever for years and the main attraction of the weekly ladies' night, when the room was briefly cleared of male clientele. Billy's big number was a stirring performance accompanying Chuck Berry's 1972 rendition of "My Ding-a-Ling," with Billy's moneymaker barely concealed beneath a small towel that he would twitch back and forth before the women.

One attendee recalled her unforgettable experience: "We went there with the girls from work for ladies' night. Billy took a rose from out of his banana pouch and gave it to Marlys, by far the most attractive girl in the group. It remained on the bulletin board at work for quite a while. As I recall we had a blast."

At a certain point in the evening on ladies' night, however, the doors would reopen, and the men would come streaming back into the room, looking for ladies to sidle. The tables quickly turned.

One woman immune to the bar's charms was the cantankerous, charismatic, and self-made political powerhouse Rosalie Butler. A St. Paul City Council member, Butler had worked her way up from nothing, married a rich Summit Avenue businessman, and ran for office on the platform of taking on St. Paul's old boys' club. She was frequently on the front page of the paper, doing verbal battle with mayors, department chiefs, or anyone else caught in her castigatory gaze.

It was because of Butler that Marv Frejlach's expansionist dreams faded and the Payne Reliever began its fall from grace. In 1977, the councilwoman spearheaded a package of "anti-pornography" ordinances aimed at taking out adult bookshops, theaters, massage parlors, and—perhaps Butler's number-one target—skin bars like the Payne Reliever. Within the year, the city unveiled an outright ban on "nude dancing in businesses that sell liquor."

Facing an existential threat to his bar, Frejlach came up with a scheme to exploit a loophole in the rules: he resegregated his club according to its three separate original addresses. Liquor would be served in one part of the bar, and nude dancing would take place in the other.

A newspaper article that year described the scene during this awkward era at the Payne Reliever:

Dallas the dancer and Lightning the snake wouldn't appear until dark, but nobody seemed to care. The businessmen, laborers, and white-haired old men who made up most of the weekday crowd still lined up outside the door to plop down their $3 and grab a good seat. It was just past noon, and the Payne Reliever Club's daily meeting was about to be called to order.

This afternoon's agenda featured, among others, "the beautiful Mary." To complement dancing Mary and her naked friends, there were soft drinks and coffee at 75 cents a shot. No reptiles this afternoon; no booze anytime. In St. Paul, nude dancing and drinking do not mix. An anti-pornography ordinance passed in July makes it illegal for bars to exhibit nude dancing.

So a little more than a week ago the Payne Reliever, which served liquor for more than 30 years, became a club. That made a lot of its patrons—who were more than willing to hand over $1 for a yearly membership—happy. It made owner Marvin Frejlach say things like "Business is surprisingly beautiful." And it made the merchant across the street at Lindahl Jewelers just shake his head.

Frejlach and Butler each made the other into villains within their respective circles—Butler in the newspaper, with her Summit Avenue friends, and in the city council chambers, and Frejlach in the working-class haunts of the East Side. "You can thank Rosalie Butler for that," he would say upon hearing the slightest criticism of the new, mandatory pasties or the Plexiglas screens that appeared between the dancers and their audience.

The legal challenges flew back and forth between the Payne Reliever and the city. In one particularly memorable moment, Frejlach's lawyer, Jerrold Hartke, invited the high-minded Judge Miles Lord to visit the establishment and see for himself its upstanding character.

Early in yesterday's hearing, Hartke suggested that Judge Lord visit the bars involved in the case.

"Are you kidding?" asked the judge.

"No, your honor, I'm serious."
"No way," said the judge vehemently. "NO WAY!"

Despite the regulation, it's no coincidence that the eventual fall of the Payne Reliever synchronized with the closing of the East Side factories. One by one, as businesses decamped or shut down, the bar's clientele diminished along with the jobs. Toward the end of the Payne Reliever's run, the business model began to shift away from titillation. Marv took a well-earned retirement, and under a new owner, the bar assumed a new identity. "The Payne Reliever / The Rockin' Eastside," as it was called. In those years, the bar had a split personality: hair-metal bands on one side and strippers on the other, neatly demarcated by Plexiglas.

The place was finally shut down in 2000, when it briefly became an Embers diner. Though the bar is now gone, to this day, if you mention the name "Payne Reliever" in a St. Paul dive, old men can still be heard muttering from the back of the room: "You can thank Rosalie Butler for that!"

Following a 1977 ordinance, the nude dancers at the Payne Reliever were separated from the portion of the bar where alcohol was served. *Photos from the* Star Tribune, *Minnesota Historical Society Collections*

"Nothing fancy.
No airs.
Just good people."

KING OF CLUBS

1950s–2001

957 CENTRAL AVENUE NORTHEAST, MINNEAPOLIS

Located in an oddly shaped beige building, the King of Clubs looked like any of about a dozen other Northeast Minneapolis joints on the inside. It had an oval-shaped bar, red carpets, neon signs, dart boards, a pool table, vinyl booths, low-hanging lights, a small dance floor, and a cigarette machine by the door. In the evenings, there may have been a bouncer or two to provide backup to the bartender orchestrating the show, while servers milled about distributing the goods.

In those days, Central Avenue and Third Avenue came together at a sharp angle, creating an oddly sliced triangular lot. The building was truncated where the two streets came together, and a massive five-foot-high playing card—the King of Clubs—was mounted on the exterior of the narrow sliver of wall. The king, with a trim beard and mustache, held a sword in one hand and a small orb in the other, the globus cruciger, symbolizing authority over the earth.

The regal image was fitting because, at least for a while in the 1970s, it seemed like the fate of the city could be made or broken in the cozy confines of the King of Clubs bar. This was especially true on Wednesday nights, when alderman Al Hofstede and his circle of Nordeast insiders gathered at the tavern for steak night, when a mere $1.95 got you a good-size cut of beef, homemade coleslaw, and dark rye bread. The bar filled with Northeast hoi polloi, factory workers, and others who had gotten their starts in the neighborhood before moving away from the factories and into quieter quarters or nearby suburbs. They always returned to the old neighborhood, pulling up to the King of Clubs in big, boxy cars for a chance to feast and mix with the folks at the heart of industrial Minneapolis. For Hofstede, who liked to boast that he "only knew how to make popcorn," Wednesday night at the King of Clubs was his favorite meal in town. And it's where he and his buddies schemed to reclaim the reins of the city.

Things had been coming to a head since 1969, when a former police officer named Charles Stenvig was elected to his first of two terms as mayor of Minneapolis. As head of the city's police union, the Republican Stenvig secured a surprising victory after running on a "law and order" platform, harnessing voters' growing anxieties around race and public safety. He declared that Minneapolis was "one of the few American cities that could be saved," and he promised to be the one who would save it.

Having a conservative in Minneapolis's highest office did not sit well with the local unions and DFLers. From the back table at the King of Clubs, alderman Hofstede and his cronies hatched plans to take back the mayor's office. Hofstede built his own campaign by working to unify the various party factions in the city, and groups of union leaders, fire and police department insiders, businessmen, and political movers made the King of Clubs Hofstede's de facto campaign headquarters. When the 1973 mayoral election rolled around, Hofstede came away victorious.

The King of Clubs, at the intersection of Central and Third Avenues in Northeast Minneapolis, 2000. *Photo by Chris Gregerson*

The next few years were a back-and-forth battle between Hofstede and Stenvig over control of the city, with the Minneapolis Police Department frequently at the center. Stenvig, who continued to stake his political fortunes on police and public safety issues, won the mayor's office back from Hofstede in 1975 before losing it again to him in 1977. How to handle the growing concerns about prostitution, smut, and nuisance bars was a constant theme on the front and editorial pages of the city papers.

But when he took office on January 1, 1974, the thirty-three-year-old Hofstede was the youngest mayor in the history of the city, and he made sure to reward his buddies from the "Club." If you were "in the Club," it meant you knew Al from back in the days at the bar, and you had a special friendship with the new mayor. (During Hofstede's time in office, he famously appointed one of the King of Clubs owners to a seat on the city's Housing and Redevelopment Authority, the body that doled out money for development projects.)

The connections became something of an issue as the years went on, especially when it came to the work done by the city's vice squad. According to some news accounts, the vice squad had gotten prostitution off the streets by moving it into certain of the city's less-esteemed taverns. The friendly connections among the mayor, the vice squad, and the city's barkeepers was a hot-button issue, and for a while the King of Clubs was right in the middle of it.

Probably the biggest charge waged against the Club was an allegation from 1977, in which a high-profile Club member from the Minneapolis Police Department blew the whistle on an undercover attempt by the county sheriff to crack down on gambling. This individual allegedly alerted the bar about a detective Decowski, who was working on the sting operations. Here's the story, which made its way to a letter to the editor in the *Minneapolis Star:*

> *A law enforcement officer who bore a marked similarity to detective Decowski entered the King of Clubs on a social visit.*
>
> *The bartender believed this police officer to be Decowski and caused the football-score "pull board" to be hastily removed from the bar.*
>
> *Upon checking with other patrons in the bar, the bartender discovered that the officer was not Decowski but rather that the officer was a "friend" of the Club (the reference being to a group of politically active policemen who frequent the King of Clubs bar).*
>
> *The bartender subsequently went over to the policeman whom he had mistaken and told him that Elmer Nordlund had been to the bar and had detailed the description of Decowski to the bartender. . . . He said that Nordlund further told him that Decowski was an undercover officer working on gambling. . . . Subsequently, I received a call from an owner of the King of Clubs, who said he was extremely upset about my opposition of Nordlund for chiefs of police and my discussion with other people of the matter that had happened at the King of Clubs. "Elmer is a friend of mine; if he hadn't, I would have been disappointed in him."*

Whether or not the story is true, folks at the King of Clubs surely relished their role at the city's political center, and the bar remained for years a cultural touchstone at the edge of Northeast Minneapolis's liquor patrol limits. The bar also remained on the edge of the city's legal and social codes, a place twenty-year-olds would go to get a drink or two when they were still underage, or where kids would sneak packs of Marlboros from the vending machine.

It wasn't all politics at the King of Clubs, though. One of the bar's co-owners was the famous Iron Range boxing champion Scott LeDoux, who made the King of Clubs his home base. After a November 1979 fight at Bloomington's Met Center, legendary *New York Daily News* sportswriter Dick Young accompanied Scott and Sandy LeDoux to the bar. LeDoux's eye was taped up from the fight, which he had lost in twelve rounds on a unanimous decision by the judges.

Young wrote how, despite LeDoux's loss, the bar was hopping:

> *Scott took Sandy and his taped eye to the "King of Clubs," their longtime hangout, a bar that is as thoroughly neighborhood as Scott LeDoux is. Nothing fancy. No airs. Just good people. The place was packed with Scott LeDoux's neighbors and friends.*
>
> *"You should see it when he wins," I remember Sandy saying that night.*

Imagining the King of Clubs after a win by either LeDoux or Hofstede, in their respective bouts in boxing or politics, is to picture the height of blue-collar revelry. Backslapping, rounds on the house, cheers for the local boy made good.

Perhaps it's fitting that, twenty years after Hofstede plotted his ascent to the mayor's office in the booths at the Club, the same bar was the setting for a scene in the Coen brothers' 1996 masterpiece, *Fargo.* For the filming, the art director added a neon sign to the outside of the bar, but most everything else about the bar remains in place when Jerry Lundegaard meets the shady Gaear and Carl onscreen to hire them to kidnap his wife. Up until the bar closed, the booth had a small plaque marking its role in the film.

The King of Clubs was torn down in 2002, the street intersection was reconfigured, and the old site became an affordable housing development for people living with HIV and AIDS.

"I can remember when people would ask 'You going to the Numbers tonight?'"

19 BAR

1956–present

19 WEST FIFTEENTH STREET, MINNEAPOLIS

Everett L. Stoltz grew up in small-town Plainview, Minnesota, a World War II navy vet living in the Loring Park neighborhood and working intermittently as an accountant. In 1956, he bought the 19 Bar, not far from the apartment he shared with his partner, George Koch. They made the purchase right about the time Loring Park was undergoing a transition, which Stoltz himself was a part of. A surplus of single-residency apartment buildings outfitted with kitchenettes and Murphy beds and, after the turn of the decade, a steady flow of gay men who had patronized the bars of Minneapolis's Gateway District until they were booted out of their old lives meant that a sizable gay population was growing in the neighborhood. It would have been hard for Stoltz to imagine at that time, but twenty years later, Loring Park would be the site of the city's first Pride Parade, and the 19 Bar the stop of choice for pre- and post-parade festivities.

Stoltz's 19 Bar had a reputation as a space where gay men and women could hang out in relative peace. There were a few other bars in town with a predominantly gay crowd that Stoltz and Koch would have been familiar with. These weren't gay bars in the sense that they're known today, but rather were mixed spaces with some gay clientele, known to each other but hiding in plain sight from straight bargoers. Kirmser's in St. Paul had a gay crowd at night that mixed with its German American blue-collar regulars, and the Persian Palms and Schiek's in the Gateway District were known to be gay hangouts. The Viking Room at the Radisson Hotel downtown had been the most prominent gay destination since the 1940s, but that was the sort of place you'd have to get dressed up to enter and be expected to appreciate the difference between a gimlet and a gibson. If you were a queer working-class person with no particular knowledge of mixed drinks, you were not going to feel welcome there.

The 19 Bar, on the other hand, was a 3.2 bar, not significantly different from the other 3.2 bars located nearby. They were all a little rough, the kinds of places you'd find old pensioners having a quiet drink, but also possibly empty whiskey bottles in the men's room and people hanging around outside, soliciting various sex acts, and who seemed to be drunk on stuff a lot stronger than near beer. Stoltz, having worked a professional white-collar job, having served as an officer in the navy, and living right in the neighborhood, at the Park Terrace Apartments, was probably able to bridge the class divide to some extent. He could run a bar that was comfortable to a variety of patrons from both the immediate neighborhood and the larger gay community.

Along with the Dugout in downtown Minneapolis, Stoltz's 19 Bar was perhaps the first in the Twin Cities to cultivate a primarily gay clientele, even if it was done mostly by word of mouth, and even if it retained a mixed crowd. (Decades later, the current owner, Gary Hallberg, installed a neon sign that read GAY BAR, to remove any lingering doubt among first timers who'd wandered in.)

Stoltz did a good job obscuring the fact that it was a gay bar from the straight world. For years, it wasn't listed as the 19 Bar in the phone book in case any would-be terrorists got the idea to call in a bomb threat; instead, it was listed as the Cat's Meow. The 19 Bar was the subject of a great deal of attention in its first decade, but very rarely did details about its clientele make it into the official record. Some Loring Park residents, wary of bargoers who'd migrated down Hennepin Avenue to the neighborhood, complained of a "growing skid row atmosphere" along the park. All four of the 3.2 bars—the 19, the Loring Tap, the Savoy, and Kit's—were put on the chopping block by the city council; only the Numbers, as the 19 Bar was affectionately known by regulars, survived. The police commissioner had earlier noted it was a "hangout for homosexuals," but during the hearing, no one present had any complaints about the 19 Bar as such. Even in early 1961, when a freak cross-country murder spree landed the bar in the headlines after two itinerant killers murdered a patron, "none of the nation's newspapers reported the killer's last stop was a homosexual hangout," according to Stewart Van Cleve in his 2009 account of queer Minnesota, *Land of 10,000 Loves.* The two killers, in fact, may not have even known it.

The contemporary gay rights movement began its life in a bar not unlike the 19: the Stonewall Inn in Greenwich Village, where in 1969 patrons fought back against police during one of the many raids on the gay bar. Throughout the 1970s, the gay community in the Twin Cities developed a more vocal and politically engaged public identity, geographically focused very much around Loring Park. An advertisement in the local LGBT paper for a bookstore noted its location at Fourteenth and Nicollet as "Gay Minneapolis 55403."

"Gay Pride means being Gay at all times, not just on a special occasion or in special places like the bars or the baths," wrote Brad Golden, coordinator of the Gay Pride Committee, on the occasion of the first Minneapolis Pride Parade in 1977. The bars, though, were key organizing spaces, the 19 in particular. In the late 1970s, after a rash of gay bashings in Loring Park that seemed to be of very little interest to the Minneapolis Police Department, the 19's owners organized safety patrols for the benefit of its patrons. The patrols were initially met with great enthusiasm, as dozens of volunteers signed up to work in groups of three, although it waned slightly over time—"present volunteers are overworked," read an advertisement to recruit more.

By the middle of the 1970s, downtown Minneapolis's Gay 90's, which had had a gay clientele going back to its earliest days, had developed into a full-blown entertainment complex, with full liquor licenses and catering almost exclusively to gays and lesbians. "The Gay 90's says it's the oldest, but they're wrong," the 19's owner at the time, Jackie Hamman, told the LGBT newspaper *Equal Time* in 1982. "I can remember when people would ask, 'You going to the Numbers tonight?'" she said. "The 19 was known as a gay bar and they were afraid to say it in public." It's not clear if the writer misquoted Hamman about whether they *were* or *weren't* afraid to say it in public. It depends, perhaps, on who the "public" is in that equation. Certainly if you were a gay man or lesbian in 1965 and you were looking for a drink and some companionship, the 19 Bar would have been at the top of your list. If you were a somewhat oblivious townie at the same time, though, you might not have noticed at all. It wasn't until the 1970s that the bar proudly noted that it was, and had been for decades, gay-owned.

The 19 Bar's status as a 3.2 joint and its relatively close distance from the hubbub of downtown gave it some other distinct advantages. It was, it pointed out in advertisements, "the only bar open after midnight Sundays." Bars with full liquor licenses were required to shut down at midnight on Sundays, even into the early 1990s. The 19 stayed open one hour later, which made it the perfect last call; lines would stretch around the block, as many as four or five hundred people piling in for the final hour.

If the gay hangouts of the pre-Stonewall era had been divided by class, the 19's no-pretense atmosphere made it a welcoming hangout for a wide range of people, both women and men. It doesn't look much different today than it did then: the pool tables were always the focal point, the clientele was mixed ("very mixed" according to one advertisement), and the music was loud but not so loud you couldn't have a conversation. There are no windows, and the walls are wood paneled. A portrait of Queen Elizabeth II, whose coronation came just a few years before the debut of the 19, sat then as now by the front entrance.

Advertisement for the 19 Bar in the *Equal Time* newspaper. *Minnesota Historical Society Collections*

The 19 has weathered the usual challenges of a neighborhood bar, often compounded by its status as the state's oldest gay bar. In the early 1980s, the ward's alderwoman apparently made a threat, during a neighborhood meeting, to "officially ask you to close," in response to complaints from nearby property owners about sex acts performed on the patio. (The property developers were said, drily, in an *Equal Time* piece, to be "proponents of upgrading, or, as critics call it, gentrifying Loring Park.") An activist named Robert Halfhill, a politically engaged expat from Kentucky then running for state senate and involved in frontline activism in the gay liberation movement, interpreted those remarks to mean the bar would be closed. He raised hell, directing calls, postcards, and letters to the city council. Halfhill downplayed opponents' more salacious claims—in reference to a report that gay men could be seen having sex "with their pants off" on nearby picnic tables, he quipped, "we must have arrived at the wrong time"—but never downplayed the 19 Bar's important role in the community for gays and lesbians. The alderwoman later backtracked, claiming she meant she'd ask the patio to close. A compromise was reached: the 19 did stay open, but with a midnight closing time, ending the bar's magic hour. Despite that setback, the city council and the developers were chastened, made to look like homophobes. "They thought they could get the public on their side by saying we were gay," said Hamman. They couldn't.

The 19 would go on to survive arson, redevelopments, and reboots, always hanging on with the support of the neighborhood and the community. "If they turn this place into a parking lot," one 19 Bar patron joked in 1980, reflecting on the gentrification of the neighborhood, "let's just say I'll never park here."

"It's too damn noisy in here. Let's go to the Black."

BLACK FOREST INN

1965–present

1 EAST TWENTY-SIXTH STREET, MINNEAPOLIS

The connection between the Black Forest Inn and artists was codified the year it opened, in 1965, when no less an authority than the director of the Minneapolis Institute of Art declared the fresco on the building's exterior a prime local example of "classic pop art."

It just so happens the fresco was painted by one of the city's best-known artists, Mike Lynch, who has made a steady career of painting quiet Twin Cities urban landscapes since the 1950s. He painted not just the frescos over the top of the Twenty-Sixth Street side, but also the wall-size mural in the parking lot in the back. "Pop art" isn't really the first thing that comes to mind when looking at Mike's work. If anything, he's a blue-collar realist, depicting liminal scenes of grain elevators and bar exteriors in the dead of night, half-remembered scenes from the lonelier stretches of the Midwest. His paintings of the Rhine River on the front of the Black Forest Inn and the sylvan expanse of Bavaria in the back are not entirely far off from his usual subjects. Maybe the Mia director was being glib. Who knows?

Standing next to the mural fifty years later, Lynch looks at it again. It's held up well, despite a spot near the street where some graffiti has been painted over, maybe ten or twenty years ago. The colors are bolder, and the forms are a little more clearly defined than those in many of Mike's scenes. "I had to simplify it. Although the deer came out pretty realistic." He remembers, after it was first painted, that a dog bounded out of a car that had just parked, looked at the wall, froze, and then started barking wildly at the deer.

The Black Forest Inn has been a hangout for artists since the 1960s, and over the years, it has accumulated one of the best collections of original and commissioned artwork around. Mike points out it wasn't just artists. That was a big part of the mix, but everyone dropped in. "Hippies and cops and all kinds in between," he says. "Not one single kind of crowd. Gay people, black and white, rich and poor. It was better than most in that way."

Part of the attraction for the artists, at least, is the proximity to the Institute of Art, as well as the Minneapolis College of Art and Design and the Children's Theatre Company, all of which have provided a steady stream of artists, actors, set designers, and more through its doors. The larger part of the bar's appeal is probably that it's a cheap, cozy spot to get a drink. There are not now, and have never been, any televisions in the place. In the spot you might expect to find a television, over the bar, there is a shimmering galaxy of hanging glassware. For years, regulars had personalized steins hanging overhead, a program that ended when they all came crashing down one night.

A magazine profile of Minneapolis nightlife from the year the Black Forest Inn opened, 1965, showed scene after scene of youth gyrating, dancing, and

The original mural on the Nicollet Avenue side of the Black Forest Inn depicted vibrant scenes of the Rhine River region of Germany. *Photo courtesy of the Black Forest Inn*

hoisting glasses of beer in bars and clubs around the city. Except for the Black: it's two guys intently playing chess, each with a stein of lager.

The Black Forest Inn is packed top to bottom with artwork, a sense of what you might recall from your freshman art history class as *horror vacui.* Even in the antechamber of the bar, a parade of hand-painted rabbit silhouettes runs along the baseboards. There has never been a formal collecting agenda, so it's all over the place.

Erich Christ behind the bar in the early years of the Black Forest Inn, with personalized steins hanging overhead. *Photo courtesy of the Black Forest Inn*

Erich Christ purchased the Black Forest Inn in 1965 with his brother Gerhard, hoping to open a German-style restaurant and bar after training as a butcher and a stint cooking in the army. The bar had most recently been known as the Swinging Door, and before that it had been known as the Flamingo, Korsmo's Club, and Nellie Stevens' Cafe, the latter owned by a woman whose suspicious death in 1944 was initially pinned on her ex-husband. The Swinging Door owner got wind of the fact that Christ was interested in a German establishment, and he renamed it the Black Forest Inn to sweeten the deal. (Ironically, if Christ had had his way, he'd have given it a flashier name, along the lines of the famed Purple Onion in San Francisco.)

Mike Lynch, who had a studio around the corner, would pop in regularly after he was done painting for the day. He met Erich and his wife, Joanne Christ, and they soon began to buy some of his work. He doesn't remember who approached whom first, but at some point, Mike got the commission to begin a beautification process.

"It's critical to this place to have artists around," Joanne Christ says today. "Every bar is good at something. We were good at incorporating artists' drive and instinct. The value of the input is hard to overstate."

The first request was for a logo: a deer's head. Mike collaborated with sculptor and employee Bruce Thomas on creating a metal version to hang above the door. Though the deer's head has remained the logo, each artist who came after changed it in some way. "That kind of pissed me off at first," says Lynch, "but that's the character of the place—no consistency! Whoever was next did whatever they wanted."

Next came the exterior: the mural by the parking lot, the scenes of southern Germany over the windows and doors. The nature scene on the Nicollet Avenue side is the piece that looks most like Mike's other work: a layer of mist enveloping a valley with a lonely church in the center. The Christs wanted German lettering for the murals, so Mike found a manual on lettering by Albrecht Dürer. The manual covered classical Italian lettering, and the Christs balked at first, worried that the effect might not be Teutonic enough. However, as Mike pointed out, "Dürer is as German as it gets." Dürer and Lynch prevailed.

For many years, the Black Forest Inn was a 3.2 bar, which allowed it to have a later closing time than full bars but was tough for a place serving German beers. The problem ultimately was solved in a very Black Forest Inn sort of way: an artist drafted up a postcard, and the Christs started a letter-writing campaign to the city council. "If the choice was mine / Wine would be fine / When we dine / At the Black Forest Inn," read the postcards. Eventually, the license was granted in the mid-1970s, though Joanne remembers an intense city council hearing at which Mama D., the matronly Dinkytown spaghetti joint proprietor, was standing and screaming, "You can pay for it like we all did!"

Getting the liquor license gave the Christs the opportunity to turn the bar into its present-day configuration and, later, to open the adjoining beer garden, which was the first German-style garden in the city in perhaps seventy-five years, since the days of the Jumbo. Inside, the bar took its place on one side of the room and the restaurant on the other. "Like cousins," is how the Christs describe the two sides of the establishment today. "Same family, but different upbringing." When Erich unpacked the bar and had it set up, he thought it didn't seem, or smell, quite right.

He opened a bottle of scotch, poured it all over the bar, and let it sit overnight. "It's smelled right ever since," he said.

The bar side could get out of hand once in a while, although sometimes people got booted for being too casual. Mike remembers Twin Cities musician Willie Murphy getting thrown out for monopolizing a round table by the entrance with his pals for too long, stretching out one or two beers to the length of an afternoon one too many times. There's another story about a fight that broke out between two painters late one night. One had the other on the floor, about to pummel her. "Fellow realist! Fellow realist!" she yelled, throwing up her hands. The other combatant relented on the grounds of shared aesthetic sensibility.

The best-known piece of bar art—not just in the Black Forest, but perhaps in the whole city—is a print of Richard Avedon's 1963 photo *The Generals of the Daughters of the American Revolution, DAR Convention, Mayflower Hotel, Washington DC*. The piece was gifted to the bar during

Avedon's show at the Minneapolis Institute of Art, one of his first major retrospectives. He enjoyed his time hanging out at the Black, and he gave the print to the Christs with a fond dedication and signature in the corner. The print in its original state is worth a quarter of a million dollars today.

It's not in its regular state, though. In one of the most famed acts of aesthetic vandalism in the city's history, in November 1986, a regular named Nelson who was sitting at the bar arose from his seat, produced a .357 Magnum pistol, and, without warning, fired three shots at the photograph, two of them hitting their mark. He hit one of the subjects right in the eye. "He became," the official complaint said, "frustrated and angry while looking at the photo."

"That photo always bugged the hell out of me," he said later. He turned himself into the Fifth Precinct down the street and was ultimately sentenced to probation. In lieu of a fine, he was required to donate three hundred dollars to arts organizations. The bullet holes remain today, poked, prodded, and examined like a holy relic. "In the wisdom of the people whose opinion we most value," Joanne says, they never repaired it. Avedon came in years later, took a look, shook his head, and left. Everyone else, though, seems to love the piece. Nelson, in his inexplicable frustration, turned the photograph into a three-dimensional object to be investigated by everyone who walks by.

Famed though the Avedon print is, three charcoal drawings by artist Birney Quick from 1980 hanging in the back of the dining room best capture the spirit of the Black Forest Inn: a festive environment, blue-checkered tablecloths, patrons sitting around with steins of beer, Erich's housemade sausages being unveiled. In the one on the right, a woman leans toward her companion, whispering conspiratorially in his ear with some piece of gossip, or observation, or something else entirely, a quiet scene of easy familiarity that is instantly recognizable to anyone who's ever hung out in a bar.

That easy familiarity is very attractive in a regular hangout. Mike remembers a night at the CC Club, just down Twenty-Sixth Street a few blocks on Lyndale Avenue. The CC is a storied hangout, too, but certainly has a different atmosphere.

"It's so noisy in there," Mike says. He remembers telling his friends, "It's too damn noisy in here. Let's go to the Black."

"As good as walking into his own living room."

HALEK'S BAR

1947–2009

2024 NORTH WASHINGTON AVENUE, MINNEAPOLIS

By all accounts, Halek's Bar was at the peak of its powers in the mid-1970s. The North Minneapolis tavern dominated rec-league sports like few bars had done before, sponsoring dozens of teams in nearly every amateur event. Halek's fearsome reputation in touch football extended not just across the city but around the state and the nation as well. Halek's barroom was lined on all sides with championship trophies, plastic gold figures frozen in every conceivable athletic gesture.

The bar was founded by Michael Halek, who had grown up working at his father's bar, Bill's Place (location unknown). In 1947, he opened Halek's Bar on a prime location at the corner of Washington and West Broadway Avenues in a dense pocket of shops in North Minneapolis. The three-story building stood less than two miles north of downtown and a long softball's throw from the Mississippi River, in the midst of the bustling industrial riverfront, an area full of warehouses, scrapyards, auto shops, small factories, and the like.

Halek passed away in 2000, and according to one eulogy, he had become obsessed with sports sometime in the 1940s when he sponsored a basketball team. The passion only grew, and over the following decades, there wasn't a team jersey he wouldn't put his name on, so long as they came back to his bar after the game. "He was a trophy nut," the eulogy continued. "Every time we won a new trophy, he put up a new shelf."

As the winning years waxed on, Halek's walls gathered ever more trophies onto these shelves. The barroom itself was a wide, long rectangle surrounding the center island of beer and spirits. Small windows looked out onto Washington Avenue on one end and the back parking lot on the other. Wedged next to a car repair place, the building was constructed in 1901 as a flophouse hotel. By the 1970s, the old hotel rooms had been transformed into about two dozen spartan apartments. At the back of Halek's, an old hotel office was used as a cashier window where area workers could cash their paychecks, which they did gladly before buying another round or two of Grain Belts.

The seven-man touch football league was probably the most competitive of Halek's many sports endeavors. The league had been set up by the Minneapolis Park and Recreation Board (then known as the Board of Park Commissioners) in the late 1950s, and by the early 1970s, the sport was booming, with more than seventy touch football teams in Minneapolis alone; game results were even reported in local sports sections as well as the official park board minutes. The rules presented a pared-down version of the bigger game: two teams played on an eighty-yard field, there were no pads, no field goals, teams had four downs to go twenty yards, and they could run or pass for extra points.

As one sportswriter described it: "Roll-out passing was the primary strategy. Offensive units consist of a center and two ends on the line, quarterback, two blocking backs, and a flanker. Defensive units include two rushers, a linebacker, two cornerbacks and two safeties. It is a fast game. Defense is the key, but sometimes things come unglued."

In 1971, the *Tribune* described one particularly heated playoff game: "a tong war, with a small Guatemalan revolution on the side. There were razzle-dazzle plays, flea-flickers, situation substitutions, and mad scrambles. [Halek's QB] Larry Wendell, skating around a la Fran Tarkenton, scrambled for almost 20 seconds before finally throwing to Bob Yurch for a score. A goal-line stand and controversial penalties, and near the end, a little blood when a Halek's rusher, Paul Marfiz, ripped open a 12-stitch cut in his forearm that he injured in an industrial accident last week."

All through the 1970s and beyond, Halek's teams played this small-scale sport like no other in the nation, recruiting former NFL players and winning national tournaments at a dizzying pace. According to longtime bartender Willey, recruiting was the secret to Halek's many championships.

"I mention the name Halek's and I get guys who played pro ball out for the team," Willey once explained. "[Former Minnesota State University standout] Kreg Kapitan played for us. Chet Anderson plays for us, and he's played for the Vikings. [Former University of Minnesota defensive back] Gary Hohman plays for us, and he isn't even a northsider. I was in Milwaukee with a couple of our football players not too long ago. We went down to a bar called

Remnants of the Halek's trophy case. *Photo by Anna Botz*

Kodric's. They beat us for the national football title last year. Not a good bar. Had one trophy in the place and that was for beating us. Big deal."

Halek's stacked the deck in every sport you could think of: bowling, golf, softball, baseball, basketball, and more. On any given night, the bar was filled with sports teams celebrating a victory and, occasionally, a crew seeking consolation after a loss. A 1975 account describes the scene one night after a tough game: "The guy stood in front of the bar at dusk, dusting off his pants where he had slid into second base about an hour earlier. He was in need of a beer, some consoling, as he walked into Halek's, which was as good as walking into his own living room. Willey, the bartender, shot the guy a Grain Belt automatically. . . . It's a second home to anybody who ever played ball on the north side."

In those days, the most unusual trophy on the wall was a four-pound carp, perhaps the only taxidermied carp on display in Minnesota. The massive, ugly fish was the result of another of Willey's creative ideas: the Halek's Carp Fishing Contest.

More than a hundred customers paid five dollars each to enter, and the winner got the whole pot. The rules were pretty simple: no spears, nets, or anything except a fishing rod and bait; no boats; and finally, "anglers are reminded that carp are not to be returned to the water or left on the banks. They should be carried away and, if not eaten, disposed of properly." Customers ran back and forth from Halek's to the river a few blocks away hoping to win the large cash pot, but they had to leave their carp outside.

Besides the carp contest, other famous Halek's tournaments included the "annual cold spring fräulein Kegle," a bowling tournament for women (a crew from South St. Paul trounced Halek's in the debut effort), and the long-lived

"Sani Flush Invitational." The latter was a golf tournament that began in 1963 with a prognostication from a local barfly, who loudly stated: "If this group had a [golf] tournament, it would be a real Toilet Bowl."

Thus the name for the tournament—the Sani-Flush Invitational—and the trophies, which featured a framed toilet seat portrait and, for one lucky winner, a bona fide working flush toilet, ready for installation. The tournament was still going strong well into the 2000s.

By the 1980s, Halek's dominant touch football teams had become victims of their own success. Fewer and fewer teams were willing to put the effort into the kind of recruiting, coaching, and competitive obsession required to compete with the crew from the northside bar. After all, there are only so many average men wanting to play beer league touch football against former Vikings players. As the beatings mounted, the number of teams dwindled, and the league, as well as Halek's dynasty, began to wane.

Michael Halek's sons took over the bar and ran it for a few decades, before they finally sold it in 2008. The bar is still there, now under the name Cliff-n-Norm's, and you can still find signs of the old trophies and faded seventies glory. Until recently, on one wall, the "asshole of the month" had their photo neatly framed at the center of a toilet seat.

The Halek's Bar space now operates as Cliff-n-Norm's Bar. *Photo by Anna Botz*

"It was the only place in St. Paul to get interesting beer."

JOHNNY'S BAR

1953–late 1990s

2251 UNIVERSITY AVENUE, ST. PAUL

Johnny's Bar was an unlikely candidate to usher in the era of Minnesota craft beer. It was a small, one-story, windowless bar on University Avenue amid the trucks and warehouses of the West Midway on the far edge of St. Paul. This was back when the neighborhood was full of working men who spent their days and nights in shops, factories, and diesel trucks. This was when the paper mill was running all day and night, recycling pulp and exhausting from its tall smokestack; when the nut company employed hundreds; when the logistics enterprises buzzed with activity; and when dozens of smaller supply and distribution centers dotted the streets behind University Avenue, delivering everything from plumbing and janitorial supplies to pressurized tanks of gas.

On Thursdays and Fridays especially, a steady stream of guys would come off their shifts and bounce into Johnny's, which was known for its generous check-cashing policy. The bar had been started by its eponymous namesake in the 1940s, and by the 1980s, Johnny's widow and two sons had taken over. The brothers, Skip and Art, ran the bar while their mother would arrive early and head down to the basement to make sandwiches.

Like many bars in the neighborhood, such as the nearby Ace Box or Cromwell's, Johnny's catered to the truckers and working stiffs from West Midway, who would slap backs and swap yarns in the bar's booths and

Line drawing of Johnny's Bar exterior. *Author Collection*

tables night after night. Architecturally speaking, Johnny's proffered a vaguely mid-century modern profile: a simple, boxy façade with a few "decorated shed" flairs, the most notable being the huge neon martini sign bearing the name *Johnny's* that stuck out on the avenue and lit up the pavement. On the side of the building, a simple mural painted on the bricks read: "Home of the Home-Made Sandwich."

The interior wasn't all that remarkable, either. There were booths along one wall, a few tables gathered around a central bar, and a Plexiglas-shielded room where Johnny, Skip, or Art would cash the checks. Skip kept a baseball bat and a gun back there, just in case, but he very rarely had to brandish them.

In the 1980s, the two main features of the rather nondescript bar were the food and the beer. The food was simple but good, consisting of sandwiches that might have been made each morning. The daily sandwich could be sliced roast beef au jus or a meatball sub or a half dozen other possibilities, but there was only one item on the menu on any given day, and you could be sure it was made fresh in the basement.

The other key feature of Johnny's was the twelve tap lines serving different and varied beers, a large number for the era. Unlike at most blue-collar bars, Johnny's didn't just serve American macro lagers. When the bar first opened a few blocks down the street, Hamm's was the only beer available. But after somebody from the brewery pissed off Johnny by raising prices and rent a bit too high, he moved to a new building and diversified the beer selection.

Art and Skip made the conscious effort to offer imported and "unusual" beers, and by the 1980s the tap lines at Johnny's were flowing with varieties that you couldn't find in most other beer joints around town. Skip, meanwhile, would bend the ear of any trucker, beer snob, or beer distributor about how they should try something new in their pint glasses.

One regular Johnny's beer connoisseur remembered it well: "I would go there weekly, and it was the only place in St. Paul to get interesting beer. I remember to this day, it was at Johnny's where I first had a Fuller's ESB. I thought, wow, this is unlike any beer I've ever had before."

Johnny's served all sorts of locally unique beers, from German and English stalwarts like Fuller's, Bass ale, Paulaner, and Hacker-Pschorr to the early wave of American craft beers like Anchor Steam from California, Sprecher from Milwaukee, or Huber from nearby Monroe, Wisconsin.

As with many things, it took St. Paul a while to join the larger trend, but Minnesota brewers eventually started producing craft ales as well. When Mark Stutrud went looking for a location for his new, craft-oriented Summit Brewery, the best spot was in a one-story warehouse located, coincidentally, across the street from Johnny's Bar. All through the construction of the brewery, the brewers and crew would come over to Johnny's to hang out, eat sandwiches, and plan the future of American beer.

Finally, the big day arrived. On September 25, 1986, the first keg of Summit beer was rolled across University Avenue from the brewery into Johnny's. It was a half barrel of Extra Pale Ale, and Johnny's regulars were the first people in the world to officially try it.

Over the next year, having Summit on tap was one of the big attractions at Johnny's Bar, local "craft" beer still being something of a novelty in the mid-1980s.

"Why does Summit cost a nickel more than Michelob?" was a common question for Skip as he worked behind the bar at Johnny's.

"It's the shipping costs," Skip would jokingly reply.

As the brewery grew across the street, the synchronicity between Johnny's and the emerging world of craft beer became even tighter. Stutrud was hanging out at Johnny's when he came up with the name for his new porter, Great Northern, a pun on the name of the railroad and the beer style.

Ultimately, though, the beer revolution was not enough to keep the bar afloat. As the truckers disappeared from the neighborhood and, eventually, the brewery moved away, Johnny's Bar followed the trend. It closed in the late 1990s and was replaced by a new apartment building some ten years later.

"You can do your part to fight provincialism."

THE NEW FRENCH BAR

1979–2001

128 NORTH FOURTH STREET, MINNEAPOLIS

When chefs Lynne Alpert and Pam Sherman opened the New French Cafe in 1977, in a part of the Warehouse District that was home mostly to art galleries and artists' studios, the plan was to serve, as the name implied, new French cuisine in an austere, postindustrial space. Not the sort of midwestern Americanized duck à l'orange you'd find at, say, the Chateau de Paris at the Hotel Dyckman or the Normandy Inn, but more contemporary, more playful: pheasant braised with endives or duck steak with Armagnac. No tacky gold fixtures or floral wallpaper, either. In lieu of these things, the space was enlivened by fresh-cut flowers.

The New French was instantly popular, and it gained a reputation not only for being a very high-quality restaurant but a place to be seen. It was where you'd take your out-of-town friends who didn't believe you could get a decent croissant between New York City and San Francisco. It was often packed and exceptionally noisy. People would be waiting in line for tables, and at a certain point, you couldn't pack any more people into the dining room. For years, reviewers complained that the space was not quiet or comfortable, but conceded that it was one of the best dinners in town, anyway.

The restaurant was connected to a small storefront space that had previously been occupied by an architect and was going unused. Sometime in 1979, the idea came up to make the storefront into a sort of antechamber, where people could wait while their table was being prepared.

Lynne and her husband, Kay Lockhart, an architect, figured that they might as well turn it into a bar.

John Marshall was a photographer who had a studio in the basement of the building, in a cavernous open room with blocked-out windows where he could pull the enormous gelatin prints he was working on. Like a lot of working artists, he had a few side hustles going, one of which was building theater sets, contracting on renovations, and otherwise using his hands to make things. Lynne and Kay approached him about building a bar. In just two weeks, they whipped up something that matched the minimal aesthetic of the main dining room: an L-shaped stand-up bar with a maple top in a storefront that was perhaps thirty to forty-five feet deep. For a bar that embodied the local arts scene, it was not particularly high concept or idiosyncratic in execution. "It's funny how vanilla it actually was," Marshall remembers. "Sheetrock, flat white paint, standard maple floors."

There was one noteworthy detail, however. In lieu of a second bay, Kay designed a long maple wood slatted bench, based on a Le Corbusier design, for the wall opposite the bar. Contoured for comfortable seating, the bench also provided a more efficient use of space, allowing for a better flow of movement between the bar and the hallway. Plus, Lynne and Kay agreed, "small is better."

"You can have five people in here, and they'll feel comfortable," Marshall remembers. "If you have 1,500 square feet, they'll feel all alone. On the occasions where it does get packed, they'll love it, too." Other than the bench, the primary décor was a bamboo tree by the front door; it would grow to fifteen feet, and its base would slowly fill with cigarette butts over the course of the night.

The New French Bar opened on July 14, 1979—the 190th anniversary of the storming of the Bastille—and for most of the 1980s and '90s, that bench was the bar's defining characteristic and focal point. "That bench was where the most interesting conversations were taking place in Minneapolis, at the time, for twenty years," says Marshall.

Initially, the New French served just beer and wine. Alpert wanted to sell aperitifs and after-dinner brandies, as well, which necessitated a liquor license. In order to be granted one, Alpert was required to rent the hallway between the bar and restaurant so that it was one contiguous space. Even then, there was some paternalistic pushback from the city. A Minneapolis cop stopped by to try to talk her out of it, alluding to the endemic corruption in doling out city liquor licenses: "Don't you know about Murder, Inc.?" he asked earnestly.

The bar was an immediate hit among the Warehouse District crowd:

The sidewalk at the New French Bar in the early 1990s. *Photo courtesy of Lynne Alpert*

lively and full of interesting people both in front of and behind the bar. The bartenders that Lynne hired, male and female, were uniformly good looking and charismatic, and each one developed a following. Susan Stavrou Riesen started at the bar in 1979 and was manager from 1986 to 1994. She recalls that women would sometimes call up and ask if a particularly attractive bartender named Michael was working. If she said no, they'd hang up in a huff.

Pam's husband, Gary, initially decreed jazz would be the bar's soundtrack, but that went out the window quickly. Instead, music was provided by a boom box from behind the bar, each bartender responsible for bringing his or her own cassettes—everything from country and western to opera, depending on the tastes of the bartender.

Alpert stocked the bar with French and Californian wines, and the occasional Spanish and Italian, while mentoring Riesen on choosing vintages. In many cases, the New French was the first bar in town to carry a particular wine. "The old guys would laugh," says Alpert of dealing with the distributors. "Wine is a passing fancy," they'd tell her. "Liquor will never go away." Liquor didn't go away, but Alpert anticipated a growing taste for wine that would become a major part of the industry. That industry was changing, and soon Alpert was able to deal with primarily female reps and salespeople.

Besides some beloved novelties like Fischer beer, the French lager that came in distinctive twenty-two-ounce green bottles, local beers began to enter the mix at New French. In a 1987 issue of the New French newsletter, a current-day fixture of the Twin Cities beer scene made its first appearance: "We are now pouring, along with our Blatz Light Cream Ale, the hot new local beer from Summit Hill, a micro brewery out of St. Paul. . . . Support your local brewery and try a glass of Summit." Susan remembers that, when they switched to James Page Brewing, another local brew a few years later, Summit had developed enough of a following that some people were extremely upset.

In that way, the New French Bar celebrated the local—local beers, local artists—and also aspired to a sort of cosmopolitanism not specific to the Twin Cities but comfortable anywhere in the world. A peek at that same

1987 newsletter gives you a sense for that aspirational quality. Alongside the invitation to try a glass of Summit, a page is given over to an editorial on taxicabs, encouraging the patrons of the New French to use them as an urbane alternative to drinking and driving, or circling the block looking for parking. "Getting around by taxi is an excellent idea, easy, fast, efficient and relatively inexpensive. Unfortunately this is a foreign concept to the Midwestern mentality."

"You can do your part to fight provincialism by taking a cab the next time you want to lunch at the NFC," the piece concludes.

These were the sorts of mundane topics you might find yourself discussing while seated at the bar of the New French: the merits of local beer, or of taking MTC transit versus driving versus hailing a Blue and White cab. The conversations would also be more rarified. The crowd drew heavily from Warehouse District artists as well as designers, art students, hangers-on, musicians (the Replacements practiced nearby), unemployable eccentrics, well-compensated yuppies hoping to impress their dates, downtown office drones, and what Marshall calls "a heavy lookie-loo element . . . people coming in from the outer-ring suburbs," especially on gallery crawl nights. Everyone was welcome, but you had to behave and be respectful of the diverse clientele. "Some people would wander in from the suburbs—you can tell," recalls Riesen. "One hot summer night, there were two women who were artists at the bar, and we were all chatting. We've all got our tank tops on. Two guys came in and were appalled that none of the three of us women had shaved our armpits. They started getting pretty belligerent. We handled it; we took care of it. We let them know they should go somewhere else. People were allowed to be who they were."

People brought their dogs and hung out with them on the loading dock in the alley. Alpert and Sherman set up tables on the sidewalk out front, too, years before sidewalk dining had caught on in Minneapolis. People sat outside drinking and looking out at the splendid isolation of the Warehouse District, a nineteenth-century industrial neighborhood stripped entirely of industry. The area was so remote in the early 1980s that you might even see deer running up from the river through vacant lots.

A 1986 *Star Tribune* feature entitled "An Eavesdropper's Guide to Night Life in Minneapolis" gave a taste for some other topics you might overhear being discussed at the New French bench, next to someone's dog and people smoking cigarettes on either side of you, conversations running the gamut from trust-fund-baby chatter to earnest discussions of art and aesthetics—words and phrases like "oral surgeon . . . Hasselblad . . . U of M film society . . . sushi . . . Lake Nokomis . . . overseas fund" floating by.

The Warehouse District gallery scene roughly followed the economic contours of the 1980s: up when banks and corporations were hiring art consultants to build their collections with local art, and down when investors and developers started buying up blocks, renovating the buildings, and pricing out artists. A logical marker of the endpoint for the whole scene is October 13, 1990, when Target Center opened on First Avenue.

The New French managed to outlast, by a few years, the scene that had birthed it. Alpert sold the bar in 1994, the same year the New French Bakery—which continues to this day in a new location in south Minneapolis (in the heart of the former "Hub of Hell)—opened next door. The bar expanded in 1995 and hung on as late as 2001. That was right in the midst of an interregnum that took place well after most of the artists and galleries had been displaced by sports bars and sex clubs and well before the Warehouse District became the go-to district for high-end bars and restaurants with cocktail programs and tasting menus—places that, in their minimalism and raw surfaces, might look a lot like the New French. In fact, from the dog-friendly patio to the sidewalk seating to the minimalist décor to the local beer on tap, the New French was remarkably prescient of twenty-first-century bar trends.

Marshall's own life was changed on the very slatted bench he'd built. One night, in 1984, he walked into the New French Bar after an afternoon shooting video at First Avenue, dressed in a pair of tight neon new-wave pants a girlfriend had made for him—"I must have looked like a total goofball." Walking in, he saw two beautiful women sitting next to each other talking. Marshall struck up a conversation with one of the women, and though it initially didn't seem to go anywhere, they exchanged numbers. A few weeks later, word got back to the woman, Lizabeth, that Marshall had been in what he describes as "a small motorcycle accident," and Lizabeth must have taken pity on the goofball from the bar. She went to visit him, and a year later, they were married.

"That bench," he says now, decades later. "People who met there, or had conversations that changed their lives, or otherwise affected them."

"People who didn't feel comfortable in other bars felt comfortable at the New French," recalls Riesen. "I can't tell you how many times women would tell me, 'I can always come to the New French and feel not threatened.' I would just hear and be involved in the most fascinating conversations at the bar. People discussing art history, the meaning of life."

"A lot of it was typical bar stuff, but it was a particular kind of crowd. It was such a special place."

"The six guys sitting around the bar look as if they've been there a long time."

THE HALF TIME REC

1910–present

1013 FRONT AVENUE, ST. PAUL

Half Time Rec on Front Avenue in St. Paul. *Photo by Anna Botz*

South of the train tracks and north of the expansive Calvary Cemetery, between Lexington Avenue and Dale Street, sits an obscure, working-class neighborhood. This quiet quarter is centered on Front Avenue, at one time in the nineteenth century the city's northern border. The street is sprinkled with remnants of the streetcar days: two-story brick buildings that then and now host a variety of small shops, and a few dozen blocks of nineteenth-century homes with mansard roofs, piano windows, DIY home expansions, and odd-angled porches. In the middle of it all stands the Half Time Rec, a thriving old-school Irish dive bar.

By the 1980s, the bar was already seventy years old and in the midst of the kind of Irish renaissance typically reserved for lyric poetry. Writing in 1986, at the dawn of the new Gaelic age in the North End, a keen-eyed reporter named R. T. Rybak chronicled the bar's dual character as the Rec transformed from a dusty sports hangout into the heart of Irish nightlife:

There aren't many people in the Half Time Rec Bar on weekday afternoons, but the six guys sitting around the bar look as if they've been there a long time. They don't move very fast, except when a stranger walks in the door; then all their heads turn in unison as the light from outside cuts through the smoke. A few seconds later, someone throws a slimy tennis ball across the room, and a mutt crawls out from under the bar to chase it, while they deal another hand.

Small saloons like these seem to be on every corner in Milwaukee and Chicago, but aren't very common in the Twin Cities. It's the social scene for the neighborhood and a hangout for the softball teams that play a few blocks away at Como Fields.

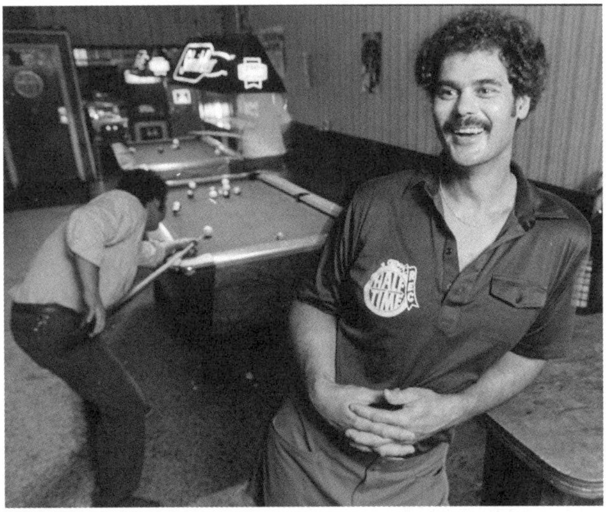

Owner Louie Walsh converted Half Time Rec into an Irish bar in the early 1980s. *Photo from the* Star Tribune, *Minnesota Historical Society Collections*

Rybak's piece was not about the slow card game or the old dog, but how, as the night grew darker, the Half Time boasted "some of the most authentic Irish music in town."

"We're not interested in pseudo-Irish music," the bar's owner, Louie Walsh, declared. "That's too Americanized. Almost all of the people who play here either live in Ireland or were born there."

For folks interested in live music, the Half Time offered ample sprawling spaces to work with. The one-story building boasted high ceilings and a large main room split down the middle into two parts. On the left-hand side as you entered through the Rec's red front door, the bar itself stretched out for fifty feet toward the back of the room. Just to the left sat a pool table and a few stools against the far wall. To the right of the bar, separated by a wood-paneled wall and the trusty popcorn machine, the rest of the room opened up around a big wooden floor. At one end stood a small stage, and a few tables were scattered around the edges.

Lurking in the corner like shadows, wooden stairways led down to the basement, where you'd find the city's least likely bocce courts, an underground Rec surprise. The two small basement courts were the brainchild of a forgotten fan of European field activities. Simple, narrow dirt encasements stretched along on either side of the wooden pillars, painted red and green, that held up the bar floor hanging low overhead. Rec visitors ventured downstairs to throw Italian balls around in the musty, limestone-walled basement. The *thunk* sounds of bocce balls hitting the pockmarked clay combined with the dancing and stomping feet on the wood floor above to create an acoustic experience you couldn't get anywhere else.

The bar's Irish renaissance began in the early 1980s, after a pub named McCaffrey's closed across town. McCaffrey's had been a hot spot for Irish music and bands like the Chieftains and the Tim Malloys. When the old place closed, the wayward musicians talked the owner of the Half Time into letting them audition.

It turned out to be a perfect fit, and over the next few years, old-school Irish music was played regularly at the Rec. Guitars, flutes, and drums filled the rooms as dancers migrated into the bar, sweeping and stomping their feet across the floor and singing along with the choruses.

On Mondays, a family-friendly version of the festivities broke out, with an ever-changing Celtic band playing reels while a ponytailed guy named Corey called out the do-si-dos for the aging hippies. On nights like this, the split configuration of the bar came in handy: regulars sat on one side, minding their own business or watching the TVs, and the other side was filled with the ponytails and skirts of spinning dancers.

Irish dancing at Half Time Rec, 1986. *Photo from the* Star Tribune, *Minnesota Historical Society Collections*

The success of the Irish music nights led to a bit of a roller-coaster ride for the Rec. On one hand, Walsh used the bar's popularity to start an Irish music festival that filled the neighborhood with revelers, and not just on St. Patrick's Day. The heyday even landed the Half Time on the big screen when, one winter night in the early 1990s, the bar was decorated to the nines, as usual, with Christmas lights and garlands. In walked a Hollywood location scout, hoping to catch some music. He was so impressed with the décor that he put the Half Time on his short list for settings in an upcoming film he was working on. A few months later, Jack Lemmon and Walter Matthau were sitting at the bar in the middle of the Rec, surrounded by cameras, fake walls, and the distinctive red door. Stills of the scene from *Grumpy Old Men* are mounted above the bar today.

On the other hand, the Irish festival put Walsh into a bit of hot water. No history of local bars would be complete without mention of pull tabs, the small cardboard gambling game that dates back to the late 1950s. Once people figured them out, pull tabs became increasingly popular in Minnesota taverns, and by the 1980s, Minnesota was by far the number-one pull-tab state in the country.

Part of the appeal was the local connection. Like meat raffles, pull tabs differ from official lotteries in that they're regulated as "charitable gambling," and each bar's proceeds largely went to individual charities designated by the establishment. In St. Paul, these charities were most often the parish church groups, sports booster leagues, and the like.

At the Half Time Rec in the 1980s, the pull tab money went to fund the Irish festival, and all was well for a time, until Walsh and his bar got caught up in a pull tab scandal. In 1989, a lobbyist named James Adams, who was connected to the Irish festival, got caught skimming money from charitable gambling proceeds for a personal slush fund. As with the pull tabs, meat raffle regulations were hardly strict, and some bars would use raffles as personal kitties, raffling off leftover meat from nearby packinghouses. Adams was caught siphoning meat-raffle proceeds from a local church, even funneling some of the money into local legislative campaigns, all while using the Half Time Rec's address as his base of operations.

The scandal and resulting backlash threw into question the sanctity of local pull tabs for months. But thanks to its reputation for good works in the community, the Half Time Rec didn't receive condemnation from the city council. One member even defended the bar on the record, arguing that it "had a reputation as a cleanly run operation." The Rec avoided closure, and the meat raffles and pull tabs returned to normal.

Though the wooden dance floor is seldom used these days for ceilidh dances, Irish music thrived at the Rec for years. And to this day, the Half Time retains its tradition of decking out the bar in holiday lights. Meanwhile, old-timers daily re-create the Matthau-Lemmon scene from *Grumpy Old Men,* holding court at the end of the bar, reading the paper, and arguing about kids today, politics, and snowplows.

“This is a real rock and roll club with a tavern attitude.”

LEE’S LIQUOR LOUNGE

1957–2019

101 GLENWOOD AVENUE, MINNEAPOLIS

The second you walked into Lee’s Liquor Lounge on Glenwood Avenue, on the “Near North” side of downtown Minneapolis, you knew you were in a different kind of establishment. For one thing, it was so damn clean. No matter what day you popped in, every surface in the place was spotless. The fake wood veneer almost gleamed, and there was barely a trace of grime on the taxidermied cougar perched in the corner.

Lee’s Liquor Lounge set a high bar when it came to the rare combination of saloon kitsch and spotlessness. Decorative Budweiser lights, with horse-drawn beer wagons going in endless circles, dangled from the ceiling, looking immaculate. Not a hint of dust blemished the surfaces of the many Elvis figurines, displaying different permutations of the King, that were mounted over the doorway arranged on terraced shelves, with a wooden plaque reading “ELVIS 1935–1977” etched in yellow.

All this gleam reflected the spirit of Lee’s longtime owner, Louie Sirian, who could often be found standing behind the Formica bar in a snug polo shirt. Louie was a firm believer in basic courtesies and social formalities. Patrons who offered “hellos,” “good nights,” and “thank yous” was the key, in Louie’s mind, to having a respectable establishment. He would size up customers in seconds, but he paired skeptical acumen with benevolence, and he would usually give newcomers the benefit of the doubt.

The apartments upstairs from Lee's provided steady customers, too. In a newspaper interview about the fate of Lee's, one upstairs tenant described his relationship with the bar downstairs: "This is my living room. There's not another place like this in town. This is a real rock and roll club with a tavern attitude. There's no dirt, not with Louie, not with this bar. Louie's the most hard-working son of a bitch I've ever met, and they don't come any better. I was on the street when I first came in here and Louie put me up."

When confronted with his tireless work ethic, Louie was fond of saying, "The last time I took a vacation, I got drafted." He had worked his way up the blue-collar ladder from the packinghouses of South St. Paul, in his younger years cleaning up the killing floors late into the nights on the third shift. Perhaps that's what inspired Louie's later penchant for mops.

Another article about the success of Lee's described Louie's distinct approach to the décor: "Louie has a favorite word: schmaltzy. He'll say something's 'almost schmaltzy,' and that's the spot-on description of the appeal of Lee's, with the careful emphasis on almost. There's certainly an element of nostalgia in the bar's appeal; the place seems to touch a familiar chord even in people who didn't grow up in the world of servicemen's clubs and small-town Saturday night dances. There's something in the bar's smoky, paneled 1950s roadhouse authenticity—with its beer signs, stuffed fish—that resonates in young urban types who've received their notions of Americana from, say, David Lynch."

The wall of mops at Lee's Liquor Lounge epitomize the bar's legendary cleanness. *Photo by Stuart Klipper*

Lee's Liquor Lounge served beer only in bottles and cans, which made it easy to tend the narrow bar that sat in the middle of the large room, ringed on all sides by stools of various heights. At some point, Louie expanded into an adjacent space (which, for a brief time, had been a liquor store owned by Vikings' defensive lineman Carl Eller) that included a large stage and a checkered black-and-white vinyl dance floor. The different seating levels offered by the bar made for perfect viewing when a band took to the stage, as was the case most nights, and Lee's transformed from a quiet neighborhood dive into a hip and swinging rockabilly and dance venue.

The dance floor was the master stroke, and likely the thing that kept the bar alive through the lean years and the second wave of freeway construction (Interstate 394) that took a meat cleaver to the neighborhood's historic building stock. By 1995, Lee's Liquor Lounge was one of the last remnants of the once-thriving industrial area north of downtown Minneapolis that had since become an industrial area featuring bus depots, a garbage burner, and homeless shelters.

Lee's Liquor Lounge was open for business on Glenwood Avenue for more than sixty years. *Photo by Stuart Klipper*

Louie bought the bar in 1976 from a guy named Lee Tremer, who had opened it in 1957. Before that, the building had been a factory of some kind dating back to the 1880s, and as late as the 1940s, Midwest Manufacturing was doing business at the location.

In the 1970s and 1980s, even after the freeway (the first one, anyway) had carved its way through the neighborhood, there were still a lot of industrial jobs in the area: Kemps milk, Munsingwear garments, McGarvey coffee, Shopmaster, the Boyer Ford Dealership, and others had facilities near Lee's. Whatever the company and wherever the worker came from, Louie would cash their paychecks and greet them with a nod. He was notoriously reliable, and reliably cheap. He'd take the checks into the back room and cash them for a buck, whether or not you were planning on sticking around and drinking.

In addition to its owner's fastidiousness and generosity, Lee's held a special place as the city's best country music and rockabilly venue. A sampling of the bar's regular acts included Jack Knife and the Sharps, Missing Numbers, the Hoot Owls, the Wringneck Mules, the Famous Volcanoes, Lazy Ike & the Daredevils, Reverse Cowgirl, Vinnie and the Stardusters, Kruddler, Cosmic Slop, Sleepy LaBeef, Marvin Rainwater, and Moonshine Willy. Of all the bands that played there, though, the rockabilly act Trailer Trash was the one that put Lee's on the music-scene map with their weekly gigs during the early 1990s.

One regular attendee described the scene: "Friday nights, we'd get all gussied up and come to Lee's. In the old days there was a jukebox with a bunch of country oldies, and maybe twice a year this band would come in and play. I think that first Wednesday with Trailer Trash there was just Ed the bartender, me, and a handful of other people. And then all of a sudden it was the place to see and be seen."

Trailer Trash was soon packing the room with relatively courteous young drunks, while also making Louie happy with his nightly till, perhaps never more so than at Christmastime, when the band held its annual "Trashy Little Xmas" show. They replaced the typical holiday tripe with rocking versions of such songs as "Please, Daddy (Don't Get Drunk This Christmas)," "I've Shopped Everywhere," and "Boogie Woogie Santa Claus."

Trailer Trash brought in a crowd that met Louie's expectations of courtesy and etiquette. "The whole group is just a bunch of fine young fellows," Louie said of the clientele. "So clean-cut and likable. The young folks have such clean good fun, and often they will say thank you as they leave."

And Louie received ample accolades himself, as is evident from the trophy case in the basement green room: it was full of shiny, polished plastic tributes to the momentary and fleeting greatness of bar culture. "To be able to distinguish yourselves in the field after all these years, that's a great honor," said Louie.

But, as Louie also liked to say, "the horse that shits the fastest don't shit for long." The forces of urban development and economics paid no heed of those trophy cases, and Lee's Liquor Lounge became a target for demolition. In 1997, the city Public Works Department was eyeing the parcel for a proposed office and garage that would be convenient to both downtown and the freeway on-ramps. But after floating the idea and getting pushback from the music community, the plans changed, and Lee's was saved from this particular wrecking ball.

As Lee's entered the twenty-first century, it also became known for its gay and lesbian scene. Every Sunday night, the country music bent slightly to make room for cowboys and cowgirls of a different stripe. On the weekly GBLT barn dance night, the dance floor was full of well-dressed cowboys and -girls dancing with each other in tight blue denim.

Like so many great bars before it, Lee's Liquor Lounge would not last forever. After Louie sold the bar to a customer and retired in 2015, Lee's stuck around for a few more years. For many people, though, it was never quite the same without Louie keeping watch over the Formica.

In 1998, Texas honkytonk musician Dale Watson had written an ode to the place called "Louie's Lee's Liquor Lounge." On the bar's final night in May 2019, Watson himself came to Minneapolis to play the final set on the Lee's stage, during which he performed the song one last time.

Well up in Minnesota
in Minneapolis,
Very near to a real bad part of town,
There's a man who's quite the legend
There on Glenwood, near 11th.
That's Louie up at Lee's Liquor Lounge.

He bought it from a man named Lee
But he didn't change that sign,
Cause Louie thinks what really counts
Was what ya got inside.

From the crowded floor
to the open door
That's the funnest place in town,
Louie's Lee's Liquor Lounge.

The music stage at
Lee's Liquor Lounge.
Photo by Stuart Klipper

"We called it 'Fall-Down Frank's.'"

STAND-UP FRANK'S

1968–2009

2202 NORTH SECOND STREET, MINNEAPOLIS

The want ad said, simply: "Accepting applications for experienced persons to tend bar at Stand-Up Frank's."

The ad did not indicate that being a bartender at Stand-Up Frank's involved a very particular set of skills, honed by men at the pinnacle of their profession. These were men who could pour a shot the way a loon dives into a lake. They served the shots with single-minded purpose. They also bounced customers, handled crowds, and dismissed the concerns of those ignorant of the ways of the famously spartan bar. Many men held the honored bartender position over the years, most of them consummate professionals. Al tended bar at Stand-Up's for twenty-five years, Red was there for fifteen, Bud was there for a long stretch, and so was Pat. One 2001 review in the *Star Tribune* described Pat thus: "A tall, lanky man with a face that's both haggard and kind. He's the kind of bartender who either recognizes you or recognizes that he doesn't recognize you, who looks after the people who walk through the door, and who—for about three bucks—will make you a gin and tonic that will just about knock you over."

Among the skills a Stand-Up Frank's barkeep might have, two were most important: the ability to make the strongest, cheapest drinks in Minneapolis, and the determination to serve these concoctions no matter what the customer really wanted. The pure potency of the drinks was the raison d'être of the place.

Stories of newcomers entering the bar and asking for the wrong kind of drink were not a bug but rather a legendary feature of the Stand-Up

Former site of Stand-Up Frank's in North Minneapolis. *Photo by Anna Botz*

Frank's experience. Here are a few tales of customer interactions with the delightfully stubborn bartenders at Frank's:

> *I was in there one night with a bunch of friends and girls from the U of M. One of the girls asked for a Tom Collins. Bartender looks up and says, "We don't serve those here," and tosses back a shot.*
>
> *We called it Fall-Down Frank's. When he mixed a drink, it would go whiskey* glug glug glug glug glug glug glug glug glug glug, *then Coke* ssppt.
>
> *My friend Kevin took me in there the first time while I was home on leave. I asked for a bourbon and water, and the bartender filled the glass with whiskey and then put an ice cube in it. I asked, "What about the water?" His reply: "What do you think the ice is?"*
>
> *The guy next to me had been drinking whiskey and ginger ale. He asked the bartender to switch to whiskey and Coke, and the bartender said, "What difference could it make?"*
>
> *I was taken out on my 21st birthday. It started at Stand-Ups for a free birthday drink. [The bartender] said, "What you havin'?" I said, "a beer." He said, "I won't give you a beer." So I ordered a real drink.*

The old bumper-pool table from Stand-Up Frank's, now located at the nearby Cliff-n-Norm's Bar. *Photo by Anna Botz*

At Stand-Up Frank's, you drank booze the way they told you to, and you liked it.

For some folks, the best way to visit Stand-Up's was after working the night shift at a nearby factory, and people regularly lined up outside the bar before it opened at 8 AM. According to some, Frank's bar got its famous nickname from the folks standing in line outside the door each morning. If you arrived for the opening, the first drink was free—continuing a time-honored tradition from Minneapolis's old Gateway District.

In addition to their potency, another surefire bet at Stand-Up's was that the drinks were damn cheap. A 1982 *Star Tribune* account of North Minneapolis bars described the whiskey regimen at Frank's:

> *"Ah, er, give me a shot of Jim Beam, water on the side."*
>
> *The bartender slides water across the bar, then plunks a rocks glass on the bar and pours it to the brim with four ounces of amber liquid.*
>
> *"That'll be $1.45."*
>
> *An elderly gent requests another hit and gets four ounces of "Wall Street," house booze that sells for $1.30.*
>
> *"A really big drink for the price," states the newcomer.*
>
> *"Yeah, but I've been coming here for 15 years and it used to be bigger—seven ounces, I think—and cheaper."*

Stand-Up Frank's had the strongest, cheapest drinks in town, and that's another possible explanation for the bar's famous nickname: it was so difficult to stand up after just a few rounds of Frank's strong concoctions.

In keeping with its laconic milieu, Frank's was not fancy. Both the building and the bar's atmosphere were as bare bones as the drinks. The bar occupied a long, narrow room in a short, rectangular building in the heart of the North Minneapolis industrial riverfront, one of many bars once clustered along West Broadway between Plymouth and Lyndale. The place had gotten its start in the 1930s, when it was known as the Walt Hobolt Bar. A guy named Frank Stalock bought it sometime in the 1940s, and around this time, Frank's Bar made a brief appearance in the local news during the mid-century crackdown on pinball machines. Stalock's bar was splashed on the front pages as one of the many dens of iniquity, targeted in a federal sting operation out to eradicate the immoral pinball contraptions, machines that supposedly encouraged gambling and were gateways to turpitude.

Despite the regulatory pressure, throughout the rest of the century, moderate risk-taking in the form of pull tabs and bumper pool bets continued to be a regular feature of Frank's. The small, windowless room was often filled with more slurred conversation than places to sit. In fact, the third, and true, explanation for why it was called Stand-Up Frank's was quite literal: for most of the first decades of its life, the bar had no stools at all; if you wanted to drink there, you had to stand up.

In addition to the drinks, Stand-Up Frank's was well known for its bumper pool—perhaps the perfect game for the addled mind. Guys at Stand-Up's would place side bets on the pool games. According to legend, one night when an old patron died at the bar, some regulars stowed the body under the pool table and finished their game while they waited for the ambulance.

For most of its life, Frank's was closely affiliated with the industrial area that surrounded it, serving shift workers from North and Northeast Minneapolis. For a brief time in the 1980s, the bar was owned by a guy who ran a machine shop in south Minneapolis. By the 1990s, Stand-Up Frank's represented a dying breed: one of the last places that still offered night-shift workers and drunks a free "wake-up" shot in the morning, one of the last places to stick to its rail-whiskey guns, one of the last places to hold out against the trend toward complex cocktails and wishy-washy mixers, and one of the last places in Minneapolis where the mere mention of the name would inspire awe.

Stand-Up Frank's finally closed for good in 2009, and the small, windowless dive was replaced by a zombie-themed bar. A bright neon sign saying "Undead Frank lives" was mounted behind the bar, a joke perhaps lost on many of the new and ironic patrons. The zombie bar closed in 2017, and Stand-Up Frank's is again waiting for its next iteration as a place to acquire a stiff drink and a good story.

“Where everybody knows your shame.”

WILLARD’S LIQUORS

1935–present

738 THOMAS AVENUE, ST. PAUL

When Frank Schweitz bought Willard’s Liquors in 1982, he might not have known what he was getting into. He had worked in bars before, and when the owner of Willard’s offered to sell it to him, he shrugged and wondered, “Why not?”

“I just did it because I was unemployed,” Schweitz explained. “I got laid off in 1981, something like that. [I thought] I’ll do it to pass some time until they call me back to work. One thing led to another, and thirty-seven years later, I’m still here.”

One of the oldest bars in St. Paul’s Frogtown neighborhood, Willard’s is a long, rectangular joint on the relatively quiet corner of Thomas Avenue and Grotto Street. The bar sits in a two-story brick building built in 1916, and the ground floor had originally been a soda fountain and grocery. During Prohibition, the owner opened a soda fountain in the space but ran a speakeasy in the back room, where select customers could enjoy alcoholic beverages under the famously benign neglect of St. Paul’s police.

After Prohibition ended, the shop became a bar, one of only a handful in the largely residential neighborhood. In the 1950s, it was known as Quinn’s, and by the 1990s, the sign hanging outside said, simply, “Willard’s Liquors.” Similar to most neighborhood joints, Willard’s featured a long wooden bar, a few tables, a jukebox, a pool table, and folks old and young swapping stories.

The bar was named after the owner's dog decades ago, a fact that led to a running joke among patrons and staff.

As Eric Dawson, a longtime Willard's bartender, explained, "If somebody needed a favor, they would come to me and say, 'I talked to Willard and he said it's okay to cash my check,' or 'Willard said it's okay for me to run a tab.'"

"So, you talked to Willard and he said it's okay?" the bartender would ask with a smile.

If the customer answered in the affirmative, Dawson would point to the picture of the dog mounted on the wall behind the bar.

"Well, that's Willard right there," he'd say, and everyone would get a good laugh out of it. The joke never got old.

Around the time that Schweitz purchased the bar, Frogtown was changing fast. It had long been a white, working-class neighborhood that lay north of the de facto "color line" along University Avenue that preserved segregation in St. Paul. For many decades, the city's African Americans were expected to stay in their place, which meant in the Rondo neighborhood, between University and Selby to the south.

Dawson grew up in St. Paul shining shoes, and he remembered well the old rules: "University was a dividing line between the black folks and the white folks. If you shopped or walked into a bar north of University, you really weren't welcome. At times, you weren't even served or you were asked to leave: 'You're not welcome here,' 'you shouldn't be here,' 'get out,' and so forth."

The unspoken but well-enforced racial lines started to shift beginning in the mid-1950s with the construction of Interstate 94, which ran through the heart of Rondo, fracturing and effectively wiping out the historic black neighborhood. At the same time, civil rights laws were beginning to take effect, and white flight to the suburbs commenced, aided by the new freeway. By the 1980s, the neighborhood had been rapidly transformed, and Willard's adapted to embrace the diversifying neighborhood.

According to Schweitz, the philosophy at Willard's was pretty simple: "We opened it up, and it was none of this white-only shit. If you can obey the rules and want to have some fun, come on in. We made everybody welcome."

Over time, the bar became the self-described "black Cheers" of St. Paul. As the regulars liked to joke, it was a place where "everybody knows your shame."

Negotiating a changing neighborhood wasn't always easy, but the bar persisted, with its regular calendar of community events. Willard's hosted things like trick or treat night on Halloween, an annual pig roast on the first day of the Vikings season, and a regular holiday party in December. Eric Dawson became famous for being Willard's own Santa Claus, with whom neighborhood kids would share their holiday wish lists.

The bar enjoyed an active social and communal environment during the rest of the year, too. Cards or dominoes tournaments might last for hours throughout the day, with older folks in the morning before the crowd got gradually younger as the night wore on.

There was also the nagging narrative, sometimes hard to forget, of crime in and around the bar. The occasional shooting or fight would put Willard's under the gaze of public scrutiny. For weeks at a time, neighborhood folks, politicians, or inspectors concerned about public safety would blame the bar.

"Once, two blocks away, a guy got in an altercation and got shot," Schweitz recalled. "He came in here wounded, and my security called the police and saved the guy's life. Well, in the newspaper and on the TV, they said 'gunfire erupts at Willard's liquors.' I called channel 11 and got them to retract the headline, because it wasn't true. But by then the damage was done."

Willard's, like many bars in working-class neighborhoods, often stood in as a symbol for larger social problems around crime or racial tensions. Bar owners often had to walk a fine line to stay in the good graces of inspectors or community groups.

"It would make me crazy," Schweitz said of the pressure on the bar to solve the problem of crime in the neighborhood. "I'd go to the community meetings and fight with them, and yell, and it doesn't do any good. We have a bartender and employee meeting every couple of months or so and we talk about all this stuff."

Frogtown continued to change over the years, and through both the good times and the bad, Willard's remained a landmark. Eventually, the neighborhood kids grew up, and the Halloween and Christmas parties faded away, as did the pig roast. These days, Willard's is known for its entourage of caterers who sling soul food or sandwiches from the back room or the food truck that's parked outside. The bar still anchors the corner of Thomas Avenue, people continue to argue over the jukebox, and the place still serves as the living room for Frogtown while boasting the best pool players in St. Paul.

"Before I quit drinking, I went to all the bars everywhere," Schweitz said. "Bars in different states, all over. I don't think you're going to find more friendly, nicer people than in here. The people I've known, for all the years I've been here, are some of the nicest people I've ever met."

"It's our policy that we do not return drinks."

RED DRAGON

1976–present

2116 LYNDALE AVENUE SOUTH, MINNEAPOLIS

In one of the far corners of the food internet sometime in the late 2000s, an anonymous poster took it upon herself to re-create, from memory, the Wanderer's Punch, the drink made famous by the erstwhile Nankin Cafe in downtown Minneapolis, and where she claimed to have worked. She was used to making the drink in huge batches, so she had to break it down for a home bar.

It's mostly rum—three kinds—with orange juice and grenadine, served in a fishbowl with some cherries. "Don't let its pretty pink color fool you," she warned. "It is called the Wanderer because when you try to get up from your barstool, you commonly find yourself unable to walk a straight line."

The Wanderer's Punch itself staggered a not-so-straight line from downtown Minneapolis to Lyndale Avenue at some point in the 1970s or '80s—shedding some a's and e's, picking up a few o's, and becoming known as the Wondrous Punch. From when it opened in 1919 to when it closed in 1999, the Nankin Cafe was one of the best-known and most beloved spots in town. It had grown out of the small but active Chinese American community that had been in Minnesota since 1876, with many of its members running restaurants. By 1910, a few years before the Nankin opened, there were ten Chinese restaurants in Minneapolis and six in Duluth.

In the years since the restaurant closed and memories of the Wanderer's

Punch become hazier, the Red Dragon's Wondrous Punch has taken its place in the local collective consciousness. At one point, a fashionable downtown bar revived the Wanderer's Punch using the original Nankin recipe provided by the Wu family, the Nankin's final owners. It was served in a branded souvenir glass. The young bar manager seemed kind of baffled by the strong response, not having any firsthand memories of the Nankin himself. He spoke reverently if broadly, a bit like describing a museum piece.

Very few locals who've spent a portion of their lives exploring the city's bars don't recognize the Wondrous Punch's name immediately. It's the drink you invoke when you want to tell a story about excess. It's a Minneapolis original that you can't believe really exists and seems redolent of another era—maybe another era of your own life, but also another era of much stronger drinks and no pretense to either ironic bemusement or mixological sophistication. The downtown bar that had revived the Wanderer's Punch only revived the recipe; they absolutely refused to sell it in a thirty-three-ounce glass like the original at Nankin. Those branded souvenir glasses are fourteen ounces. More than that just seemed too . . . much.

The Red Dragon has never worried about crossing such a line. You order a Wondrous Punch at the bar, and you get twenty ounces. It is, like the blogger said, a pretty shade of pink. In the dimly lit environment of the Red Dragon, it almost seems to glow. "It's our policy," the neon green laminated bar menu reminds you, "that we do not return drinks!!" That extra exclamation mark lets you know you're truly on your own. Ask people who remember the Wanderer's Punch, and they'll tell you that, despite the similarities in size and ingredients, the potency of the Red Dragon's version makes the Nankin original seem like a box of apple juice from a schoolkid's lunch bag.

The twenty-ounce goblets at the Red Dragon are also their own kind of souvenir. A bouncer's job is always to keep rough characters from coming in, but the Red Dragon bouncers occasionally need to stop drunk patrons from sneaking out with the cherished goblets. It's long been a problem for a place that, by midnight, can be as tightly packed as any bar in the city, and where the bartenders need every piece of glassware they can get. The rows of fishbowls hanging above the bar shrink steadily over the course of a Saturday night.

Lai Wong opened the Red Dragon in early 1977 in a former dance academy on Lyndale Avenue, where Norwegian ballerina and film star Vera Zorina once rehearsed. Wong had been the head chef at the Nankin Cafe for many years, and he brought with him his culinary expertise—as well as a few cocktail recipes. The dining room side in particular retains

The Red Dragon Restaurant and Lounge on Lyndale Avenue. *Photo by Anna Botz*

the spacious, high ceilings of its earlier iteration. The Dragon held a grand opening celebration on Super Bowl Sunday, offering free orchids to the first hundred ladies in the restaurant side and free beers in the bar side for every Vikings touchdown during Super Bowl XI, which was being shown on the bar's TV. (Everyone present presumably received two free beers and a sense of crippling disappointment: the Vikings lost to the Oakland Raiders 32–14, in their fourth and, to date, final Super Bowl appearance.)

The sign on the side of the building read "Polynesian Drinks—Cantonese Food—Szechuan Cuisine." By 1976, the tiki cocktail trend was fading a bit nationally from its postwar heyday, though it had really only been established in the Midwest for ten or fifteen years, having slowly moved eastward from Hawaii and California. The Sheraton Hotel downtown had a Kon-Tiki Lounge where you could get mai tais, but the Red Dragon was perhaps the first to offer such fare outside the downtown core. It was tiki culture directed at locals living in bungalows and apartments on Bryant and Grand more than at traveling businessmen slurping down zombies on corporate expense accounts. The Red Dragon had the standard tiki bar staples, but it dispensed with the mid-century modern bamboo-and-teak cocktail lounge look of a Trader Vic's and instead went for a more traditional decorative motif that is nonetheless touched with a distinctly mid-seventies sense of weird, unselfconscious excess.

The Dragon is divided into two sections: the bar side and the restaurant side. People drink in both, but the restaurant side tends to shut down earlier, leaving the bar side buzzing until closing time. It all looks very much like it might have in 1976, '86, or '96, with the exception of an ATM, some local beers that didn't exist at the time, and a few flat-screen TVs. The TVs are fine and all, but just as entrancing is the wallpaper, a repeating tableau of gold figures from Chinese mythology on a black background, all of which seems to move across the wall the longer you stare at it.

Regulars may be drinking beers at the bar, under the red gabled Chinese-style roof that sits above it, or in the booths along the wall. The main attraction, as ever, is the specialty drink menu. The Wondrous Punch sits at the top, but a whole mix of other similarly sized and apportioned drinks are available, ranging from classics like the Mai Tai and the Zombie to Dragon-specific innovations like the Purple Rain and Molly Ringwald. The namesakes of the latter two are well chosen. They both place the drink's origin straight in the middle of the 1980s, but also within a timeless pop cultural continuum that feels less dated than classic.

A 1998 newspaper profile summarized the scene in a way that still feels familiar today. The bar was notoriously smoky, even for the time. The TV was usually set to westerns or *Xena: Warrior Princess*, while Prince and Sade could frequently be heard on the jukebox. The former is less true these days, but the latter is still broadly true, with a lot more hip-hop mixed in. "This is the only place I can go to find skinheads, lawyers, gangsters, yuppies, and people with piercings and tattoos all together," said one regular, who identified himself as a law student. "It's like an escape from Uptown," said another. "Intimate" is how yet another described it.

The lack of windows and the emphasis on red—in the wall coverings and trim, the lanterns, the upholstery—gives it an almost womb-like quality. That, mixed with the fuzzy potency of the drinks and the unwelcoming climate outside for half of the year, make the Dragon a bar that feels inviting to an almost transcendent degree. It's easy to picture yourself at the Red Dragon on a snowy winter evening at 8 PM, right before the evening rush, taking it all in and bathed in a red glow, with a fishbowl of booze and a plate of cream cheese wontons (another Minnesota innovation, courtesy of Leeann Chin) in front of you at the bar. It would be hard to think of a more quintessentially Minneapolis setting of the past forty years.

"I don't want people acting like they're in Paree."

THE BLUE NILE

1997–2015

2116 LYNDALE AVENUE SOUTH, MINNEAPOLIS

For eight weeks in 1948, a psychic named Prince Yoco performed nightly on a stage in the large back room of the Tempo Bar. The Tempo was a Franklin Avenue hot spot complete with singing waitresses, a three-piece band, and a thriving scene of young University of Minnesota collegians trying to impress their dates. Prince Yoco wore a white suit and elaborate jeweled turban and sported a thin mustache on his upper lip. He would stand before a complex of astrological charts and amaze the crowd with his carnivalesque prognostications, "reading the stars" and "answering the important questions with amazing accuracy."

If Yoco could have predicted the future of the Tempo Bar, it would have been an impressive feat indeed, enough to make anyone a believer in the powers of the so-called "clock of destiny" through which the astrological signs foretold the fates. Over the years, the bar rode a roller coaster of conflicting identities on its way to becoming another vacant lot on the edge of East Franklin and Minnehaha Avenues.

The Tempo had fallen on hard times by the late 1970s. Its owner, Earl Montpetit, had a rather dubious reputation at city hall and in the neighborhood, and the 1950s-era remodel that had covered the building in Formstone was starting to show its age. One newspaper account from the time made it sound like something out of dystopian urban films of the period, like the *French Connection* or *Mean Streets:* "'[The Tempo] was not the kind of place that you'd take your wife, if you know what I mean,' said D. C. Zierden, a Minneapolis police officer who has worked on East Franklin for ten years. It wasn't all bad, he said. If he or his partner needed information about a fencing operation or a burglary, they could usually get it from "'known burglars' who made the bar their home away from home during the day."

The 1970s-era Tempo was really two bars in one: in the foreground was a peanut bar full of "motorcycle types," anchoring the stretch of biker hangouts on Cedar Avenue, a haven for guys rolling around Minneapolis in leather and denim.

The other half was a thriving disco and dance club. As one report described it: "The crowd, which sometimes numbered more than a thousand, was as black as the one in the peanut bar was white. No jean jackets here. What you had were generally well-dressed customers moving in the near

The ornately painted Blue Nile on Franklin Avenue in Minneapolis. *Photo by Alexius Horatius, CC-BY-SA-3.0*

darkness to the thud-a-thud, heavy-on-the-funk disco beat."

The Tempo finally closed in early 1980 after one too many altercations and ongoing pressure from neighborhood folks fed up with the fights and late-night chaos. Montpetit then remade the building into an elaborate Mexican restaurant named Montanita's, which lasted a little over a decade selling margaritas and fajitas. The modernist exterior was re-covered with stucco, and the doorways were turned into arches in the classic style of New World Spanish architecture. After Montanita's closed down, the cavernous building sat empty on Franklin for a few years, until it was bought in 1997 by an Ethiopian entrepreneur named Fahmi Katabay, who had lost his lease on a restaurant space on Lyndale Avenue.

Named after the branch of the Nile River that flows from Ethiopia's Lake Tana, Katabay's Blue Nile restaurant became a hot spot for Minneapolis's burgeoning East African community, the first groups of which began arriving in Minnesota in large numbers in the late 1980s and early 1990s. Immigrants from Ethiopia, Eritrea, Somalia, and other countries were making their homes in the city's Seward and Cedar-Riverside neighborhoods, within walking distance of the new restaurant and bar.

The Blue Nile soon transformed into a kind of global hub—in both the drinks it served and the clientele it attracted—a place where, according to a 1998 *Star Tribune* review, you could "travel the world in a cushy throne-like chair." The bar offered beers from all over the world, everything from Singha of Thailand to Castle Lager of Zimbabwe to the latest American craft beers from Minnesota and beyond, as well as all kinds of cocktails.

Katabay wanted his bar to be a place where people could engage in reasoned political debate. "If America bombs Iraq," he said in the *Star Tribune* piece, "I want this to be a place where people will feel comfortable discussing the pros and cons in an intellectual way." He didn't want "poseurs," and the reporter described Katabay rolling his eyes and lifting an invisible cup of tea with his pinkie in the air, saying, "I don't want people acting like they're in Paree."

The review described Katabay as a "friendly, soft-spoken man" who wanted to create an establishment both cosmopolitan and local, a mix of a neighborhood bar and world-beat disco.

The Blue Nile's musical offerings fed a diverse mix of tastes, from straight-ahead jazz to fusion to blues to a dozen stripes of world music—Brazilian beat, reggae, African rock, Afro-pop dance music, and more—bringing in bands and musical styles that were well known in their home countries but less so in Minneapolis. Whenever an Afro-pop dance band came through, the place was transformed into what one reviewer described as a scene similar to "crashing an Egyptian wedding."

On the building's stucco exterior, an elaborate mural depicted grass huts, odd sculptures, and savanna landscapes in strong colors. Inside, the restaurant's byzantine spaces opened in strange ways, as arches folded through the drop-ceilinged rooms full of tall, deep booths. The walls, previously decorated in Mexican themes, were repurposed with new murals of palm trees, tropical ferns, coffee plantations, waterfalls, and the ancient hills of Ethiopia. The Blue Nile's distinctive vibe attracted both curious white Minnesotans and new immigrants from all over the global South. On good days, you'd find diners learning about *injera*, pouring back pints of beer, and listening to live music. On slow days, you'd be hard pressed to find the bartender.

In the 2000s, the Blue Nile became an early adopter of local craft beer. Longtime bartender Al McCarty began devoting more and more of his tap lines to the city's brave new breweries, like now-defunct Harriet Brewing and Surly, as well as a bunch of other breweries from around the Midwest.

The place eventually fell victim to bad credit, changing tastes, allegations of mismanagement, and the lingering effects of years on the margins of respectability. Meanwhile, the awkward location near the unpleasant intersection of East Franklin, Minnehaha, and Cedar Avenues surely did not do the bar any favors. As cosmopolitan pan-African culture and craft beer went on to thrive elsewhere in Minneapolis, in 2018, the building that had once housed the Tempo Bar, Montanita's, and the Blue Nile became a vacant lot.

"Any publicity, good or bad, is okay with me."

NYE'S POLONAISE

1950–2016

112 EAST HENNEPIN AVENUE, MINNEAPOLIS

Nye's Polonaise was what they called a "union house," one of the last in Northeast Minneapolis; at one time, the staffs of most of the bars in Northeast had been completely unionized, until those bars began to close down or change hands. Nye's was one until the end—when Al Nye opened it in 1950, expanded it in 1964, and sold it in 1994, and even after that, right up until it closed in the spring of 2016. As a result, a lot of union guys hung out there.

Back when Al Nye owned the place, the head of the International Brotherhood of Electrical Workers local happened to walk in after work one afternoon. He noticed that Al had a couple of electricians outside, doing some work on one of the buzzy red neon signs that anchored the corner of East Hennepin and Lourdes Place. He didn't recognize them.

He walked up to Al, who was sitting at the bar, drinking a Diet Coke. "Al, come on," he said. "You got some non-union guys doing the electrical work out there. Do you want to get them off the job and get some union guys in there? Otherwise, we might have to picket the place."

Al shrugged. "You picket, and the newspaper and TV crews will show up. We'll be all over the TV. And hey, any publicity, good or bad, is okay with me."

The relationship between bars and the media has been a long and

Nye's Polonaise was a Minneapolis institution for more than sixty years. *Photo by Alan Turkus, CC-BY-SA-2.0*

fruitful one. The only reason we know as much as we do about some of the establishments covered in this book, especially those out of living memory, is because newspaper guys showed up so regularly and wrote about them in such depth. We know what the saloon at the American House was like, down to the wall fixtures, because the writers from the *Globe* were in there all the time.

Corky Heisel tended bar at Nye's from 1990 until it closed in 2016. He remembers a few distinct eras, connected, at least in part, by external factors driven by media coverage.

"When I started there in 1990, it really wasn't all that busy. It was a sleepy old passed-by kind of supper club," he remembers. "And then, you know what happened: we were frequented by the people who ran *City Pages*, and that's when they started doing the 'best of' kind of stuff. They liked to sing at the piano. So they started nominating Nye's as 'best piano bar.'"

"And that was when things started picking up."

To hear Corky tell it, there was a sort of sine wave of publicity that waxed and waned every few years: next was when Twin Cities Public Television came in and did a documentary on Al, and that brought in more people. After that, Ruth Adams and the World's Most Dangerous Polka Band appeared on the *Jon Stewart Show*, and people came in asking about that. In 2006, long after Al Nye had sold the bar, *Esquire* magazine named it the best bar in America—full stop—in a rhapsodic feature that

The Old Side at Nye's. *Photo by Becca Dilley*

danced right to the edge of hyperbole. Something about Nye's brought that out in people. "The best bar in America occupies a corner where the path to righteousness and the road to perdition run parallel, east to west, perpendicular to the muddy river that cuts this country in two, north to south," wrote Chris Jones.

"But don't go," he added. "You'll just ruin it."

Well, maybe, but Nye's would be a hard place to ruin. Nye's Polonaise Room was built to withstand an enormous amount of pressure from the outside. Any night, there were no fewer than three or four different nodes of activity: dancing to polka, singing at the piano bar, having pierogies with your family in the Chopin Room, drinking grasshoppers on the New Side, downing shots of whiskey on the Old Side. For most of its existence, Nye's was in fact two separate and distinct bars, each with its own individual character. In 1950, Al Nye, the son of Polish and Austrian immigrants from North Minneapolis, bought a workingman's corner bar with his brother on East Hennepin called Heffron's. It was a typical beer and whiskey joint, with one exception: off in a side room, next to the restrooms, Al kept a little two-burner hot plate where he'd make sauerkraut and Polish sausages to serve. Corky remembers seeing the hot plate gathering dust as late as the 1990s in the back room.

That part of the bar was variously known as the Polka Room, the Old Bar, or the Old Side. Even after he'd sold Nye's, Al still came in. The new buyers had offered him free drinks for life, not knowing that Al was a teetotaler. So he was offered free Diet Cokes for life.

"He'd always make damn sure he got his Diet Coke for free," says Jenean Gilmer, who was the bar's first female bartender and worked there for a few years during the mid-2000s. "He was a penny pincher. That's how he bought that whole block up."

Tales of Al's carefulness with money were legendary. Corky remembers hearing about a mailman who claimed he saw Al count out $60,000 in cash, by hand, to pay a liquor distributor while the guy stood there waiting—he didn't trust anyone else to do it. Al could sit at the bar and watch his bartender for two hours, unbroken, just to make sure he wasn't taking any of his money.

That thriftiness *did* allow Al to buy up the whole block. A three-story building on the corner, with a lunch counter on the first floor and SRO apartments upstairs, went up for sale in the early 1960s, and he purchased that. In the vacant lot between the buildings, he built an elaborate dining room, with a painting of Polish national hero Frédéric Chopin on the exterior and "Nye's Polonaise" painted across the front. It opened for business on Christmas Eve, 1964. Inside, Sweet Lou Snider operated a piano bar. The restaurant also offered a full bar with table service, a full kitchen, and a menu that was expanded from Al's original sauerkraut recipe to include pierogies and prime rib. That became the New Side, referred to as such even after it had been a fixture of the neighborhood for forty years, a place for wedding anniversaries, graduation parties, and retirement celebrations.

Opposite: The New Side at Nye's. *Photo by Becca Dilley*

Regardless of what newspaper articles or magazine features were bringing in new clientele, none of the hype had much effect on the regulars. "In Northeast, the bars are like the community centers," says Gilmer. "It's a very big deal when you go into your dad's regular when you were twenty-one. You can't do it beforehand, because you've been going in there since you were two years old, and everyone knows who you are."

The Old Side remained where the regulars went. For years, Al cashed paychecks at the bar, and the drinks were strong. Until the end, you could make any drink a Jumbo—fourteen ounces of mostly booze and ice, with maybe a splash of tonic as an afterthought. The bar was open late, too, right up until the 1 AM closing time, and rarely a minute before. When the downtown bars closed shop at 12:30, there'd be a rush across the river for last call at Nye's. Even after Al sold it and subsequent owners raised the prices to keep up with the times, Nye's was a place to get a cheap drink anytime.

Most everyone on the Old Side had been coming in for thirty or forty years: Northeast lifers, second- or third-generation, or nominally retired

business guys who would drive their LeSabres and Cadillacs from their downtown offices, drink a few martinis over lunch, and drive back over the Hennepin Avenue bridge. But there were always influxes of new clients coming in and mixing with the old, whether it was college-age kids looking for a good deal, new arrivals in town who'd heard Nye's was something to see, or tourists who'd seen it on a travel website or TV show. On the Old Side, a younger crowd would often be mingling with old-timers, who were, in fact, thrilled to be the center of attention, telling the same stories with an unending enthusiasm. Or, on the New Side, you'd see nervous couples on dates alternating with seasoned pros at the piano bar, or "frat boys who just wanted to sing 'Sweet Caroline' over and over and over again," according to Jenean. "Eventually, Sweet Lou Snider was just, *No way, I'm not doing that song anymore.* She was sweet, but she could be not sweet, for sure."

Most of the longtimers had their regular seats at the bar, and, especially if you came in earlier in the day, you'd probably meet them. I remember getting a drink there with a friend after work one day, and one of the regulars sidled up to us. I found out later he was one of a set of twins who hung out there for decades, whose matching accordions hung over the door between the Old and New Sides.

He launched right in, asking me if I was an asshole or not. I said I probably wasn't, but he wasn't convinced, and he wanted to be sure. "No, you might be an asshole. I've written extensively on this. I've got a tract about it," he said. He offered to mail me a copy so I could check for myself. I gave him my address with a sense of both annoyance and amusement, he went back to his drink, and I didn't think of it again.

Six months later, an envelope containing a Xeroxed and stapled document entitled "The Ordering of Assholes," with no other explanatory material, arrived at my apartment. It took me a few minutes to recall where it might have come from. *Of course. That guy at Nye's.*

Nye's did come to an end in 2016, after a protracted and undignified death rattle when the owners announced plans to sell the building and have the site converted into condos—the air above Nye's in this densely populated part of the city was simply too valuable. A few years later, a zombie version of Nye's popped up on the corner where the Old Bar had been. It still had a piano and a mural of Al Nye on the wall, but it had little to do with what made Nye's worthwhile, and more to do with selling nostalgia. Not a lot of new memories seemed to be forming in there.

After the *Esquire* article, a banner was hung outside of Nye's that spelled it out in huge letters: BEST BAR IN AMERICA. I remember sitting with a few friends, chuckling about it. "The best bar in America," we smiled. It seemed incredibly over the top, especially for this little corner of a medium-size

Ruth Adams and the World's Most Dangerous Polka Band performed weekly on the bar's Old Side for decades. *Photo by Becca Dilley*

pair of cities in the middle of America. To live in Minneapolis is to come to terms with the feeling of being completely embarrassed by attention like this, but also burningly, secretly proud of it.

Then we all got quiet and looked down at our drinks. We were thinking about the various evenings we'd had there over the years. I may have been thinking about "The Ordering of Assholes," or the time during the 2008 Republican convention when I sang "Ghost Riders in the Sky" to a roomful of drunken GOP political operatives, trying to bait them by changing the word "Ghost Riders" to "Ted Kennedy." Or the fact the cathode ray tube TV set, later given a "Lifetime Achievement Award" by a local website, was so old that the tracking warped whatever baseball game was on into a kind of pixelated ghost transmission. Or the décor in the Chopin Room, with its golden upholstered booths and chunky glass mosaic light fixtures hanging overhead, suitable for bringing your mom because it reminded her of the 1960s, friends from other cities because they couldn't believe something like this still existed, and second dates because it showed what a good sense of humor you had as you serenaded them with ABBA's "Fernando."

"You know," said one of us, after a moment. "It's funny. Maybe it's *not* the best bar in America. But I can't really think of one that's better."

“No place took being laid back more seriously than we did.”

TOWN TALK DINER

2006–2011

2707 EAST LAKE STREET, MINNEAPOLIS

“That bar was special, right?”

Nick Kosevich is talking about the bar at the Town Talk, where he worked in 2006 and 2007 with his colleague Aaron Johnson on the beverage side. He's speaking not of the establishment as a whole, but the actual, physical bar you'd sit at to enjoy a beverage.

“It was six inches lower than a legal bar could be. It was an old dining table. The way that the guest sits and the way the bartender stands—that interaction is not a normal physical interaction in terms of space. It's different than in a normal bar, so there's something magical. You're looking at them eye to eye. You're closer into everyone's conversations. When I bartended there, the best nights I'd remember were ones where I'd be having six different conversations going with six different groups.”

The Town Talk was originally an old lunch counter, situated on Lake Street across from the train yards and factories that once clustered around Lake and Hiawatha Avenue. The largest of these factories, Minneapolis-Moline, turned out scores of hungry workers at the end of their shifts building tractors. The diner was built in 1946, a sliver of an alley filled in with bright metal surfaces and wedged between two larger buildings, a lunch counter down the middle. Paul Pearson, the owner, had been part of a restaurant family going back a generation, and he knew how to bring

The Town Talk Diner sign is a registered historic landmark. *Photo by Max Sparber*

in customers. The sign he commissioned out front was the greatest creation by Naegele Outdoor Advertising, the Minneapolis sign makers who furnished much of the Hennepin Avenue loop district with its more notable neon displays. This one was their masterpiece, though, and the only one that is now historically protected: TOWN TALK DINER in bulbs, against a fizzy aqua metal backdrop, blocky, playful letters in the Streamline Moderne style. That sign would ensure that whatever business went in there would, at the very least, have visibility on Lake Street.

Two sisters named Barb Link and Vicki Brever were the final owners of the original iteration, running the diner from 1978 to 2002. When Johnson and his team, chef David Vlach and general manager Tim Niver, bought the building in 2006, the space had been vacant for four years.

The Town Talk Diner added a dining room on the side, but the lunch counter was the focal point. The new owners retained the counter's original fixtures and dimensions: fixed seats, a little lower than a standard bar, not much room in front of the bar for people to linger, and even less room in the back for the bartenders. Kosevich and Johnson, two bigger guys, would slide back and forth behind the bar with a third guy between the well bar, the mid-bar, and the point person by the kitchen who kept the lists. "Our next bar back, he's got to be skinny, man!" Johnson remembers yelling one night after a near-collision at the mid-bar. "No one our size!"

That arrangement did create the sort of atmosphere that encouraged people to lean forward, chat with the bartenders, talk to each other—or yell: the Town Talk, on weekend nights, was cacophonously loud. Indeed, it

The Town Talk Diner was an early pioneer in Minneapolis's craft-cocktail scene. *Photo by Max Sparber*

could be one of the noisiest places you'd ever been; the walls and surfaces of the room were all brushed metal, and shouts and laughter bounced off every surface. People coming in from the street, especially in winter, would have kind of a dazed look on their faces. They'd enter through a red velvet curtain protecting the bar from the cold and be tossed into this warm, loud, dimly lit space, everyone packed against the counter, three bartenders in white aprons running back and forth, pointing, shouting, mixing drinks, and generally holding court. Typically, when a person entered, the bartenders (and some of the people sitting at the bar) would turn to the door and break into applause, even if no one had ever seen them before.

It was the kind of spot where, upon walking in, you could tell instantly if you wanted to be there or not. "No place," says Kosevich now, "took being laid back more seriously than we did."

In the early 2000s, cocktail culture in the Twin Cities was still a little hungover from the 1980s and '90s. Cocktail menus in high-end restaurants and lounges tended to involve bright, synthetic liquors, neon colors, and various types of -tinis. Johnson had come out of the fine-dining world, classically trained in French cuisine in New York. He was interested in doing with drinks what cooks were already doing with food. "Why do people not focus on the composition of a cocktail in the way they do with a plate of food?" he asks now. "There's all the same factors in place: layering, acidity, sugars. If you take a real classic rum and Coke, there's a reason why it works so well. It's got layers, a composition. Why not take the tricks that you've learned in the back of the house and bring it to the front of the house?"

The Town Talk gave him a perfect platform to try out some of those tricks. It was a neighborhood hangout, located in a residential part of town, a small, easygoing joint where the food was well thought out but not prohibitively priced. They bought the same fish as the high-end restaurants downtown but sold it for a lot less. With a side of fried cheese curds, if you wanted. You couldn't be too pretentious in that context.

And so, Johnson and Kosevich came up with a spread of cocktails that emphasized playfulness and creativity as well as taste, sometimes starting with a great name and working backward. The Jackson Pollock, for example, involved a garnish of basil oil applied with an eye dropper over gin, grapefruit juice, simple syrup, and wine, the oil beading up and making miniature painting-style splatters over the surface.

When the bar wasn't too slammed—or even occasionally when it was—you could have a drink mixed up on the spot. "It wasn't a bar where it was like, okay, what do you want?" says Johnson. "You'd start a conversation: How's it going? What do you like to eat? You like vodka, rum, bourbon? You like bourbon? Okay—you go and mix something up—try this. How do you like it? It was an inquisitive thing, challenging ourselves to be creative. We're grabbing pickle juice out of the kitchen and building cocktails on the fly."

"And much quicker than some bartenders do it today," he adds. That's true: for all the care that went into the drinks, there wasn't time to be precious. These drinks were mixed up efficiently and quickly.

As noted, space was tight behind the bar. In fact, too tight for extra lines, so the Town Talk did not have taps; beer was served only in bottles. And as with a wine list at a fancy restaurant, Town Talk offered bottles of beer in various sizes—seven-ounce ponies, magnums. On the larger side, they started offering forty-ounce beers like Miller High Life and solved the problem of how to keep it cool by serving it in wine buckets. You get the practical aspect of keeping the beer cool and the added absurd flair of having the server present you with the "Champagne of Beers" in a wine bucket and a towel draped over his or her arm.

"Too much art and ego, and you lose the sense of why are we doing this," says Kosevich. "We would do weird stuff, but it was done in a playful way that was approachable."

Johnson and Kosevich both departed Town Talk in 2007. Kosevich took the work he began there—coming up with fresh ingredients and, ultimately, a wide variety of bitters—and applied it on a nearly industrial scale with a bitters company called Bittercube.

Town Talk itself went through a few more owners before closing in 2011. Since then, the space has gone through several different iterations, including, briefly, a French-inspired one called Le Town Talk, with a neon "Le" inserted above the Town Talk signage. The original sign was designated a historic landmark in 2013, ensuring that whatever iterations come in the future, they will be called Town Talk, in some fashion, as well.

The Town Talk of 2006 and 2007 was the beginning of a lineage of bartenders and bar runners that continues to spread throughout the Twin Cities bar and restaurant scene. The bartenders who trained at Town Talk with Johnson and Kosevich took a lot of the DNA of the place with them. Today, there is no shortage of bars and restaurants with imaginative cocktail programs. Many of them are fun places to hang out, but few have quite the theatrical blend of absurdity and hospitality that Town Talk offered people wandering in from Lake Street.

"If you can throw a successful party every night," Johnson says, "people will come."

Kosevich adds, "People would say, well, I'm going to Town Talk on Friday. Then what? You hopefully get a seat and see what happens. It's like theater."

"Come fool around like monkeys and laugh like hyenas. Come and experience life, here at Malina's."

MALINA'S SPORTS BAR

2002–2018

693 DALE STREET, ST. PAUL

When Malina's Sports Bar opened in 2002, it made the front pages of the Hmong newspapers, because a Hmong-owned bar was a rarity in St. Paul. Named after the oldest daughter of the owners, it took the place of an older, abandoned Dale Street bar that once stood at the same location in the north end of Frogtown, brushing up against the old industrial areas and vacant lots of the neighborhood.

The *Hmong Times* described the newly opened bar in 2002: "Ever walk into a Caucasian Sports Bar with the intention of wanting to watch one's favorite sports team, but felt out of place? No more feeling out of place now, because an Asian Sports Bar has just recently opened. Now all you sports fans can get together to cheer for your favorite sports team and feel right at home!"

The owners, Vone and Mee Moua, were both former social workers, and, like a lot of immigrant entrepreneurs, they wore a lot of hats. Vone

Malina's Sports Bar was located on a once-vibrant stretch of North Dale Street in St. Paul. *Photo by Bill Lindeke*

had worked as a mental health counselor, and Mee had been a therapist, but they quickly turned Malina's into their second home. The telephone pole on the sidewalk outside even bore the pencil-line markings noting the heights and ages of the various Moua children over the years, like the wall of a family kitchen.

Decades earlier, Dale Street had been a dense and vibrant commercial street lined with businesses and shops, a main drag running north and south through the heart of the city. The Malina's building was just one of many early twentieth-century two-story brick structures on Dale, with shops below and apartments above. Built in 1911, it served as a grocery store for the first decades of its life, until, during Prohibition, the owners got caught in a sting selling bootleg booze out of the back. Both the father and son ended up in the federal pen for short stretches due to the bootlegging.

In the subsequent decades, the place turned into a bar. It was called Len Nielsen's Bar for a while in the 1960s and became the Bourbon Bar by the 1990s. Along the way, this stretch of Dale was widened during the freeway era, and the east side of the street was leveled, the old buildings replaced with more pavement and a row of vacant lots. The asymmetry of the resulting streetscape gave Dale Street a windswept feel and a touch of pathos. In the midst of it sat the old beige building with a plain white door and a pale sign reading "Malina's Sports Bar," two palm trees on either side. It made it seem like an oasis.

Malina's was almost always either packed or empty, and very little in between. Vone Moua was usually there, quietly tending bar, performing social work of a different kind. He would greet most everyone with a small smile, a drink, and a platitude. Malina's had high ceilings, dark red walls, a pool table on your left, a small U-shaped bar in front of the kitchen, and a booth tucked into the far corner. The room's incongruous decorations included sports pennants hanging from the ceiling, a handmade wooden sign, a poster of Marilyn Monroe on the wall, and a two-foot statue of Betty Boop in the middle of the bar. On one wall, there was a small framed poem that read:

There's a place I go
To sit and think;
It's also a place where
I can have a drink.

I like to watch the people,
Short, big, beautiful, or tall.
Here at the bar
You can see it all.

You might see guys
Who are big, tough fellas.
But they might prefer drinks
With little umbrellas.

You may even see women
Giving all that they got,
Glued to the bar
Taking shot after shot.

Whatever you like
They've got it here,
Champagne, wine,
Hard liquor, or beer.

So come fool around like monkeys,
And laugh like hyenas.
Come and experience life . . .
Here at Malina's.

Sign outside Malina's Sports Bar. *Photo by Bill Lindeke*

Despite the name, most people at Malina's Sports Bar were not there to watch sports on television. Instead, playing pool was popular, as were the video games. A main attraction for many of Malina's patrons was the nightly karaoke, when the small stage along the wall was transformed into one of the city's finest karaoke spots. Long into the evening, a slow parade of women and men took turns belting out old pop jams, slaying Céline Dion, Bonnie Tyler, Journey, and more.

Vone's wife, Mee, spent most of her time in the kitchen, and by bar standards, Malina's menu was extensive and the food was solid. There were a few different kinds of larb (a meat salad), Hmong papaya salad, pickled eggs, and other Southeast Asian treats.

The far room at Malina's, past the bar on the left, was once a separate store with a separate entrance. After being incorporated with the bar, it was used mostly for events. On some nights, the entire place would be full of people, maybe a family celebrating an event, with a band on the stage and couples dancing, filling the place with life. The rooms were often decorated with shiny cellophane fringe and brightly colored disco lights illuminating the dance floor.

Tap beer was not Malina's forté, and most people drank Heineken or Rolling Rock out of bottles. Shots and mixed drinks were the focus. High on the shelf behind the bar stood a bottle of snake whiskey, a Thai concoction in which a snake is clearly visible inside the bottle. In Malina's final years, they had a special shot called the Dalai Lama, a mix of four types of whiskey and 151-proof rum, which was lit on fire. It was impossibly strong and could make a large man instantly drunk, and it was one of many specials served up on the bar with great fanfare.

Not all bar stories end happily, and in 2014 Vone Moua was shot by a patron in a dispute over a twenty-dollar game of pool. The bar sat empty for a while after his death, and then it was reopened for a few years with a new owner. Today, like a lot of the buildings along the west side of Dale Street, Malina's is shuttered, waiting for crowds and activity to revitalize the old place once more.

"This is Rice Street, and we're tough."

HOOVER'S PUB

1960–present

755 JACKSON STREET, ST. PAUL

Hoover's Pub sits in a small, windowless, square building on a quiet intersection in a quiet part of town, tucked among the machine shops and cemeteries. The bar occupies the northwest corner of Jackson and Acker Streets, an obscure intersection at the southern edge of St. Paul's North End, just past the train tracks and over the hill from Capitol Heights. It's safe to say that, at least until the birth of the smartphone, most people in St. Paul didn't know about it, had never heard of it, and couldn't have found it if they tried. And most people did not try.

Hoover's is the kind of bar that can only be found if someone takes you there. People might happen upon it by accident, wandering down Jackson Street and noticing the dim glow of the light in the doorway alcove, but

Hoover's Pub at 755 Jackson Street in St. Paul. *Photo by Anna Botz*

since the bar lacks windows, nobody is likely to even know whether it's open. The entrance to the bar, angled to face the intersection, looks out toward a bridge over the railroad tracks and toward the old roundhouse, an elaborate, weather-beaten hemispherical structure that now houses a railroad museum.

The building directly across Jackson Street from Hoover's is nearly a mirror image, and it, too, used to be a beer joint, once called the Mount Airy Bar, named for the hill that rises just to the south. Together, these two bars formed a gateway of sorts to the North End for most of a century, and over the years they fought off various intruders, withstood holdups by gunmen, welcomed wandering dupes, and endured tragic losses.

Hoover's Pub occupies land that, in 1890, was home to a Scandinavian family that was proper enough to employ a maid. But that was then, and today, the industrial area around the bar offers a mishmash of enterprise, everything from the rusty, city-owned asphalt plant that churns out the pothole-patching mix every spring to machine shops, supply sheds, auto parts yards, metal warehouses, and elaborate garages housing engines in various states of completion. On these battered back streets, there's a real sense of the self-reliance and independence that hearkens back to the earliest days of St. Paul, when people built their own homes and had tight grips on their bootstraps. It is also home to the city's oldest cemetery.

Hoover's itself dates to 1963. Back then, it was a convenient hangout for the city's "breadmen," guys who drove delivery trucks for the nearby Taystee Bakery on the edge of downtown. A half century later, much of the interior décor seems unchanged. For a while in the 1970s the bar was owned by Larry Bowie, a former offensive lineman for the Minnesota Vikings who originally hailed from West Virginia and surely had a bit of a mountain sensibility. After Bowie sold it, the bar became Buddy's, then Diamond Lou's, then (allegedly) Blood n' Guts, then Scooter's, and finally Hoover's—so named because the current owner is (allegedly) an excellent third baseman in his softball league, scooping up every ground ball as if he's a vacuum.

Among the paraphernalia inside the bar is a legitimate, wall-mounted rotary phone. It's not the only phone in the place, but the beige rotary contraption somehow still functions, and when someone calls the bar, its analog ring is a siren call from another age.

Just to the left of the door inside Hoover's is another odd sight: a large, wooden setup that looks like a wall-mounted roulette wheel. It is a rare dive-bar gambling game called Tri-Wheel that involves picking numbers roulette-style, marking your initials on a slip of paper, and waiting to see how the big wheel spins.

The Tri-Wheel game (visible on the left in the photo) is a popular activity at Hoover's. *Photo by Anna Botz*

The life of the bar revolves somewhat around the television schedule, with *Wheel of Fortune* mirroring the local Tri-Wheel on the far wall, *Jeopardy* or *Family Feud* offering mental challenges, or the nightly airing of the local news. Each broadcast is watched from the corners of the eyes of the folks bellied up to the bar, drinking bottles of Michelob and pausing conversations just long enough to deliver snide commentary about the mayor, the new Vikings' kicker, traffic on 35E, or the state of the city's potholes.

Otherwise, unless someone is feeding dollar bills into the jukebox, the ambience at Hoover's is an irrepressible cacophony of conversation, amplified by the closeness of the wooden walls and the low drop ceiling. A bar without music has a music of its own, and in the intimate confines of Hoover's, the organic soundtrack is made up of voices, laughter, and slaps on the back of the men and women at the bar or clustered in corners. The constant stream of stories, jokes, and ribbing covers everything from tales of the workday to vacations to odes to old Rice Street and the routine complaints about how much worse things are today. In this manner, you become a regular, and to acquire a nickname at Hoover's is a badge of honor—the bartender herself went by Lambchop—and having a name is to be welcomed into the small club, received only once you survive the gauntlet of jabs. A typical self-deprecating slag: "Why don't you go back to Hoagie's on the East Side? This is Rice Street, and we're tough. I was raised when men were men and sheep were nervous. They could hear a zipper at a hundred yards."

Afternoon crowd at Hoover's Pub.
Photo by Anna Botz

Every afternoon and evening at Hoover's Pub, in between the coughing, the claps, the laughter, and the periodic spinning of the Tri-Wheel, voices bump together to create a social orchestra, mixing like a cocktail and blending together into the musty air, the low, raspy voices of old men and high throbs of laughter from women planted like flowers on the barstools around the front of the room. Without seeing the television or glimpsing people's cell phones, it would be impossible to tell what year it was in the windowless bar. Something timeless is conjured, and folks chatting in the back corner of the room go up to have another drink.

"I just wanted to be in that scene so bad."

CC CLUB

1934–present

2600 LYNDALE AVENUE SOUTH, MINNEAPOLIS

"Well a person can work up a mean, mean thirst / After a hard day of nothin' much at all." This is maybe the introductory quote you were expecting for the CC Club.

Of all the bars mentioned in this book, only one has had a song written about it, and then had that song performed on national television. That bar is the CC Club, and that song is the Replacements' 1985 album cut "Here Comes a Regular." It summarizes the bleary-eyed sense of warmth tinged with melancholy that comes with being a bar regular better than just about any other song. Paul Westerberg was about twenty-six years old when he wrote it, and having lived in the neighborhood for some time, he had likely been going to the CC Club for at least a few years. People in the neighborhood had been going there since Clarence Campbell, the CC of the bar's name, opened it as the CC Tap in 1934.

Funny thing about the CC, though: the years go by, but for the most part, those regulars remain the same age as Westerberg was when he wrote the song. Sure, you can wander into the CC today at 4 PM and find someone sitting at the bar who's been going there for twenty or thirty years, since the days when Oar Folkjokeopus record store was across the street. But if you wander in after 9 PM on a weekend, you'll find it's full of kids in their early to mid-twenties, fresh out of college, working crappy jobs, living on their own in Minneapolis for the first time. That's who's been coming to the CC for the past thirty years, at least.

The CC Club was sold in 2013 to the owners of the French Meadow, an upscale organic bistro nearby on Lyndale Avenue. The purchase was made for a variety of reasons, though some insist that it was because it gave the French Meadow access to the CC's parking lot, a valuable asset in this crowded, chic part of the city. The new owners vowed not to change anything about the bar, and they've kept their word. Not much is different from the old days, with a few exceptions: the storied jukebox is now an internet-connected model, and of course the smoke is gone. Any other changes are barely perceptible, just floating in the atmosphere.

The CC Tap in 1967, before it became the CC Club. *Minnesota Historical Society Collections*

That same year, the *New York Times* ran a story on the dating scene in Minneapolis, one of those stories they write every so often that seem calculated to drive clicks from non–East Coast parts of the country obsessed with reading about themselves in the "Paper of Record" (which is to say, every part of the country). The article was much ridiculed on social media in certain circles around town, but as these types of stories tend to do, it struck a nerve in depicting something familiar. The piece followed a group of men and women in their mid-twenties out for a night on the town, and they wound up at the CC Club. While it was easy to laugh and roll your eyes at the article, at least part of it resonated with anyone who had moved to Minneapolis from whatever small town in Minnesota or Wisconsin or North Dakota they had come from. It was a tale you hear in the Twin Cities over and over again, this time from a young teacher named Kathleen. "I totally dreamed about Minneapolis when I was growing up," she told the reporter. "I grew up in the suburbs and got so sick of it. I remember going to Uptown when I was in high school. It was so cool. I just wanted to be in that scene so bad."

A little bit of knowledge is always transmitted orally through a community about these sorts of scenes. In 2013, even a twenty-two-year-old out for some beers who didn't know (or care) anything in particular about the Replacements had a sense that the CC Club was the sort of place you treated with a little bit of respect, knowing that it had been a noteworthy hangout of some kind for longer than you'd been alive. During the CC Club's 1980s heyday, the musicians and hangers-on who frequented it considered it an old neighborhood dive bar, the kind of place their working-class dads and moms and aunts and uncles would have frequented after work in the 1940s and '50s. A young person in 1985 might not have known anything about the bar's previous life as the CC Tap, or its softball team, or the western swing combos that performed on weekends, but they, too, would have had a sense that this bar was a very Minneapolis kind of bar. They may have intuited through a haze of whiskey and cigarette smoke that there was something to be respected about that, bringing a sense of civic ownership that could be shared with everyone else drinking there.

Moe Emard, who co-owned the CC Club with his wife, Sharon, from 1985 to 2013, knew about the bar for years before he bought it. "It was a beer joint, the most well-known beer joint in the five-state area," he said later, on the eve of his retirement. "Any kid from North Dakota, South Dakota, Iowa, Wisconsin would come into town, [and] first place they knew about when they were in high school was the CC Tap."

In the same way, the stories of the Replacements and the crowd from Oar Folkjokeopus and David Carr and Tom Arnold trickled down through the decades, and the CC Club has long inspired more reverence than the standard neighborhood dive. "It doesn't matter what era it is, it's the kind of place that young people like coming to," Emard said. "It's always been a place you could find somebody, somebody you were looking for or someone you knew."

For Molly Davy, the CC Club was the focal point of her and her friends' weekend nights in the early part of the 2010s ("purple lipstick and two-for-ones" is how she summarized the era). The CC wasn't where you spent your whole night, necessarily, but where you went at the beginning of the night to get a cheap pitcher and then again at the end to partake in the late-night culture. "My first impression," she said, "was that it was firmly established as the cool bar to go to. Somehow that was the place for a while."

Molly grew up in the southwest suburbs, but her father was raised in the city, and she remembers that he—a veteran of many 3.2 bars in and around St. Louis Park—was slightly horrified that the CC was her hangout. "His impression was that it was this dangerous biker bar," she says, something along the lines of the Hexagon, where guys in leather jackets would break pool cues over each other's heads.

The CC Club of 2013 was not the sort of bar where you'd see any sort of biker bar fight. You'd certainly see an older biker or two, especially earlier in the day, but it was one of the few places outside of the chicest parts of the city where you also might find that most midwestern of thrills: the low-level celebrity. Molly remembers seeing singer Aaron Carter ("his manager really loved the CC, apparently") and Justin Kirk from *Weeds* there.

For the most part, though, the CC has been the destination of choice for twenty-six-year-olds in south Minneapolis because of how it's laid out: framed around nodes of activity, the kind that encourage people to circulate or to group together in little clusters, almost like a high school cafeteria. The emphasis is on hanging out. For one thing, there are no performances at the CC Club—or at least the kind that appear on a stage. "Anywhere else, the night was framed around when the next set started, or if someone had started or just finished playing," Molly remembers. "Or there was karaoke. That didn't dictate the space at the CC." Here, the jukebox was the primary diversion.

The regulars get the bar up front. In the back, tables fill the middle of the space, and booths line the walls leading to the bathrooms and jukebox. Farther back are the pool tables ("a whole different social world of young men being assholes," Molly remembers). The tables and booths are full of people, and you'll probably know somebody at one or two of them if you've been living in the city for a year or two—and probably quite a few more than that if you've been here for five or twenty-five or fifty years. There's a constant flow of people coming in to start their night or on their way out to try their luck somewhere else. "You'd run into random people you hadn't seen in a long time," Molly says. "I had that experience a lot more there than other bars I was hanging out in."

The things that Westerberg liked—and maybe resented a little—about the bar are the same things that twenty-six-year-olds in 2013, and twenty-six-year-olds today, like and maybe resent a little about it. It looks and feels the way a Minneapolis or St. Paul bar should look: beat-up vinyl seats, a wooden horseshoe bar with bags of potato chips lined up behind it, dark wood paneling and beer swag on the walls. In the summer, the back door is open, and the inside feels like it goes on forever. In the winter, it's dark and warm and a place you could spend all of February and March. You walk in, through the weird little airlock that so many neighborhood bars have, and wipe the snow off your feet. You show the bouncer your ID, and you sit down at the bar and get a pitcher of Premium and maybe a Heggies pizza. You text your friends and let them know you're at the Cha-Cha, or you just sit by yourself and hope you run into someone you know. Or maybe you hope you don't: "And sometimes I just ain't in the mood / To take my place in back with the loudmouths," as Westerberg sang.

Whatever you're doing there, whenever you're there, you have a sense that the CC Club is a place you might have gone ten or twenty-five or fifty years ago. And it might not be a lot different. But you also know a lot has changed, some of it for the worse, some of it for the better. Maybe next year is the year it will all change for good, and they'll be putting wheat germ in the beer or they'll start serving fifteen-dollar salads and none of our friends will feel welcome anymore.

But none of that means you're not enjoying it right now. It's your time, and it's your bar. It's been a lot of other people's bar over the years, and it still belongs to them. But it's yours now. That's why you keep coming back.

Evening crowd at the CC Club. *Photo by Aaron Brethorst/Flickr*

ACKNOWLEDGMENTS

Bill Lindeke would like to thank and acknowledge the following individuals for their assistance and insights: James Eli Shiffer, Peter Majerle, Phil Platt, Shadey Chavez, Gilbert de la O, Frank Schweitz, Eric Dawson, Mark Stutrud, Dick Westby, Dave Thune, Tim Gallivan, Art Eddleston, Annette Fleming, James Hathaway, Tom Schroeder, Peter Rachleff, the organizers of the Stupor Bowl, and the countless people who help Twin Cities Facebook history groups thrive.

Andy Sturdevant adds his thanks and appreciation to Ta-coumba Aiken, Frank Atlas, Susan Riesen, Karl Raschke, John Marshall, Janine Sherry, Jeanne Anderson, Lynne Alpert, Nick Kosevich, Aaron Johnson, Jeanine Gilmer, Corky Heisel, Erica Christ, Joanne Christ, Paul Maccabee, Mike Lynch, Brad Zellar, Jackie Beckey, Nancy Wong, Molly Davy, and Bailey Diers.

Both authors further thank the Gale Family Library at the Minnesota Historical Society, the Ramsey County Historical Society, the Quatrefoil Library, the University of Minnesota libraries, the St. Paul Public Library, and the Minneapolis Central Library.

INDEX

Italicized page numbers indicate a photograph, illustration, or caption.

ABOUT THE AUTHORS

BILL LINDEKE is an urban geographer and writer who focuses on how our environments shape our lives. He currently writes MinnPost's Cityscapes column as well as a local urban blog at Twin City Sidewalks. He has contributed articles on local food and drink history for *City Pages* and the *Growler* and is the author of *Minneapolis–Saint Paul: Then and Now.* Bill is a member of the Saint Paul Planning Commission. He lives in St. Paul.

ANDY STURDEVANT is an artist and writer who has written about art, history, and culture for a variety of publications, including *City Pages, Belt,* and *Mpls.St.Paul.* For five years, Andy wrote "The Stroll," a weekly column on Twin Cities neighborhoods, art, history, and architecture for MinnPost. He currently writes a regular column for *Architecture MN.* He is the author of *Potluck Supper with Meeting to Follow* and *Downtown: Minneapolis in the '70s.* Andy lives in Minneapolis.

COLOPHON / CREDITS

The text of *Closing Time* is set primarily in Minion Pro, an OpenType update of the original Minion family designed by Robert Slimbach and released in 1990 by Adobe Systems. It has been described as "balanced. . . clean. . . handsome. . . easy to like" and criticized for being so "noncontroversially good-looking" that it is, in fact, rather dull.[1] Additional typefaces used in the design of this book include Neutraface (created for House Industries by Christian Schwartz in 2002, inspired by the design principles of architect Richard Neutra) in various weights and styles, including Display, Text, and Condenced; as well as Serifa (created by Adrian Frutiger in 1967, featured most prominently in the logo of Montgomery Ward from 1982–92, and also used in candidate Ross Perot's 1992 presidential campaign ads[2]). Spot illustrations in *Closing Time* were hand drawn by Minnesota Historical Society Press interns Pader Fang and Amelia Thompson. Cover art and design is by Adam Demers, as is the interior design and layout. No alcohol was consumed and no bar fights erupted during the making of this book.[3]

1. Wikipedia: Matthew Butterick, "Minion," *Typography for Lawyers*. Archived from the original on 1 May 2015. Retrieved 15 August 2015.
2. Wikipedia: Serifa. Last edited on 19 August 2018, at 10:57 (UTC).
3. Cannot be substantiated.